I BUILT NO SCHOOLS IN KENYA

I BUILT NO SCHOOLS IN KENYA

A YEAR OF UNMITIGATED MADNESS

Kirsten Drysdale

VINTAGE BOOKS
Australia

A Vintage Australia book
Published by Penguin Random House Australia Pty Ltd
Level 3, 100 Pacific Highway, North Sydney NSW 2060
penguin.com.au

First published by Vintage Australia in 2019

Copyright © Kirsten Drysdale 2019

The moral right of the author has been asserted.

All rights reserved. No part of this publication may be reproduced, modified, stored or distributed in any form or by any means without prior written permission from Penguin Random House Australia Pty Ltd or its authorised licensees.

Addresses for the Penguin Random House group of companies can be found at global.penguinrandomhouse.com/offices.

Names in this book have been changed.

 A catalogue record for this book is available from the National Library of Australia

ISBN 978 0 85798 854 6

Cover design and images by Alex Ross © Penguin Random House Australia Pty Ltd
Typeset in 12.5/16 pt Centaur by Midland Typesetters, Australia
Printed in Australia by Griffin Press, an accredited ISO AS/NZS 14001:2004 Environmental Management System printer

CONTENTS

Prologue: The Nine Iron — I

1. The Situation — 5
2. The Place — 12
3. The Routine — 25
4. Alice — 38
5. The Wife — 57
6. The Club — 67
7. The Great Escape — 108
8. The Ruse — 120
9. Fiona Returns — 142
10. Blood & Beers — 160
11. The Final Straw — 190
12. Touchdown Take 2 — 207
13. Shortcomings — 234
14. Fun Run — 296
15. Nytol — 306
16. Things Fall Apart — 321
17. Pammy — 329

Epilogue: Reckoning — 337

Prologue
THE NINE IRON

Nairobi, Kenya – November 2011

The man whose murder I've been asked to prevent is trying to kill me. His name is Walter, and he's coming at me with a nine iron. He's threatened me before, but it's different this time. I can tell by the way his jaw is set and the unusual quickness in his hips. This time he really, *really* means it. And the guy survived a lion attack once – that unlucky cat's taxidermied corpse is hanging on the dining-room wall, glass-eyed proof that Walt is not a man to be messed with. I could do with some back-up but, as per usual, there's no one else around when I need them.

I whistle for Walt's 'pedigree cur', his 'mucky dog', his 'lovely mutt'. She usually licks him calm, but right now she's busy haranguing the troop of monkeys in the trees at the bottom of the garden, hackles up and teeth out, not paying me any attention. The guard hut at the front gate is empty: Patrick, the *askari*, has gone to have a crack at the monkeys too. He lobs gravel from the driveway at them with a handmade slingshot, while the monkeys return fire with small red berries. He flinches and ducks, swearing in Swahili and struggling to reload. The monkeys are winning this round.

Walt is coming at me with a nine iron because I won't give him the goddamn car keys. He's *always* trying to get his hands on the goddamn car keys, but he's not allowed to drive anymore. He doesn't know what year it is or what country he's in; how's he supposed to make it through Nairobi traffic unscathed? Not to mention the rest of us.

A call to prayer sails out of a nearby mosque. I glance towards it, my eyes catching on a bamboo thicket where two owls have made a nest. Half an hour ago, Walt was fondly showing it to me. Before his mood turned dark, the wrinkles on his face were crinkle-soft like crepe paper. Now, they are sharp and hard and angry around his eyes, and he is starting to frighten me. 'Give me those keys, you little bitch!' he spits, showering my face in tiny droplets of fury that cool my skin as they dry in the sunshine. Well, he's not fucking getting them.

I hold my arm behind me and shuffle backwards with my fist clenched tight around the little jangle of metal. The bright red plastic Peugeot tag is peeking out from between my second and third fingers. Walt sees it. He lines up the nub of my wrist with the polished toe of his golf club. There's a backswing.

'Walt, wait!' I plead, relieved when he lowers the club slightly.

I'm fuming that he's got a club to swing at all. After the garden hoe incident, his daughter, Fiona, sent an email ordering us to remove all 'potential weapons' from Walt's reach, including golf clubs. Apparently she's already locked the garden tools away in the shed and hidden his walking sticks under my bed. Talk about cold comfort.

Fiona is in charge around here even when she's not around — which is most of the time, given she lives in England. She rules via text message fiats and email edicts and makes semi-regular site inspections, visiting every couple of months. I don't know who left the golf clubs out today, but Walt spotted them on his way to the garage. On his way to attack whoever he suspects has been driving his car without his permission.

Through the kitchen window I see three staff members with their faces pressed to the glass, eyes and mouths wide in shock. This scene must be vaudeville to them. A pink-faced pair of loons, sixty years apart, running in circles around the driveway.

'Esther!' I hiss to the maid at the window. 'Esther, get James. We need help!'

The faces peel away from the glass, and I hear Esther call for James. He's one of the few people Walt will listen to when he gets like this.

'*Bwana! Bwana!*' James comes running from the garden. He wipes the rich red soil off his hands down his navy overalls as he calls gently to Walt.

But Walt doesn't seem to hear him. He's still glaring at me and coming at me and waving that nine iron at me.

My right heel butts up against the garden bed. I manage to stagger to the other side of the Peugeot, putting it between me and the madman. Fuck breaking an arm over this shit.

That's when I hear the Mazda engine idling at the gates. It's Walt's wife, back from her golf game, but Patrick isn't there to open up: he's still slinging rocks at the monkeys. What a bloody racket. Patrick shouts at the barking dog, '*Hapana!*' The Mazda's horn blasts: *bip-beep!* The muezzin calls '*Allahu Akbar!*' James pleads, '*Bwana, kuja hapa – bwana, tafadhali!*' but Walt ignores him, peering into the Peugeot.

'Ah-ho-*ho!*' he says in a tone of bitter vindication. 'I see you've all been out and about again.' He must have noticed the odometer reading has increased by several thousand kilometres, proof that someone's been joyriding in his car since he last parked it however many decades ago in his mind. 'Well, no more, chaps,' he announces, grabbing the locked door handle.

Patrick fires one last rock at the monkeys, and finally lopes back to the gate in long, uneven strides. He jams the slingshot into the back pocket of his uniform, rattles the keys out of another and unlocks the padlock, then he pulls the gates open. '*Jambo, memsahib! Karibu!*' he says, saluting the grey-haired white woman in the passenger seat and nodding at her African driver.

The Mazda pulls up around the side of a bougainvillea, and Walt's wife climbs out. 'Hell-*ooooo*, my darling!' she calls to him, as he adjusts his grip on the end of the club and lines me up again. 'Are you having more car trouble?'

He pauses mid-swing to squint at her, but he doesn't see his wife of forty years. He sees an old lady in a sun visor. God, I feel for this woman.

Turning to me, she asks the bleeding obvious. 'Oh dear, is he having another one of those "turns"?'

I hold the car keys up in silent reply, as we hear the thwack of a nine iron bouncing off laminated glass.

It might be time for me to resign again.

I
THE SITUATION

Nairobi, Kenya – October 2010
So here's how it is: I'm a live-in carer for Walter Smyth. He is very rich, very old, very sick and very senile. Over the next eight years, dozens of people will occupy this role. Most of them won't last long. Some of them will literally run away in the dead of night after just a few weeks. In comparison, I'll be here quite a while. Eleven months all up. But I don't know that yet. I can't imagine what's to come.

Walt doesn't know it, but he has employed three women to look after him. There's me; there's my mate from high school, Alice; and there's Millicent, a sweet old woman who is very into God. The three of us tag-team around the clock in eight-hour shifts, supervising Walt's meals, his morning walks, his medication, his showers, his shits and his sleep. Alice and I are also supposed to spy on his wife, Marguerite, for his daughter, Fiona, who thinks Marguerite's trying to kill him, even though she's not. I didn't know the whole imaginary-murder-surveillance thing was part of the job description until I got here.

Millicent is an old family friend of the Smyths, a fellow former colonial, a couple of decades Walt's junior. She blends in a bit better than Alice and me. We're in our mid-twenties and come from Mackay, a town in regional Queensland. We've had to learn the ways of this world.

The Kenyan household staff are just getting on with things as best they can. There's Esther, the maid, James, the gardener, Khamisi, the cook, Peter, the driver and Patrick, the security guard. There's also David, who looks after the granny flat out the back, and Frank, the night shift guard – but we don't see as much of them. Most of them have been working for the Smyths for a very long time – though I don't think it's ever been quite the punish it is now that Walt's sick and surrounded by a team of meddling *mzungus*. Not that they ever complain.

Walt's house is in one of Nairobi's nicer suburbs. It's one of the area's older, more modest homes, surrounded by hedge-hemmed mansions boasting tennis courts and swimming pools. Someone very important has a place just down the road – in the evenings you can hear their helicopter coming in to land. When I jog past their high gates I'm watched by camera lenses and rifle sights, and barking dogs that scare me over to the other side of the road.

As for Walt himself – well, he's an anachronism. An old-school colonial from early establishment stock. His father was one of the first white men out here, one of those guys you imagine arriving with a sack of Union Jacks slung over his shoulder, marching along in a pith helmet from the coast to the Nile, laying claim to land with every few steps on behalf of the Empire and promising to 'civilise' the 'natives', as though there's anything 'civilised' about subjugating people in their own country. On Walt's mantelpiece is a photograph of Teddy Roosevelt when he came to Kenya on a hunting safari in 1909. Except it wasn't called Kenya back then; it was still the 'British East Africa Protectorate', one of the many pink patches on the map.

THE SITUATION

So you see, these people are a big deal around here. At least, they used to be. Modern-day Kenya barely knows or cares that they exist. Old colonials are literally a dying breed.

Walt has so much money it will never run out. It's partly inherited and partly self-made. He was a farmer, of tea and coffee and cattle. I'm told by the household staff that he worked hard to turn unproductive land around, and was nearly bankrupted doing so. Daniel arap Moi, Kenya's second president, admired Walt's farm so much he compulsorily acquired it from him in the 1980s. Walt was lucky to receive a good price. Independent Kenya, for the most part, made a point of being relatively gentle with its former colonial masters. Whether that was for better or worse depends on who you speak to.

Anyhow. Now Walter Smyth's in his eighties, and his mind is falling apart. He's got vascular dementia: a demolition team of tiny strokes and little wrecking balls of sticky protein are destroying his brain, leaving a rickety frame of consciousness behind. Walt grasps at the past and hallucinates much of the present. His body isn't quite as shaky as his mind, but he does have a pacemaker and a dodgy liver and kidneys that need keeping an eye on. Most days, Walt thinks he's in England, where he lived half his life. He thinks it's 1942 and he's collecting Second World War bomb shrapnel from the fields near his school. Or he thinks it's 1985 and his mother has just died and he needs to get his suit ready for her funeral in Dover. Some days he *does* think he's in Kenya – but that it's 1956, in the middle of the Kenya Emergency, and he's up on the tea farm, and needs to drive to the city for supplies, and might be attacked by Mau Mau terrorists on the road to Nairobi, and so needs to find his guns. He never thinks it's 2010 and he's already at his house in Nairobi, the one he's had for thirty years. Even that lion hanging on the dining-room wall doesn't jog his memory. You'd think it would – he's got scars all the way down his legs from its claws. Those yellow teeth were sunk deep into Walt's foot when he finally managed to unjam his rifle and send a bullet through the side of its skull. Now the lion watches him eat, its jaw frozen in a silent roar.

There's no good reason for my being here (though there are plenty of bad ones). I have no nursing experience. All I know about dementia is what I saw as my grandmother's mind crumbled to dust in the latter years of her life: the way she would conduct orchestras at the dinner table using chicken bones as batons, or cut pictures of puppies out of tissue boxes and glue them to the back of her couch because they were 'sweet'.

More than anything else, this whole story is the result of cosmic timing.

In September 2010, I'd just started working in television, back home in Australia. But *Hungry Beast* – the show I worked on – had finished and we weren't sure it would get another season. Having uprooted my life and moved to Sydney for the once-in-a-lifetime opportunity of working for Andrew Denton, I was in a weird place. In one sense, I felt I had the world at my feet. But I wasn't at home in Sydney. I was lonely, a bit lost, and in hindsight probably mildly depressed.

Just as I'd decided to move back to my family's farm in Mackay for a while, Alice called from Nairobi with a somewhat intriguing proposal. She'd been hired by the Smyths through a carers agency while she was living in London, and when they decided to return to their home in Nairobi, she agreed to go with them. But the job was too much for one person alone – they needed more help.

'They just want someone white, female, slim and switched on,' she said.

'Those first three seem a bit . . . icky, dude.'

'No, no, no – it's not like that. The thing is, we're *living* in the house with Walt. So even though he doesn't know what's going on, we need to *look* like people he might have had in his home throughout his life. That's why they can't hire black carers – he'd never stand for it. And he's terrible with fat people. Would comment on their weight all the time. Like, repeatedly, 'cos he forgets what he's just said. It'd be way too awkward. But with me, he just assumes I'm some friend of the family or whatever. You'd fit right in.'

'He sounds like a total arsehole.'

'Oh no, he's really quite sweet! Well, most of the time. I mean, obviously he's a bit racist. And sexist. But that's to be expected. He's a product of his time! And look, he can get a bit cranky and frustrated now and then, but it's easy enough to calm him down by flirting with him and making him laugh.'

'Mm,' I said, slightly revolted. 'And all we have to do is make sure he doesn't run off and get lost?'

'Yeah it's cruisey as! You pretty much just have to help him get dressed in the morning, sit and read the papers with him on the patio, and make sure he takes his pills. He can go to the toilet on his own and all that – it's just keeping him company, really. Giving him someone to talk to, ya know?'

'So, does this guy *know* he's got carers? I mean, how did he hire you in the first place?'

'His daughter, Fiona, is organising everything for him. She's the one who found me through the agency. Walt's wife – that's Marguerite – is still in England. She'll come over to join us in a few weeks.'

'Right . . . And how long are you planning to stay?'

'Just a few months, then I'll go on safari. Fiona wants me to help recruit other carers 'cos we really need to have someone on duty at all times and she's really keen on Aussies. Reckons we've got the "thick skins and nous" for the job.'

I can see how someone might draw that conclusion from Alice. She is one of the most robust people I know: a Muay Thai kickboxer with no time for nonsense and niceties, while remaining empathetic and perceptive. She's like a kindly nurse with a six-pack. But I did think it seemed odd to apply that singular character assessment to an entire nationality. And to bring someone to the other side of the world without vetting them first.

'Doesn't Fiona want to interview me or anything?' I asked.

'Nah, she trusts my judgement! So you'll do it? They'll fly you over and everything. It's a decent daily rate and you won't have any living expenses – all meals are provided, unless you want to go out of course. And you'll be able to go travelling around a bit too, in time off.'

Well. There were a few hurdles for my conscience to clear. Taking a job I'd been offered explicitly because of my skin colour? That job being to care for a man whose riches were partly colonial spoils?

I pondered, then I did what white people are so good at doing: I pushed all those niggling issues into the corner of my mind. I told myself it was hard to refuse a proposition this odd. But a few additional factors pushed me to accept it. Maybe, I told myself, I could get a bit of journalism work over there. Pitch some articles, bone up on my writing. Yes! It would actually *be* a career move. I also happened to have good friends – a couple – working for the Department of Foreign Affairs, who had just been posted to the Australian High Commission in Nairobi. Knowing I'd be able to tag along with them in my free time made the prospect of developing a social life and making good contacts in the country much more likely.

The third factor – the main thing, really, feeding my curiosity – was my own connection to Africa. My parents and most of their immediate families left Zimbabwe for Australia in the early eighties, but all our history – for several generations, on both sides of the family – is back there, somewhere, scattered across the continent along with a few remaining distant relatives.

I've always been fascinated and appalled by my family's stories of life in Africa. That exciting and romantic but fundamentally unjust colonial life was so many miles and years from my upbringing in sleepy little Mackay – and my progressive millennial persuasion – that it seemed as though it couldn't possibly be real, couldn't have ever been real. Still, I had an overwhelming longing to see it. The Finnish have a word for this strange emotion: *kaukokaipuu*. A feeling of homesickness for a place you've never been.

So. Although Kenya is a different country, thousands of kilometres from Zimbabwe, it is still Africa, and the time-warp colonial world of the Smyth household would be *something* akin to the one my parents had known. This was a pretty rare chance to see it up close. Probably as close as I would ever get.

I told Alice to book my flights, and I landed in Nairobi a week later.

The thing is, when my good friend Alice called to offer me a job on the other side of the world, she didn't give me the full story.

Not even close.

Big chunks were missing. Huge chunks. Crucial chunks, you might say. Chunks you can be sure a person would want to know about before signing up to a gig like this.

So when I first arrived at the Smyths' house in Nairobi, I was more than a little baffled when the first thing Fiona – who was visiting at the time – said to me wasn't 'Hello!', or 'How was your flight?', or 'You must be tired! What a long way you've come.' Nope. Nothing like that.

The very first thing Fiona said to me, in a low voice while looking at me sideways, was simply: 'You're brave.'

2
THE PLACE

I fly down the Queensland coastline to Brisbane, then west over the Northern Territory, then over Indonesia and Malaysia and the Bay of Bengal, and across the guts of India and the Arabian Sea.

From Dubai I fly south through a cloudless sky, over Saudi Arabia and Yemen. I look out the window as we pass over blue-violet water where the Gulf of Aden meets the Red Sea, and then over the seas of red sand in Djibouti and Ethiopia. The desert gives way to pocky scrub, then rocky mountains, then more of that dead dry desert, as I crosscheck the view from the window with a map showing the flight path on the screen in front of me, alternating between English and Arabic text every few seconds. The beautiful strange places below have ancient names like Berbera, Hargeisa, Dire Dawa, Awasa and Arba Minch. The only one I recognise is Addis Ababa.

Inside the cabin, the modern world closes in.

The young Kenyan sitting next to me, Leo, could be from anywhere. The Killers wail through the Sony headphones plugged into his iPhone. He's wearing a black Adidas flat cap with a logo embroidered in metallic rainbow thread, a pair of baggy blue denim jeans and a white singlet with a red flannelette shirt open over the top, sleeves rolled to the elbow. Leo and I chat about music as we wash down our lunch with Heineken. He tells me the band Gorillaz are rumoured to be playing a music festival the following month, at Lake Naivasha, only a couple of hours' drive from Nairobi. I should go! He has a friend organising the event who booked one of the DJs. Leo can't get there, though. He'll be on holiday 'either in Phuket or Cape Town'. He's still deciding.

God fills the row in front of us. Three African nuns in full kit: white coifs, black tunics, rosaries, the lot. *Where have they just been?* I wonder. Not so long ago it was one-way traffic, white missionaries bringing His Word to the newly encountered heathens of the Dark Continent. Have they been so successful that the message is now being returned to sender? I hope so. I really, really hope so. I love the thought of these sweet African ladies strolling through an Iowan cornfield, climbing up to knock on the farmer's air-conditioned tractor cab and introducing him to the Holy Spirit.

In the middle aisles, a group of Irish teenagers in orange shirts chat excitedly. Their chaperone tells me they've come for a two-week charity project, to dig wells for a local school. I don't tell him I've come to care for the wealthy. There doesn't seem a good way to put it.

On our descent to Nairobi, the ground turns much greener. It sprouts combed rows of emerald and clumps of wet jade, while fine networks of yellow-brown veins crawl across the swathes of pale green grass that stretch west towards the East African Rift, that aching great rent in the Earth's crust where humanity began. I catch my breath as we drop lower; the ground sparkles with tin roofs and windscreens, buildings and buses, and then suddenly it's a blur of bitumen black.

And still, I don't know what I'm in for.

Jomo Kenyatta International Airport is the hub of East Africa, and – whether by design or by accident – does a great job of preparing you for the place you're about to experience. In this case: a perplexing mix of the ancient and modern worlds, of dysfunction and achievement, of tribalism and globalism, of poverty and wealth, of racial tension and harmony, hope and frustration.

In posters along the corridor walls, telcos called Safaricom and Airtel and Orange implore me to buy one of their SIM cards. *'Jambo! Karibu to Kenya!'* they read in cartoon speech bubbles, next to photographs of jumping Masai men holding spears and smartphones, or Warhol'd portraits of pink giraffes poking out neon green tongues.

I pinball around the arrivals hall, looking for my luggage in a messy throng of people: there are Somali families, tall and slender, the women in jeans and colourful headscarves, the men in white tunics and loose pants, their children wearing sequinned denim jackets and getting tangled up in strangers' legs as they chase fluorescent rubber balls; Indian families, the men in jeans and polo shirts, the women in glittering saris, their children squabbling over huge cardboard boxes secured with flimsy dollar-shop string; all types of whites – European diplomats and American soldiers, NGO do-gooders and Bible-backed aid-bringers, and rosy-cheeked safari groups, dragging guitar cases and backpacks and camera bags across the tired concrete floor. Here and there, somehow seeming less welcome than anyone else, are small clusters of apprehensive Chinese men; they're labourers, I later learn, there to build Kenya's new highways. And, of course, among it all are Kenyans: high-flying businessmen and women, expats on home visits, ground staff and security guards, cleaners and taxi touts and money traders, all of them apparently well accustomed to the influx of visitors to their country and enduring it with weary grace.

Just as I'm about to give up on my bags, they show up, and a moment later so does Alice.

'Oi!' she hollers, grabbing me by the arm as I exit through a customs bay. 'Give that to Peter, he's our driver.'

A slight, round-faced man in a grimy Shell Oil baseball cap grins at me. He's otherwise impeccably dressed, in a Ralph Lauren shirt and pressed pants, with polished leather shoes. Aside from his worn-out teeth, he looks to be in his forties. *'Jambo!'* he says, shaking my hand, then, before I can stop him, he takes my suitcase out of my hands and races out of the terminal with it balanced on one shoulder. Alice and I chase after him to the car park where an old, olive-green Peugeot sits double-parked and gleaming in the sun.

It's in the middle back seat of that car, as we drive down Mombasa Road past the giraffes and zebras gathered at the edge of Nairobi National Park, that Alice fills me in on the missing chunks of the story she'd first told me.

I'm told that Marguerite is Walt's *second* wife (of forty years, mind), and *stepmother* to Fiona, and that there is no love lost between the two women.

'Marguerite's a real piece of work, you'll see,' Alice said. It's clear that we are to be on Fiona's side, even though she'll soon be returning to England, and we'll be here with Marguerite.

I learn that Walt's being here in Kenya at all is ... *contentious.* Two weeks earlier, he'd been in hospital in London, recovering from a heart attack. Fiona, shocked at how frail he had become, had then unilaterally decided that The Wife wasn't looking after him properly and that he'd fare much better back in his African home with the 'sun and slaves' to keep him warm and waited on.

'She actually says that?'

'Well, only to Walt,' says Alice. 'Just, like, to muck around with him. He thinks those sorts of jokes are funny.'

Walt and Marguerite had been living between the two continents for decades, returning to Kenya each year to escape the English winter. But after a lifetime enjoying the best of both worlds,

Fiona felt it was time her father went back to Africa for good. And so, without telling The Wife, she discharged him from hospital and put him on a plane to Nairobi – first class, oxygen canister in tow.

'The one time in my life I get to fly first class and it was a fucking nightmare!' says Alice. 'Walt fretted about having his passport and ticket the whole way. He didn't realise we were already on the plane. Wouldn't keep his mask on, kept trying to get up and walk around. A fucking nightmare. Seriously.'

I discover that while Alice and Walt and Fiona were being handed hot towels in the air over the Mediterranean Sea, The Wife, upon discovering her husband had vanished, was filing a kidnapping complaint with the London police.

'But she's decided to drop the charges, thank God. She's gonna join us here instead.'

And *then* I'm told that Fiona suspects The Wife has been 'doping Walt up' on antidepressants and sedatives, in an attempt to make him easier for her to manage.

'And you're telling me all this *now*?' I say to Alice.

'Yeah, well . . .' she says with a guilty grin, 'I didn't want to put you off coming.'

'Jesus,' I say, reeling. I'm not sure whether to be pissed off or impressed.

As we approach the city, the national park falls away and buildings and people creep in. Out the window is a whirring tableau of yellow jerry cans and squashed spinach leaves and plastic crates strapped to the backs of rusting bicycles with bungee cords that look like they'll give out at any second. Sinewed men strain to pull a car-tyre rickshaw through an intersection, their necks cushioned by grey-stained rags wrapped around its yoke; street hawkers leap out of their way at the last possible moment. Sagging shade-cloth roofs hang over market stalls, sheltering towers of tomatoes and piles of limes from the sting of the sun; bright wraps of fabric swaddle the bodies of busy women, all buying and selling, counting cash, swatting vervet monkeys away with long sticks. And right next to all that colour and movement is an OiLibya petrol station, where a fat man in a grey suit and sunglasses climbs out of a silver Mercedes.

We come to a stop. A truck full of nervous goats is about to tip over – it has somehow backed into a power pole and is stuck with one back wheel spinning across the top of a retaining wall and the other wedged into the gutter. The front axle groans under the weight and the goats bleat over it. I'd pay good money to see how they manage to get out of this mess, but the driver hangs out of his window and waves us around impatiently.

Peter grins into the rear-view mirror, acknowledging my disappointment. 'Don't worry, you'll see something like that every day,' he assures me. 'Welcome to Nairobi traffic!'

What strikes me most about the city isn't those developing-world quirks, but the surprising familiarity of everything else. Sofa-filled furniture showrooms and billboards advertising insurance, 'designer living' apartments for sale overlooking newly landscaped gardens. Dettol and Nivea and Samsung logos – Kenya is full of all the same overhyped consumerist-capitalist-corporatist promises as home, only here the faces beaming with fraudulent salesman grins are brown, instead of peach-yoghurt-white.

As we crawl along the Uhuru Highway I look up at a twenty-foot Johnnie Walker strutting along the side of a skyscraper. 'Keep Walking' the smartarse tells us, as we're overtaken by streams of pedestrians on the side of the road who easily outpace the bumper-to-bumper traffic.

This feels like the real Nairobi, the beating heart of twenty-first century Kenya, where Google and IBM and the United Nations have their African headquarters. But we're going back in time, to a much quieter part of town where people live in beautiful old houses on huge tree-filled plots. A place where residents 'take tea' on the verandah and play tennis behind eight-foot-high brick walls topped with jagged shards of glass, and go to bed every night knowing that even the barbed wire and electrified loops of razor ribbon on their perimeter won't keep the most determined or desperate away.

We pull up at an iron gate on a gravel driveway and Peter taps the horn. For a moment, nothing happens. My heart skips a beat.

This, my parents had warned me, is where you are most likely to be car-jacked or kidnapped or killed in Africa. 'Waiting at a bloody gate,' Dad had muttered, during the personal safety lecture he'd given me on the way to Mackay Airport. My parents have quite a roster of murdered friends, and a good many of them breathed their last in the seat of an idling vehicle. 'Listen, if you pull up at a gate and there's any delay, especially at night, you don't get out of the car,' Dad said. 'You put your foot down and get the hell out of there.'

I'm just about to suggest this course of action when a lopsided giant of a man lumbers over in a navy-blue trench coat, heavy black boots, and an empty pistol holster. He looks to be about sixty. He has the friendliest face I've ever seen.

'This is Patrick – the *askari*,' Alice says, 'the security guard.' I add *askari* to my mental list of Swahili words, using the mnemonic 'a-scary security guard': how can this man possibly be an effective deterrent? He looks like he's about to hand out ice creams.

It takes Patrick a long, fumbling moment to find the right key to the padlock. He waves apologetically as the keys elude his fingers. Finally, having hooked the right one and cleared the way for our passage, he stands to attention and salutes as we drive past, a giddy grin spanning his face when we pull up beside him. Alice introduces me and lets him know I'm an approved visitor.

He takes my hand through the wound-down window in both of his and shakes it like a snow globe. '*Jambo*, Madam!' he says, nodding so furiously I worry he'll hurt his neck. '*Jambo, jambo! Karibu!*'

'*Jambo!*' I say, wanting to hug him in return, and wondering how on earth he ended up with this job.

'And what's he saying? "Carry-boo?"' I ask Alice and Peter as we drive on towards the house.

'Yeah, *karibu*,' Alice says.

'It means "welcome"!' Peter adds, turning around to repeat it. '*Karibu* to Kenya.'

Huge bougainvillea line the driveway, erupting in fountains of fuchsia. Smooth green terraced lawns step behind them, rainbow-striped with flower beds. Springing out of the red earth are purple agapanthus, yellow daylilies, orange spikes of strelitzia, and white daisies with pink-tipped petals. Climbing night jasmine and shocks of bamboo stretch along the back fence; palm trees off-set acacias and, everywhere I turn, roses of every colour.

The house looks like an English country manor, what with its peaking, shingled roof, softly smoking chimney, and walls of grey-brown stonework that crawl with ivy. Neat green hedges frame white lattice casement windows. Decorative metalwork gates enclose a small portico at the steps up to the front door, and beside them is the apparently recent addition of a gently sloping access ramp. I half expect a red-fezzed butler to appear and offer us tall glasses of iced tea, but no one is there to greet us.

Before I can step inside, Alice sends me around the side to find Fiona and Walt on their afternoon stroll and let them know I've arrived. Fiona is guiding Walt along by the elbow when I walk over to say hello.

That's when I'm met with 'You're brave.'

I don't quite know how to answer this, which isn't a problem — Fiona doesn't expect a response.

She puts a finger to her lips and nods at the old man bent double beside her; he's squinting at the inscription on the cement lid to a septic system embedded in the lawn. Walt hasn't noticed me yet, and it seems his daughter wants to keep it that way. She shoos me away, whispering, 'Ask Alice to show you your room. The staff will bring your bags in and unpack for you.'

So I do what I'm told and go quietly inside, following Alice across polished floorboards through rooms full of ivory lampstands and Persian rugs, down a carpeted hallway to the twin bedroom we're to share until Fiona returns to England, and where, sure enough, a maid — in a pink gingham uniform — is unpacking my suitcase.

'This is Esther,' Alice says, as the maid puts a stack of my underwear into a drawer in the dresser. She's a slender woman, she doesn't look to be much older than us — maybe in her thirties. Her hair is pulled back in a tidy bun, and her skin glows with a copper sheen. 'Esther, this is Kirsten.'

'Hello, Miss Kirsten,' Esther says, giggling shyly, eyes downcast.

I look at the now neatly folded piles of clothes she has laid on the end of the bed, and cringe. My bag was not 'packed' so much as aggressively stuffed — I wasn't expecting anyone else to have to deal with it.

'Oh — it's okay — I can do that!' I say. Esther looks at Alice for guidance, as though she's not sure it really *is* okay to let me do it for myself, or maybe she's worried I don't want her touching my things? It's the first of many small moments of cultural confusion.

'Yeah, you really don't need to do this sort of thing for us,' Alice says, picking up one of the piles from the bed to prove we're capable of moving clothes around ourselves.

'Okay then, okay,' says Esther, smiling. I don't think she's offended.

'But thank you very much!' I add, as she leaves the room.

I look at Alice. We were meant to *be* 'the help', not *have* it. Although I suppose this is the taste of colonial Africa I asked for. *I've never felt more white in my life.*

'Yeah, it's pretty weird,' Alice says. 'But it's how things are here. You just have to tell them if you don't want them to do all the things they normally would.'

Esther, Alice explains, is the only woman on staff because Marguerite believes having too many women is 'asking for trouble', that they 'compete for attention from all the chaps'.

'I'm pretty sure that's bullshit,' Alice says, 'but I'm not sure Esther is thrilled we're all here. It's made a lot more work for her! Come on – I'll introduce you to the rest of the staff.'

We find Patrick walking around the bottom of the garden with two dogs, all of them looking up at the tree canopy.

'Are you taking care of the monkeys again, Patrick?' Alice asks, startling him.

'Oh yes, madam, yes, yes,' he says, rushing over to greet us, again with that affable smile. I get the sense the man is physically incapable of frowning.

He's got a handful of pebbles, and a slingshot made of wonky strips of old tyre-tube rubber wrapped around a forked piece of wood.

'The monkeys come through here every afternoon,' Alice explains. 'They stir the dogs right up. Patrick's our first line of defence. You should see how good he is with that thing!'

Patrick laughs. 'They are very naughty monkeys!' he says.

One of the dogs – a brown bitzer – comes over to lick my hand.

'This is "Shujaa",' Patrick says, and then pointing at the golden retriever scratching at the base of a tree, 'and that is "Jua".'

'They're lovely,' Alice says, 'but Jua can be a little bit confusing for Walt. He's got a golden retriever in England too. So . . . it's not very helpful when we're trying to make him understand he's in Kenya.'

The sound of tumbling rocks distracts us. We turn to see a short, stocky man tipping out a wheelbarrow full of stones next to a small sandpit.

'Oh – that's James. Let's go say hi,' Alice says. 'James is Walt's favourite,' she whispers, as we walk towards him. 'He's been with the family for years, and his father was their gardener before him.'

'Hello, Alice!' James says. 'How are you today?'

'Very good, thank you, James! This is Kirsten – my friend from Australia.'

'Hi James, nice to meet you,' I say, shaking his hand.

'*Jambo*, Kirsten,' he says, smiling. '*Karibu*.'

'She's here to help us with the *mzee* too,' Alice says.

'*Ma-zay?*' I ask.

'It means like, "old man", right, James?' Alice says.

'Yes,' James says. 'It is to be respectful to say *mzee*.'

'So it's different to *bwana* then?' I ask.

'Mmm, yes,' James says, head tilted, pondering how to explain his language to us. 'A *bwana* is a boss. But a *mzee* is any older person.'

'Right. So Walt is a *bwana* and a *mzee* then?'

'Yes,' James laughs. 'He is both.'

'*Mzee* when he's being nice, *bwana* when he's being bossy,' Alice says.

James laughs again. 'Yes. That is okay.'

I suddenly realise how dark it's getting, how tired I am. I try to stifle a yawn.

'You must be buggered,' says Alice. 'Come on, let's go inside. It'll be time to get ready for dinner soon.'

But I just cannot stay awake. I don't make it to dinner.

I walk back down the hallway to the room I'm sharing with Alice, climb into the bed closest to the window, pull a mint green duvet up to my chin, and fade to black.

It's three in the morning when I wake up in a pinched-sphincter panic.

There's a silhouette in the bedroom doorway. It's a man. He's holding a gun and saying he's going to blow my bloody head off.

My mind scrambles through the sleep fog for a foothold and then it comes to me – Kenya. I'm in Kenya. With Alice. And the crazy old man. And this is a home invasion.

Terror has me pinned flat to the bed, clammy and mute, while my insides scream and my heart thumps so hard my ribs hurt.

Alice jumps up from her bed and lunges at the intruder.

I scream. Surely it's all over. Everything I've ever known about to be exploded out of my skull in fragments of brain and blood and bone. I spend the split second before my death thinking about how mad my parents will be – about how the whole reason they left Africa was to make sure this sort of shit didn't happen to their kids.

But that brief eternity passes, and I realise there's been some kind of mistake: my head is still intact, my heart is still beating.

Alice slaps the wall and the light comes on.

The man in the doorway is Walt. He's wearing a striped tie over flannelette pyjamas and pointing a vacuum cleaner at us.

I nearly choke when I remember to start breathing again.

He blinks into the light, looking back and forth between Alice and me. Then he pulls his wallet out of his pocket, holding it open to show us it's empty.

'Where's my fucking money?' he snarls. 'And who the hell are *you*? What are you doing in *my house!*?'

I hear a door fling open, somewhere down the hallway, and footsteps approaching. Walt turns to aim his plastic pipe at them.

'Oh, Dad,' Fiona says, in a playful tone, 'you silly old bugger! What are you doing up at this ungodly hour?'

He looks at her as though it should be obvious. 'I'm blasting these thieving scoundrels away!'

'Here, give me that.' She prises the vacuum free of his clutches. 'After all, cleaning is *women's work*, isn't it?'

The rage falls away from his face and his empty wallet falls to the floor. The murderous bastard is laughing. 'Christ, yes! I wouldn't be caught dead standing on *your* toes in that department,' he teases, wagging his finger in his daughter's face as she walks him back to his room.

I smell my own acrid death-sweat, as Alice rolls back into bed. 'That was lucky,' she says, 'we only put the guns into storage last week.'

3
THE ROUTINE

When I next wake, it's dawn. Somewhere nearby, a muezzin wails into a megaphone, waking the birds and the faithful. I draw the curtains and lie back in bed, watching the sky come to life and everything between me and it slowly take shape through the window. A honeyed smoke tinges the air, its scent lighting up a memory of a family trip to Zimbabwe in 1995 when I was eleven years old. My parents wanted me and my two younger sisters to see where they were from. Or as they put it: 'So that you brats know how bloody lucky you are!' But their plan backfired. The excitement of a place teeming with monkeys and elephants and lions led us to conclude we'd have been much luckier growing up there than in boring Mackay, where all there was to see was sugar cane and dumped shopping trolleys.

Mum has always said that sweet smoke is the smell of Africa for her, and that the sound is the cry of a fish eagle. And here I am, thirty years after they left the continent, breathing that same hazy air. Only *my* Africa sound will be the incessant beeping of a pager.

It first starts going off at about half-past six.

'Jesus Christ, what is that noise?' I ask.

Alice rolls over and hands me a pager. 'It's connected to a pressure sensor under Walt's mattress that detects when he gets out of bed,' she says, reaching to grab a baby monitor from the table between our beds. 'Although, as you saw last night, it's not *entirely* reliable.' She flicks on the monitor screen: it shows a grainy image of Walt standing beside his bed, one hand resting impatiently on his crotch. She watches him for a moment. 'It's okay, he's just going for a piss,' she says, settling back onto her pillows.

There are, in fact, *two* cameras connected to the baby monitor, operating on separate channels. One is in Walt's bedroom, hidden beside a faded photo frame on the top of his dresser; it captures most of his bedroom, from the hallway to the ensuite, but leaves a blind spot in the far corner. The other camera is on a windowsill in the bathroom; it films the shower and the toilet. The monitor also transmits sound, and automatically switches to night vision when the lights go out. Whoever is on duty has to carry the pager and baby monitor with them at all times, switching between the two channels as Walt's pixelated spectre floats from one side of the little screen to the other – our own geriatric version of *The Truman Show*.

I watch as he flushes the toilet and climbs back into bed.

'He always does this,' Alice tells me. 'He'll usually go back to sleep for a bit. But if he does try to get *up*-up before seven, go into his room and convince him to have more of a "zizz". You can usually get him to lie down again for a while if you say, "Everyone's having a sleep-in after the big party we had last night." That helps to put him in a good mood, too. But once he's decided he's getting up, there's no turning him around. You'll have to go in there to help get him ready for the day.'

Half an hour later, the pager starts beeping again. On the monitor I see that Walt has swung his legs out from under the blankets and is shuffling his feet into a pair of slippers. He rubs his face with both hands, then runs them over the back of his head and looks around the room. A man in his own home, but totally lost. I feel a sudden pang of pity for him, and resentment at the injustice of old age.

'Yeah, he's *up*-up now,' Alice says, heaving herself out of bed. 'You can tell when he starts looking around the place like that, trying to work out where he is.'

And so begins my induction into the 'cruisey' job of looking after Walter Smyth.

While Alice guides Walt through his morning routine, I hang back to watch with Fiona so that she can 'explain things in a bit more detail'. I soon find myself wondering if I should take notes.

'You must place Dad's razor and soap brush on the ledge above the basin there – just to the right of the soap. Only turn the hot tap thirty degrees to the left – that will get it to just the right temperature. We don't want him scalding his hands when he takes the plug out. And don't forget to put his comb out – he's very fussy about making his hair neat in the morning.'

Fiona talks in that low, intense voice she'd first greeted me with, all the while watching her father, seemingly poised to intervene should she need to at any moment. She's a tall, athletic woman, with a practical haircut and practical clothes, whose default expression is like that of a tennis player waiting to receive a serve. She's spent the last few weeks completely overhauling the house to better suit Walt's needs – the access ramp I'd noticed out the front was thanks to her. The ensuite itself had just been remodelled and fitted out with handrails, the toilet replaced with a raised seat and arm rests, and the door widened to make room for a commode or wheelchair, if and when the time should come. She strikes me as the kind of person you'd be thankful for in an emergency – but also as the kind of person who makes everything *feel* like an emergency.

'Now. When you lay his clothes out for the day, put them here on the end of the bed – so they're the first thing he sees when he turns around after shaving. Lay them out in reverse order of how he needs to put them on.' She places his cashmere pullover, his trousers, then his shirt, singlet, underpants and socks on the bed. 'Roll his belt up beside them – buckle on the outside – and tuck a clean hanky into his pocket. Everything's here in this dresser, see? You'll have to help him keep his balance while he steps into his pants. And do his buttons up if they're too tight and fiddly – his hands can get a little stiff. Pyjamas should go into the wash every second day, please. Hang his dressing-gown here on the back of the door.'

Up close like this, without the dehumanising fuzz of a monitor screen masking the detail of his ageing skin and thinning hair and cloudy eyes, I see how vulnerable poor Walt is. He doesn't even seem to notice we're there, live-commentating the minutiae of his life. He looks right through me, and it's only when Fiona directly addresses him that he responds.

I'm reminded of my own grandmother when her dementia was starting to take hold – of all the little things we knew to do to help her life run smoothly when her mind was coming to a spluttering halt. My mother would go around to visit her at her retirement village flat at least every second day. Mum stuck a whiteboard next to the phone, with all the important names and numbers on it, and wrote out Granny's schedule for the week.

On Fridays we'd pick Granny up and bring her out to stay with us on the farm for the weekend. When we took her back on Sunday nights, we'd make sure she had fresh milk, take the rotting soup bones out of the fridge, and run the dirty clothes she'd hung back in her wardrobe through the washing machine. But no one was there with her every second of every minute of every hour of every day, to make sure she didn't stash Scotch Finger biscuits under her pillows, or to remove the family of mice nesting in her underwear drawer.

Eventually, we moved her to a high-care nursing home. It was only a matter of months before we had to move her again, to the hospital ward where she lay for three weeks, refusing food, having fluids administered intravenously, her stomach blown up like a basketball against her emaciated frame as her organs shut down and her bladder closed up, until finally, with her face twisted into a grimace and my mother holding her hand, she died.

It still makes me furious. That a woman who was so against any creature suffering she refused to kill even spiders – would gently remove such unwelcome intruders by hand and release them into the garden while the rest of us screamed profanities – should be made to die that way. My grandmother was a lifelong member of the RSPCA. She'd spent her life hand-rearing the orphaned wildlife her game ranger husband brought home from the bush. Had she seen an animal forced to endure the sort of physical pain she had to, she'd have reported animal cruelty. It makes me wild with rage that we couldn't do more to help her in her final years, and her final moment.

I find myself wondering how much more we *would* have done if we had the kind of money the Smyths have. If we'd have modified her house and moved in round-the-clock carers trained to cater to her every idiosyncrasy and rigged up a surveillance system to keep her monitored. Maybe we would have. Maybe Fiona isn't being over the top at all – maybe Walter Smyth's golden years in Nairobi is the ultimate case study in how to help someone die when money's not an issue. Playing out in a place where for most people it very much is.

By seven-thirty that morning we're sitting at a breakfast table festooned with tropical abundance. Honestly, it's an orgy of fruit, bordering on obscene. Clutches of lady finger bananas fan the ends of a platter filled with diced mango cheeks and thick slivers of pawpaw, topped with wedges of lime and halved granadillas and a scattering of strawberries. A toaster on the sideboard has a springy fresh loaf of brown bread sliced beside it, crumbs tumbling over the long wooden slab. Toasted muesli and natural yoghurt and honey sit in their store-bought containers, the garish branding out of place against the rawness of the surrounding spread. There is a white linen tablecloth, silver cutlery, glasses that wait for the chilled orange juice in a carafe beading with condensation, and teacups for the porcelain milk jug that is draped with a square of white gauze, weighed down at the edges with colourful beads.

For eggs or more coffee, we're simply to ring a little brass bell and Esther will come through from the kitchen in the next room to take the order. (After a few days, I hide that bell. I just can't bear it.)

Walt sits at the head of his table, with Fiona to one side of him, Alice to the other, and Millicent and I across from each other at the end. He looks around as he unrolls his napkin, trying to work out who all these people are, and where in the world he is. I'm feeling much the same way.

Millicent intrigues me. She's the daughter of a long-time friend of the Smyth family, and lives with her elderly mother elsewhere in Nairobi. It's just that bit too far to travel every day, so she stays in the house with us when she's on the morning or night shift, sleeping in the sunroom. Millicent evidently has nowhere near the Smyths' kind of money. She makes her living doing this sort of thing all over the world. 'Only Commonwealth countries, though,' she says sagely, as though I should know what that means. She wears huge thick glasses with tinted lenses and rusting gold frames, and has tawny-grey hair that reaches nearly to her waist but is always pinned up in a topknot. I imagine that a street blog would deem her style – a reliable combination of ankle-length skirts and sturdy linen blouses in clashing palettes and patterns – 'rustic Mormon chic'. Millicent says 'bless' and 'dear' a lot. She must be about sixty-something? It's hard to say: the whites here have all had so much sun damage.

Fiona's running commentary continues. 'Dad's not to have any caffeine, so Esther will prepare a separate pot of decaf coffee for him – make sure you don't get it mixed up at the table with yours. In fact, I think I'd rather you girls didn't even have a pot of the regular stuff in here. Make your own in the kitchen out of sight if you absolutely must have it. Safer that way. And watch how much sugar he tries to put into his cup. We're trying to cut down. Aren't we, Dad?'

'Hmmm?' Walt isn't paying attention. He's fiddling with his watch. It must be a strange thing to know the hour of the day but not the decade you're in.

'He forgets he's done it. I've seen him put five spoons in before. *Five!* Can you imagine? He'll end up with diabetes. We *really* don't want that. Best you put the sugar in for him so that you can keep it under control. Just *one* teaspoon of the stevia blend, please. Keep it in the sugar bowl so that he doesn't realise.'

Alice loads up a plate of food for Walt, and Fiona continues. 'He'll probably just have a piece of pawpaw and a banana and a slice of toast with marmalade for breakfast. Encourage the banana – the potassium is good for him. Watch him with the sugar, though! He'll want to sprinkle it all over his pawpaw. You mustn't let him – I can't stress enough how much we don't want him to get diabetes. He can have as many refills of coffee as he likes. Just remember to watch the sugar. And best to pour it for him – his wrists are a little weak.'

Walt protests as Alice takes the pot out of his hands. I wonder whether not letting him do anything for himself is a good strategy.

'Now. Pills. He has a good dozen or so to take each day. Six in the morning, then another lot with lunch and again at dinner. I'll go through them with you later. Sometimes he'll take them happily enough, but I'm sorry to say that often enough he won't. You're going to need to get creative.'

Walt takes a mouthful of pawpaw, and we hear what sounds like sand being ground between teeth.

'Bugger.' Fiona spots a stray sugar bowl and moves it out of his reach. 'Anyway – pills. Put them next to his coffee at the beginning of breakfast on this sweet little hippo dish, and don't make a big deal about it. It helps if you can take your own in front of him – that way he thinks we're all in this together.' It doesn't matter that I don't have any pills of my own to take: there are a whole stack of multivitamins in the pantry I can use as props. 'They won't do you any harm,' Fiona assures me. '"Doctor's orders!" is a good catchphrase for this one, I've found. But look, if he flat-out refuses, don't push it and get him all wound up. He's a stubborn old coot. Just put them aside and try again later, when he's forgotten about it.'

Breakfast is followed by time sitting on the patio, while Fiona explains that Walt's teeth should be brushed both before and after breakfast. 'I don't want them going rotten. It helps if you go in and brush yours with him. Keep a second toothbrush in his bathroom, if that's easier. Once that's done you can sit out here in the morning sun. No! Not on that chair – that's Dad's. I've put an extra pillow under the base so that he doesn't have to bend his knees so far to get in and out of it, see? Let's pull it out a bit so that the sun's on his back. Yes, that's how he likes it. Just there.'

Three newspapers are laid out neatly on the table. Walt scowls at the front pages, deciding which one to pick up first. The Kenyan papers – the *Daily Nation* and the *Standard* – are both all about the country's recent constitutional referendum. They have photographs of local politicians and advertisements for money transfer companies. The *Telegraph* – flown in from the UK so that Walt can read about the future a day late – has a picture of Naomi Campbell testifying at former Liberian President Charles Taylor's war crimes trial at The Hague. The story tells of how after a fancy dinner she'd attended with him years earlier, two men had come to her hotel room in the middle of the night and presented her with 'a pouch', simply described as 'a gift for you'. It was only the next morning, she says, that she opened the pouch to find a few 'dirty-looking stones', and assumed they'd been sent by the warlord.

There's no news from Britain about Kenya's recent election. Just Africa's blood diamonds and bloody dictators.

'Oh, he does *loooove* sitting here in the morning, with all the birds,' Fiona whispers, tearing up while she gazes at her father.

Esther appears, carrying the pawpaw and mango skins left from breakfast.

'Morning, Esther,' says Fiona, jumping up to help her spread the fruit along the edge of the patio wall and scatter some birdseed around. '*Habari?*'

'*Mzuri sana*, Madam. Good morning, *bwana*,' Esther replies.

'Morning,' says Walt, not looking up from his newspaper.

And then the birds arrive.

They stream in along gold-flecked sunbeams, no less. Noisy yellow weavers, with red eyes and dark heads and wings splashed with black lacquer. Goofy grey mousebirds with fluffy spiked crests and pale cheeks, tripping mid-air over the long tail feathers that drag behind them. Sparrows and pied wagtails and even the occasional little bee-eater; he looks like a feathered superhero, with his golden chest and a wedge of bright yellow tucked under his throat, a green cloak on his back and stripes of aquamarine over the black bandana that covers his eyes. Then the tiny little firefinches, my favourites, always the shyest and last to arrive; they're bright red and put together with dainty curves and cusps, like a collection of Scandinavian ornaments. We all sit there, quietly watching, as the birds chirp and chirrup, tweet and trill, and are briefly spooked when a family of squirrels scamper in along the railing.

Walt scolds the weavers as they bully the finches off the seed. 'Cut it out, you nasty buggers!' he says, shooing them with his hanky. He watches the mousebirds balance on the edge of the fruit skins to tear the last bits of flesh from them, and chortles when one flips a skin over entirely, briefly trapping itself underneath in a flapping panic. 'Oh, you bloody fool!' he laughs, delighted by such idiocy. (I'll soon learn that on a good day, Walt can sit for an hour and a half watching the birds. It's the happiest he ever seems. Bird Time is the highlight of Walt's days. But Bird Time never lasts.)

All those cups of decaf coffee in Walt's gut eventually filter through to his bladder, and he stirs in his chair. He folds his newspaper over, stands up and startles at the sight of me, before tapping the side of his nose and saying with feigned familiarity, 'Now, my dear, if you'll excuse me a moment, I think I might just go around the corner.' He shuffles into the house.

Fiona takes the opportunity to warn me about Marguerite, The Wife. 'I want us to get everything running smoothly before she arrives next week. All of this will become more complicated once *she's* here.'

'How so?' I ask.

'She'll interfere and nag and do everything she can to stir him up,' Fiona says. 'She's awful. Dad hates her. Always has.'

'Oh ... so ... why did he marry her in the first place?' I ask. 'And why hasn't he divorced her?' Forty years is a long time to stay with someone you can't stand.

'She bullied him into it. It's what she does. He's tried to leave her, several times. She's got him completely under her thumb. You'll see.' Fiona checks the monitor: Walt is still at the toilet. 'I just — I want Dad to live the rest of his days in comfort. And with the right care, I think he's got a great many more days left. Marguerite doesn't look after him properly — he's a drain on her lifestyle. We just need to stay on top of his medications and diet and he'll be well enough to enjoy life, here in Kenya. This is his home. But she hates it here — much prefers to be socialising back in England.'

'So why is she coming back then?'

'Oh, she can't have it *look* like she doesn't love her husband. And she doesn't want to risk her right to his money. Honestly, if he dropped dead tomorrow I think she'd be delighted. That's why she's trying to push him along.'

'Push him along?' I ask, wondering how literally she means it, but we're interrupted before I can find out.

Walt returns from his trip around the corner with his wallet and a frown. It's a dummy wallet, full of old library cards and a few hundred Kenyan shillings cash, for when he needs to see that he has means. But it isn't always enough to placate him. He pulls the notes out, rubs them between his fingers.

'What's the matter, Dad? Has that horrid wife of yours been raiding the coffers again?'

'What?' Walt looks up, startled, as though surprised to hear another voice.

'Has Marguerite been shopping again?'

'Marguerite?'

'Yes, Dad. *Marguerite.* Your *wife.* You know.' Fiona leans over to whisper in her father's ear. '*The Serpent.*'

Fiona loops her arm through his and helps him back into his chair. He rubs his hands over his face and looks up to the sky as though searching for divine assistance, the same way he did after he first woke up this morning.

'Oh, her,' he says. 'Yes. Well. It would appear so.' He pats the wallet into his pocket.

But I'm not sure if Walt knows who 'The Serpent' is at all.

Fiona shows me how to steer Walt on walks around the garden, 'never too far away – you need to be able to catch him if he loses his balance', how to help him in and out of chairs, and tells me to make sure I watch him on the baby monitor every time he goes to the toilet for a shit. 'It's one of the most common places for people in his condition to have a heart attack,' Fiona explains. 'That's why we don't want him getting constipated. You've got to make sure he's getting enough fibre. Watch him carefully when he goes to the loo. If it looks like he's straining, you might need to introduce some Metamucil to his diet.'

Apart from his regular medical appointments (cardiologist, dentist, podiatrist) there aren't too many places we can take Walt for outings: the country club, the golf club, or the homes of a few pre-approved friends. (Anyone with too many stairs or small dogs is out. 'Tripping hazards,' Fiona tells me. 'Just not worth the risk.') But whatever we do with him, he is to be home and showered by six each evening. We're to help him out of his clothes and turn the taps on for him so that he doesn't burn himself, to pass him the soap and a washcloth. Every three days, at least, we're supposed to wash his hair.

'He absolutely *hates* washing his hair, but if you tell him he looks like "a greasy *dago*" you can usually convince him to do it,' Fiona says one evening, showing me how she squeezes shampoo onto the top of Walt's head as he bends down to scrub his knees.

'Sorry, what's a "*dago*"?' I ask.

'A wog!' Walt replies, squeezing his eyes shut to avoid the suds.

'Yes, Dad, an *Italian gentleman*.'

'A *dago*. Or *Di-ego* if you're being polite.' Walt is delighted to be able to fill me in on the etymology of his favourite slur. And I have to admit, Fiona's tactic has worked: it distracted him long enough for her to work up a lather in his hair.

'You must be ready and waiting with a towel – we don't want him walking across the wet tiles to find one himself. And have another spread over a plastic chair for him to sit on as we help him dry off. Check him over for any bumps and bruises, and to see that his moles haven't got nasty. There's a big one on his back here, and a few down his arms. Clip his nails if they need doing. Not too short — squared and filed at the edges please, as we don't want him getting an ingrown toenail.' Walt's skin is old and delicate, dry and prone to eczema. He needs two types of cream rubbed into his legs and arms each evening: three big pumps of sorbolene and one of an emollient for each limb, and the leftovers dabbed onto the scaly patches around his hairline. For any sores or spots, there's a small tube of medicated ointment.

Walt is to be helped into his pyjamas *left arm first*. He's less flexible on that side since getting the pacemaker.

Then we're to help him into his bed socks, slippers and silk robe, and take him through to the living room, where Esther will have the fire roaring and the day's newspapers laid out (again) and a small bowl of Indian crackers on the table beside his armchair. He has a 'G&T' which is actually just a tall glass of tonic and fresh-squeezed limes, with a little gin wiped around the rim to give him a whiff of booze with each sip. 'Only three ice cubes, please. *Three*. Any more and he'll scoop them out of the glass and throw them into the fire.'

Then, for the half-hour or so until we're called for supper, we can 'listen to the wireless'. Fiona's managed to find a modern stereo designed to look like a vintage radio. There are three choices of soundtrack: Walt's two favourite CDs — *Dreams of Ireland* or *Classic Operas* — or the radio's BBC Africa News Hour.

News hour is unfailingly dire. But let me tell you now: it doesn't take long for stories about mass rape in the Congo and violence in Sudan to become more tolerable than hearing 'Danny Boy' for the fifteenth time.

4
ALICE

Here's the thing I've come to realise about my friend Alice: she's odd.

I mean, we all are, in our own special way. But Alice's way of being odd is to not seem to notice how odd everyone else is. The woman is utterly unfazed by the sheer insanity of other people. Me? I walk around every day marvelling at how nuts everyone else on the planet is and wondering why they're not all normal like me. But Alice? She knows that everyone is nuts – she just accepts it as part of the physical reality of the universe. Doesn't even see fit to pass comment, unless probed. Then she'll think about it for a moment, concede you might have a point, perhaps even add a few observations of her own in support of your theory, and just get on with her day. She did spend several months training with Thai monks at a Muay Thai school once; maybe that's where she learned how to be so zen.

Look, it's an admirable quality. But frankly, here and now, I feel like she's gaslighting me.

One night, in our room after dinner, I find Millicent has left a missionary magazine on the end of my bed, open at a page about discovering Jesus 'where you least expect him'.

I say to Alice, 'Ah . . . so . . . what is the deal with these people?'

And Alice, shadow boxing in the corner of the room, abs rippling like the back of an egg carton, just says, 'What do you mean?'

'Are you serious?' I say. She's serious.

I check the door is shut. There's no lock, so I prop up a chair against it. Fiona's in the next room putting Walt to bed, and it's already clear she's not much of a knocker.

'Let me get this straight,' I say. 'We're here not just to "look after" a nutty old man who was kidnapped from England by his daughter, but to protect him from his own wife, and to *spy* on said wife and report back to the daughter on her every move, *and* the wife doesn't actually know we've been hired, are living in her house, and that she's going to have to pay us.'

'Well, she knows about me,' Alice says, starting a round of sit-ups. 'But yeah . . . you're going to be a surprise.'

'What if she kicks us out?'

'She won't!'

'Fiona reckons she's trying to do away with Walt. What if she tries to "do away" with us?'

'Oh, she is not. Fiona's just exaggerating,' says Alice.

'And yet she hired me without even interviewing me. I could be anyone!'

'I told you! She trusts my judgement!'

'You can see what I'm saying though, right? This is bananas. These people are bananas.'

'Yeah,' Alice says, stopping mid-crunch to think about it. 'But you know, they're really rich.' She shrugs. 'Money makes people weird.'

'So you admit it! They're weird!'

'Yeah, but it's not weird that they're weird.'

'Fuck me. You've got a bad case of Stockholm syndrome. What did they do to you in England?'

Alice is getting exasperated with me. 'You don't understand. The doctors had said he had to come here. He wasn't in good shape – he wouldn't have survived the winter. Marguerite wasn't looking after him properly. He was so frail. Like, he was in a wheelchair and on an oxygen tank and everything. You don't realise how much better he is now than he was even a month ago. Trust me. All this would make more sense if you could have seen how he was back in England.'

Later that night, just after we've turned the lights off, I remember the cherry on top.

'Oh, and let us not forget about the evangelist across the hallway,' I say to Alice in the dark. 'Let it be known that I have called it early: this place is totally fucked up.'

I've got the morning shift. It's my first time with Walt on my own. Well, sort of on my own. No doubt Fiona is hovering over a monitor in another room.

I'm surprised – and relieved – at how readily Walt accepts my presence. Even though he has no idea who I am, he seems to feed off my confidence, as though if I act like I know him well and am meant to be there, he'll figure that he knows me. We get almost all the way through the pre-breakfast routine without incident – then there's a hiccup.

Walt has two pairs of shoes on the ground beside the chair in the corner. We're supposed to alternate them every few days, so they don't rub in the same spots and give him blisters.

We're also to make sure his orthotics are in them, and to remember the separator for his bunions – a squishy piece of pink plastic, like a piece of chewed bubblegum, that we mould to fit between his toes.

But I can't remember which shoes he wore yesterday.

I hesitate.

I decide the pair of shoes the bubblegum is currently in must be the pair he wore yesterday, so I pull the other ones forward.

I'm wrong. Before I can get Walt's toes in, Fiona comes tearing in to correct me.

'And you must tie his laces for him,' she says, 'so he doesn't have to bend down too far. Double knots! He'll try to stop you doing it for him but you've just got to cheerfully insist.'

'What are you women doing down there?' Walt asks, reaching to take over. 'I can manage that.'

'No, Dad! Just sit back, we're nearly done. Don't you know what a lucky old man you are? You've got a young blonde kneeling at your feet!'

Gross.

'A bit of flirting always helps,' she whispers to me. I can see that it does. But I don't much like it.

The rest of my shift runs smoothly. We have breakfast, he takes his pills, we do Bird Time, we walk around the garden. At lunch I remember all the benevolent trickery I was taught the day before: Walt isn't allowed too much salt, so the 'table salt' is actually caster sugar, which he sprinkles liberally on his meals in a frustrated quest for flavour. We can't substitute it with the stevia blend, because the granules are too fine and he'd notice the difference. ('All the more reason to cut down on the sugar elsewhere,' Fiona says.) He isn't allowed alcohol, so the 'red wine' we have with lunch and dinner is actually Ribena, decanted into an old merlot bottle and carefully recorked. The sundowner 'shandy' we're to make him each afternoon involves a special non-alcoholic beer you can only buy at a few stores in town. We have to be careful not to let him see the cans with the big '0.0%' logo on the label. 'If he asks, it's Tusker. There are some empty bottles in the bottom of the pantry you can show him as proof if he ever gets suss.' I have to give Fiona credit. She's thought of everything.

That afternoon, when Alice takes over, I have a chance to Skype my family to explain the situation I have arrived to is not quite the situation I was expecting.

Esther is vacuuming in our room, and Walt, Alice and Fiona are having tea on the patio, so I find myself huddled over my laptop in the study, whispering my unlikely predicament into the microphone and listening through headphones to muffle the incredulous responses.

'What!?' my sisters say. '*Whaaaaaaaat?* You need to get out of there. You need to come home.'

My parents roar with laughter.

'So, what,' says Mum, 'are these people part of the "Happy Valley set" or something?'

'The what-set?'

'You know, all those wife-swapping murderers they had running around up there in "British East Africa",' says Dad, in a tone that suggests Rhodesian colonials didn't think much of their equatorial counterparts. 'Lord Delamere and that mad bloody bunch.'

I don't know what they're talking about.

Later, I look it up. The 'Happy Valley set' was a group of early colonial aristocrats who settled in the Wanjohi Valley, at the edge of the Aberdare ranges. Legend has it these lords and ladies lived large. From the 1920s through to the 1940s, while the rest of the world was recovering from the Great War and the Great Depression, they were enjoying a Great Gatsby lifestyle under the African sun. They did heroin and cocaine. They threw wild parties. They slept with one another's partners and occasionally murdered one another's partners, in fits of jealous rage. One notable member, Kiki Preston – an American socialite who'd moved to Kenya with her big-game hunter husband – allegedly had an affair with Prince George, introduced him to drugs, and spawned him an illegitimate son. Her own drug habit was so conspicuous that she was nicknamed 'the girl with the silver syringe'. Kiki ended up jumping out of a window in New York City. Not many of the Happy Valley set had happy endings.

I can see why people like my parents have never thought much of these types. And neither, apparently, did the rest of the colonial community in Kenya. Hard-working settlers and administrative types were embarrassed by the raucous tales of horses being ridden through dining rooms and chandeliers being shot to pieces. They didn't see Africa as a playground: they saw it as Serious Empire-Building Business. A wild and dangerous land that needed to be tamed in order to reach its — and its people's — full potential. Its people, no doubt, have always had a different view.

I don't think Walt and Marguerite were part of that hedonistic crew. But they certainly seem to share some measure of the madness that many in the Motherland put down to Kenya's altitude and sunshine.

'Just be careful, hey?' Mum says. 'Really, you must. And if you think you're not safe there, you need to come home.'

'Yah,' says Dad. 'Watch out for *nyamazanes*. And don't you be a bloody *nyamazane!*'

(Not-being-a-bloody-*nyamazane* was our parents' golden rule when we were growing up. The word means 'wild animal' in Zulu — they used it to describe anyone who behaves foolishly. 'Like a "badly behaved bloody bogan",' was my father's translation.)

Fiona bursts into the study, reeking of contained panic. 'Quickly, I need you to go around the side of the house. Dad's on the move.'

I say a rushed goodbye to Mum and Dad, close my computer and head through to the garage. *On the move? Where can he possibly move to?* The gates are padlocked shut. He's an octogenarian, for god's sake. He's hardly going to scale the fence and mongrel his way over broken glass and through electrified barbed wire.

I get to the garage and spot him — strolling, calmly, past the gardenias near the granny flat, hands clasped behind his back. He stops, tilts his face towards the sun and shuts his eyes, soaking in the warmth.

Walt is fine.

Fiona is not.

She pokes her head from around the corner. 'Go!' she mouths, urgently waving me over to Walt, like a commando sending soldiers into a cleared area.

I follow orders. I walk over to him. 'Hi, Walt,' I say.

He opens his eyes and turns to face me, smiling. 'Oh, hello there.' He chuckles. 'I was just enjoying this lovely sunshine.' He takes my arm and we carry on with his loop of the garden.

I look back at Fiona. She gives me the thumbs up, then signals that she'll meet us back at the patio. I can't figure it out – is this a test or something? Why am I chaperoning him around the lawn? Why can't we let him be? Surely we can't lose him if we keep him in sight.

On our way past the bougainvillea, Walt snaps off a few overgrown branches and nicks the back of his hand on a thorn.

It's the first thing Fiona notices when we get back to the patio. 'Now what have you done there, Dad?' she says, dabbing at the fine stripe of crimson on his knuckle.

'No idea,' says Walt, 'no need to make a fuss!'

'I think it's a scratch from the bougainvillea,' I say.

'Yes,' Fiona says. 'Go and get the medi-kit, if you wouldn't mind? It's in the cupboard in your room.'

I bring her the medi-kit. Ignoring his protestations, she wipes Walt's hand down with antiseptic and sticks a bandaid over the tiny cut. 'That's why we must be so careful with him in the garden,' she says to me once he's gone back to reading his newspaper. 'His skin is so delicate – any little bump can cause a bleed. And with all the blood thinners he's on, he won't be able to clot so well.'

Ah, so it *was* a test. And I failed.

Oops.

It's not for another few days, when Fiona and Alice take Walt out for a doctor's appointment and Millicent goes home across town to check on her mother, that I get a chance to nose around the property. Some of the staff, I discover, live in a small block of rooms in the back corner of the garden. Esther, Patrick, David and James have a room each, and only go home to visit their families in nearby towns every other weekend, while Khamisi, Peter and Frank live in outer suburbs of Nairobi, and travel to and from the house each day by *matatu*. I haven't been told not to go into the staff quarters, but I get the sense that I shouldn't. That it's their space, their one patch of privacy to retreat to at the end of a working day. *Hopefully,* I think, *once we've got to know each other better, I'll be able to have a look.* But for now I think I should keep a respectful distance.

The house itself is less grand than I was expecting. There are signs of wealth, but no ostentatiousness. It's a slightly rambling old place full of homely tones, chintz and oiled oak, polished silver and brass and china. Worn Persian rugs over polished parquetry. Reupholstered furniture and mug rings covered with doilies. Uncoordinated pastels and floral patterns on curtains, bedspreads, sheets; tartan blankets, a cabinet of crystal, a storeroom, a fireplace. It's decidedly English, though seasoned with African touches: carvings and beads and sculptures and ornaments that decorate sideboards and occasional tables and windowsills.

In a strange way, it reminds me of home. I grew up in a creaky, hundred-year-old Queenslander that had miraculously survived the Mackay cyclone of 1918. By the time we moved in, termites had all but eaten away its stumps, the corrugated-iron roof was rusted red, and possums patrolled the rafters. In a few places, where the boughs of the six mango trees in the yard hung close enough to drop fruit onto it, the roof looked as though it had been shelled. The gaps between the floorboards in my bedroom were so big we had to cover them with gauze to stop the mosquitoes and carpet snakes from getting in. My parents couldn't afford to fix it up – let alone renovate or put in air conditioning – so we sweltered through summer, deafened by a chorus of green frogs and surrounded by sickening armies of cane toads.

It was about as ocker a place as you could get – and filled to the brim with African-colonial furnishings. Oil paintings of elephants having dust baths. A knee-high soapstone statue of a rhinoceros. Decorative ostrich eggs. Antique ivory lampstands with fringed silk shades. (The lampstands are family heirlooms. They're from a time when killing elephants for their tusks was seen as an admirable pursuit, not the barbaric, cowardly abomination it is. We see them as a talking point – not a point of pride.) Silverware that tarnished with the humidity and dust. Copper that turned green in the humidity and dust. Did I mention the humidity and dust? There were days the air felt like warm soup, while tractors pulling sugarcane bins up and down the road filled the atmosphere with ash and topsoil.

For a long while, my mother tried to keep on top of the housework these trappings demanded: the dusting, the polishing, the removing of spiderwebs and hornets' nests. Until one day, the dining table strewn with Brasso-stained felt rags and miniature salt shakers clogged up with wet grit, she threw it in. 'Fuck it,' she said. We knew she must be mad – she never said 'fuck'. 'I've had a gutful of this shit. Fuck, fuck, *fuck* it.' 'Then don't bloody do it!' said Dad. He'd never cared for finishings. 'I won't!' said Mum. And she didn't, ever again. I reckon that's the day they truly became fully fledged, fair dinkum, unpretentious Aussies. But here in actual colonial Africa, where people have the help of 'the help' to keep everything sparkling, it all makes much more sense.

Looking after Walt can be intense, but I find it also involves a lot of quiet time just sitting, being, contemplating the world around me. It's nice. I can feel myself catching my breath.

I start to understand things about my parents' life in Africa in a way I didn't before. They're things I'd known to expect, but I'm appreciating them on a visceral level now. Most striking is the sense of danger. Growing up in north Queensland we had a permanently unlocked house: a home we couldn't have secured even if we'd wanted to — we literally did not have a set of keys for the doors. We left car keys in the ignitions of vehicles; we casually left handbags and wallets on café tables. In most parts of Australia, you can freely walk around at night with only a half-serious fear that something bad might happen, knowing how rare such incidents are.

Here in Nairobi, beneath the surface, the threat to personal safety is ever-present. The police can't be relied upon; instead, private security companies like G4S, KK and Hatari boast about their 'rapid response' times, promising that their people will arrive within minutes of a call, decked out in paramilitary uniforms. There are big red panic buttons on the walls of every room of the house; they summon the twenty-four-hour armed security patrols that coast the neighbourhood streets, their vans packed with squads of German shepherds barking viciously through bars. Home invasions aren't uncommon, especially in wealthy areas. Theft is usually the primary motivation, but break-ins often feature gratuitous violence.

After sundown, we lock and chock every door and window. Slide heavy brass bars across the main entrance. Pull shut a deadlocked iron gate that separates the back half of the house from the front, cocooning the bedrooms in an extra layer of security. Here, we hide passports and an emergency stash of cash in a safe under the floor, because 'you never know when a revolution might break out'. We wind the windows up and lock the doors before we drive out the front gate. We are patted down before entering shopping centres, and use ATMs inside locked cubicles, and don't stop for *anyone* on the road after dark.

I am also acutely aware of my status as a member of a privileged racial group. My white skin makes me part of a comfortable minority in Kenya, a position that somehow feels simultaneously safer *and* more vulnerable than most, as it casts me as a valuable target for thugs and opportunists.

Having so many people around the house also takes some getting used to. The staff are rostered on six days a week, from seven in the morning through to seven at night with a two-hour break in the afternoon, except for Saturdays when they finish at noon. They take turns covering Sundays.

Alice and I occasionally join them on their breaks, sipping sweet tea in the shade of the jacaranda tree around the side of the garage, but I'm sure this isn't usually the 'done thing' and it takes us some time to work out where we fit into this strange arrangement. On the one hand, we're supposed to blend in as 'part of the family' when Walt's around, so we're imbued with their status. On the other, we're uncomfortable with being waited on – not least because we're staff too. Our solution is to accept the domestic staff's service when we're on duty with Walt, for the sake of the charade, but to help with chores like clearing tables or washing up when we aren't. I worry that our wanting to 'pitch in and do our bit' might actually be standing on someone else's toes – or implying that the staff aren't doing a good enough job. But after a time, it means we're able to chip away at the barriers between us and them, and can start building a more personal rapport.

Even so, there are all kinds of customs and protocols to learn in order to ensure the smooth running of day-to-day life.

Things like, you know, proper underwear etiquette.

'You mustn't put them in with the rest of the wash,' my mother lectures me over Skype one afternoon, while the house is quiet during Walt's post-lunch zizz and I'm sitting on the patio. 'They don't like it. It's disrespectful. You must hand-wash them yourself.'

'Disrespectful to who?' I ask.

'To the staff! How would you like to wash someone else's knickers?'

'What do you mean? I've washed plenty of other people's jocks in my time. As long as they don't have skid marks, what's the big deal?'

'*Ag sies*, man!' she said, breaking into the Afrikaans slang she and Dad always used to express disgust.

'Jesus, Mum, it's not 1960s Rhodesia anymore. It's not like they're doing it by hand. There's a washing machine here. Everyone else puts theirs in.'

'It's not about that – it's a boundaries thing. Personal items should be kept personal.'

'But what if they think *I'm* being weird by not putting them in with the rest of the washing? Like it's because *I* don't want *them* touching my underwear? Like it's a weird racial hang-up? Isn't that just as offensive?'

'No, please man. *Please* promise me you'll wash them yourself. You just do it in the sink and hang them to dry in the shower once everyone's gone to bed.'

'Ugh, *fine*, Mum. I promise.'

'And another thing – you know there were people who refused to leave Zimbabwe, saying, "We'd rather be murdered in our beds than have to make them ourselves"? Well, some of them were. You must make your bed yourself. Every morning. Don't become a bloody princess.'

So, obedient child that I am, that's what I start doing. Getting up early every morning to make my bed and bring my never-quite-dry underwear in from the bathroom.

Until one day, when Fiona catches me wringing a pair into the basin, and insists I put them in the wash. 'Dad will have a fit if he comes to have a piddle in here and there are women's knickers hanging off the taps!'

'Oh – ah, my mum told me I should do them myself, though?'

'No, that's nonsense. Besides, you need to have them ironed.'

'Ironed?'

Fiona opens a cupboard in the hallway to show me where stacks of freshly pressed and folded clothes, towels, sheets and smalls sit in an aura of warm soapy air. It takes less than twenty-four hours for dirty washing to make its way from the wicker hamper in the bathroom to this pristine state in the airing cupboard. And, as it turns out, there's a very good reason for ironing everything – including underwear.

There's a type of blowfly in East Africa known to entomologists as *Cordylobia anthropophaga*, and to the rest of us as the 'tumbu fly', the 'putzi fly' or, most tellingly, the 'skin-maggot fly'. This wonderful creature likes to lay its eggs on damp washing while it's hanging out to dry, so that three days later when you put your pants on, the larvae can burrow into the warm flesh of your buttock and spend a week feasting on your blood and meat and fat. Then, that sore red bump you thought was just a pimple or mosquito bite ulcerates into a hideously painful boil, out of which wriggles a corpulent little grub and a lifetime of nightmares. If the eggs are laid on a pillowcase, the worms will emerge from your face. (Look it up on YouTube, if you can bear to.)

'So, yes,' Fiona says, 'we iron *everything* here. With an iron as hot as the fabric can bear.'

I don't want to break my promise to Mum, but I also don't want a butt full of maggots, so I compromise. I wash my underwear in the shower then hang them inside my wardrobe where they drip all night into a bucket. Once they're dry, I sneak them through to the laundry to throw them in with the clean washing, although every so often I miss the opportunity and have to 'iron' them myself with a hair straightener.

ALICE

Esther catches me one day. She comes into our room to put fresh sheets on the bed and finds me sitting on the end of it, a pile of damp cotton briefs in my lap, one pair steaming from between the ceramic tongs.

'Sorry! Sorry, sorry!' Esther mutters, reversing through the door as though she's walked in on me masturbating.

'No, no, it's fine, Esther – it's fine! Come in, please!' She eyes the hair straightener warily. 'I'm just – I'm ironing them,' I explain. 'To kill the tumbu fly eggs.'

'Ohh . . . okay.' She still looks confused.

Fuck it, I think. *I'll just ask her straight up.*

'Hey, Esther, tell me: is it okay for me to put my underpants in the wash basket?'

She looks at me, processes the question.

'Yes, it's okay.'

'You sure? You don't mind?'

'It's okay,' she repeats, in a tone suggesting she can't think why it wouldn't be.

After Esther leaves my room I send Mum a message, vindicated:

Asked Esther re underpants. She said it's FINE to put them in wash. YOU'RE the weirdo.

My victory is short-lived. Mum writes back:

You can't do that! They are too polite – they'll say yes to anything u ask.

Me: *But I told her I could do them myself and she said it was fine!*

Mum: *No!!!!!! HAND. WASH. YOURSELF. BRAT.*

Alice says I'm being insane, but that night I see Millicent smuggling what I'm sure are her own wet knickers back to her room after showering. Maybe it is an outdated colonial habit, but I reluctantly carry on with my secret underwear routine for the entirety of my stay.

Walt's personal care isn't the only thing that keeps him going. Every day, we pump a cocktail of life-preserving chemicals into him.

Walt is on beta-blockers and alpha-blockers, steroids and aspirin. He has pills for his cholesterol, for reflux, for angina. One tablet lowers his heart rate but increases his blood pressure, so that's got to be offset by *another* tablet that lowers his blood pressure but is contraindicated in people with renal impairment, so *that* has to be offset by yet *another* tablet that helps prevent fluid retention. We give him pills to prevent heart attacks, pills to widen his blood vessels, and pills to inhibit the beta-oxidation of fatty acids by blocking acetyl-coenzymes to enhance glucose oxidation in his ischaemic cells, whatever that means.

Red pills and blue pills, white pills and yellow pills, pills that can't be taken together and others that ideally should, pills for the morning and pills for just before bed, pills that are crucial and pills that can be skipped: a carefully titrated extension of life expectancy, rattling around in plastic.

The night before Marguerite arrives, while Alice puts Walt down to bed, Fiona sits me down on the floor of our bedroom to take me through the process of managing Walt's pills. Alice is already across what he needs to take, it had been part of her job in England. But now that we're in Kenya, Fiona wants to establish a new routine. 'Doing Walt's Pills' is to always take place in this room – his medication is kept inside a padlocked suitcase in the top of the cupboard.

'Marguerite can't be trusted, so we need a good place to hide the key,' she says, then – without asking – opens my underwear drawer, rifles past my jocks, and pulls out a box of tampons. 'How about in here?'

Sure. Fine. Why not, I think, giving up any last hope of personal space or privacy.

Fiona takes a plastic binder full of documents out of the suitcase. She spreads the documents out on the carpet around us – years' worth of Walt's medical records, doctors' letters, prescriptions and test results.

She says she wants me to understand the backstory to what's been going on – why it's so important we keep such a close eye on him here.

'I went to see Dad at their house after he started becoming unwell, and I swear he was drugged. He was a zombie – a vegetable!' she says. 'He wasn't at all himself. Even his eyes – you could see. They were so dull and grey. It was horrible.'

Then, Fiona discovered he'd been taking an antidepressant.

'This one.' She hands me a printout of the Wikipedia article on 'Citalopram'. Sections of the text are highlighted in yellow. She lists the possible side effects as I look over the pages.

'*Drowsiness . . . insomnia . . . fatigue . . . cardiac arrhythmia . . .* I mean, with *his* heart condition! Can you believe it? *Blood pressure changes . . . anxiety . . . mood swings . . . dizziness . . .* he shouldn't be on anything like this.'

Fiona draws my attention to a section double underlined in red pen: *increased apathy and emotional flattening.*

'That is *exactly* what Dad was like. Flat. Absolutely *flat.*'

Well, he had just had a heart attack, I think. *You wouldn't expect him to be bouncing off the walls.*

'So why was he put on this in the first place?' I ask.

'Because he'd finally mustered the courage to tell Marguerite he'd had a gutful of her! He tried to kick her out of the house – he's wanted to for years – so she took him off to see her doctor about getting him sedated. Just doped him up on this stuff so that he was easier to control.'

Fiona pulls out a letter from Marguerite's doctor to the Smyth family trust which gives a slightly different version of events. This doctor reports that Walt's behaviour was becoming increasingly erratic and aggressive – that his declining mental state was causing him great distress and serious difficulties at home. It says that on a number of occasions he had lashed out at Marguerite – sometimes physically – and was a potential danger to her and to others.

'Rubbish!' Fiona says. 'Dad wouldn't hurt a fly!'

The letter says it is common practice to prescribe dementia patients a mild antidepressant to help manage these sorts of symptoms at this phase of the disease, and that the 'extremely low dose' of ten milligrams would simply 'take the edge off' his anxiety, lowering the risk of violent outbursts.

It's all bullshit, according to Fiona.

'Marguerite's got that doctor in her back pocket,' she says. 'He'll say whatever she tells him to.'

I quietly note the part in the Wikipedia article that says:

There are studies suggesting that citalopram can be useful in reducing aggressive and impulsive behaviour. It appears to be superior to placebo for behavioural disturbances associated with dementia.

'I got a second opinion,' Fiona says, handing me another doctor's letter. '*This* doctor says the Citalopram is "completely unnecessary". It says that the focus should be on "creating a safe and supportive living environment" and that he should cease taking the Citalopram immediately, especially given its interaction with all the other medication he's on.

'So I tipped the whole lot down the loo. But I wouldn't put it past her to have a stash hidden away somewhere. We'll have to have a snoop when she gets here.'

It starts to rain outside. Fat gusts of damp and dusty air billow out from behind the linen curtains, blowing the papers across the floor. While Fiona gathers them up and shuts the windows, I pull out my laptop to read more about Citalopram.

I flick through drug information sheets and patient reviews and health forums, trying to get a handle on how the drug – an SSRI antidepressant – works, and what effect ten milligrams is likely to have.

I mention to Fiona that the therapeutic dose range is ten milligrams to forty milligrams, so he was on the lower end of the scale. Was it really possible for that to turn him into a 'zombie'?

Fiona sets me straight.

'She was giving him much more than ten milligrams.'

Fiona grits her teeth, angry tears pool in the corner of her eyes as she looks through the papers for her next piece of evidence.

She hands me a photocopy of a scrap of lined paper. It's a hand-written list of Walt's medications. She points to a figure scrawled beside the word 'Citalopram'.

It says '75mg'.

'No bloody wonder he was so unwell! It's a miracle he was even *conscious*. I will never, ever forgive her.'

The bed alarm starts beeping. Fiona unclips the baby monitor from her waistband, sees that Walt is up, pacing in his room. 'Bugger,' she says, wiping her eyes. 'I'll go and take over from Alice. She can fill you in on the rest.'

But as she leaves the room, I notice something else about the photocopied handwritten list Fiona thinks is a smoking gun.

'Citalopram' falls between 'Aspirin' and 'Clopidogrel', both of which have '75mg' listed — correctly — as the dosage beside them. I check every other list of medication in the folder — the prescriptions, the pharmaceutical receipts, the hospital discharge summaries. Nowhere else is the Citalopram listed as '75mg'. It's always down as '10mg'.

I do some sums: *if* Marguerite *had* been giving Walt seventy-five milligrams of Citalopram per day, she'd have been going through an entire box of pills every four days. It's impossible that she'd have been able to get away with that without raising suspicions somewhere along the line.

It seems vastly more likely that a seventy-something-year-old woman was jotting down a list of her husband's medications and absentmindedly wrote '75mg' between the two drugs that *were* meant to be '75mg'.

It seems to me Marguerite is guilty of nothing more than a mistake. I point it out to Alice, who concedes my point then returns us to the task at hand, apparently not as keen to play Nancy Drew as I am. She pulls out a pair of plastic pill dispensers. 'Here – these need to be restocked every fortnight,' she says. The Monday-to-Sunday tubs of colourful beads rattle like an advent calendar of death-defying Skittles. 'And we've got to make sure we've got reserves of everything for at least another three months. Fiona says it's good to have a buffer, in case anything "goes down" in Kenya and it's hard to get things in from England.'

Alice and I pull everything out of the suitcase. In addition to the medicines there's an old rolled-up sock, an asthma inhaler and some tubs of Vaseline that we put aside. We remove the rubber bands holding boxes of capsules and tablets together, and lay them out across the floor, arranged in alphabetical order. We work our way through the list on the spreadsheet, pull out the foiled blister packs and pop out the required number of pills. Some don't come in the exact dosage Walt requires – we have to halve or quarter them using a pill splitter.

The pill splitter sucks. Alice goes to get a sharp knife and cutting board – that's not much better. Tiny bits of tablets are pinging across the room and we're on all fours sweeping our hands over the carpet trying to find them, grasping for crumbling half-moons hiding under the bed or behind the dresser, or caught in the piles of crumpled pharmaceutical blurbs. And all the while, I'm trying to cross-reference what's gone into the dispenser and how much is left and update the spreadsheet as we go.

Alice had warned me that it took 'a while' to do Walt's pills. Turns out she underplayed that too. It takes hours, literally *hours* to get the job done. I knew coming to Africa to look after a rich old man would involve some dullness, but I didn't expect to be doing stocktakes until midnight.

5
THE WIFE

'Yoo-hoo! *Yoooooo-hooooooo!*' An alarming, high-pitched cry torpedoes down the passageway from the front door. It takes me a moment to recognise it as a human voice – it sounds like the cry of a demented bird.

'She's here,' Fiona says, poking her head into my room as I'm doing up my bra. Alice has taken Walt out for the morning – Fiona said Marguerite's arrival would be too disruptive for him, but thought it would be good if I were here. 'Come, let's wait for her in the living room.'

I'm expecting a cool, coiffed, sharp-tongued socialite: someone buttoned-up and bossy, the sort of person who takes tea without milk or sugar, says 'no' to cake and shoos friendly animals away. A wicked, money-grubbing bitch. I'm certainly not expecting Marguerite to be quite so . . . *bubbly*.

'Yoo-hooooooooo! It's meeeeeeee!'

Six suitcases roll into the house behind her, as she yodels about how 'terribly suffocating' Virgin Atlantic's first-class seating arrangements are.

'Fancy having a *divider* all the way up between you and the chap beside you!? I mean, *really*. How jolly awful if you'd like to talk to each other. And you know, I *do* like to talk to people and find out their business. Well. It didn't matter in the end, did it? I took one of those *wonnnnnnnnderful* Temaze tablets and blipped through the whole thing. Oof! It *did* fly by. I was almost sorry it was over when we landed – I didn't even get to wear my aeroplane pyjamas! *Such* a shame. Now where's Esther? Esther! *Esther! Yooo-hoooo!* Oh, Esther, do come here, won't you? Quickly. *Quickly* now. I have a *lo-ver-ly* pressie for you!'

I find myself smiling – I can't help it. Marguerite's the most British person I've ever met. She somehow combines the plummy voice of Hyacinth Bucket from *Keeping Up Appearances* with the scatty demeanour of Eddie from *Absolutely Fabulous*. It's like seeing Big Ben for the first time and finding it's held together with licorice allsorts.

I feel Fiona watching me, trying to work out whether I can resist Marguerite's spell. I reset my face, stand up straight, try not to appear quite so . . . entertained.

Marguerite can't stand still. She paces figure eights around the living room, directing David and James to leave her various bags in various corners, where they spring open with the pressure of her colourful wardrobe, jack-in-the-boxes full of embroidered handkerchiefs and resort-wear flying around the room, catching on floor lamps and armchairs and picture frames. Fiona and I stand silently with our backs against the wall on the far side of the room, trying to follow Marguerite's frenzied index finger as it assigns the order in which her bags are to be unpacked.

When Esther appears at the door, Marguerite presses into her hands the complementary set of pyjamas she was given on the flight. 'Ohhhh, Esther, *there* you are. Now. I've brought these in *just* for you – they're *super*! Don't you think?'

Esther, I suspect, does *not* think the set of stretch cotton tights and top is all that super. Nonetheless, she dutifully expresses gratitude – '*Ohhhhhh, asante sana, memsahib, asante!*' – before retreating to the kitchen, leaving Marguerite elated by her own generosity.

'Oh, they *do* like it when I bring things back for them,' she gushes, bouncing on the spot with joy, fairy clapping herself. I'm transfixed.

It's like watching someone offer a homeless person a doggy bag full of leftover lobster.

Then – for apparently the first time since entering the room – Marguerite spots me. 'And now, who might *you* be?' She makes a beeline for me, pulling up mere inches from my face, retrieving a crumpled tissue from under her bra strap and holding it up to the corner of her mouth. I glance over at Fiona for guidance but before I have a chance to answer, Marguerite squeals, 'Ooooh! I know – don't tell me – you must be *Kirsten*, the other *Or-stray-lyan* girl! Did I guess right?' She taps my shoulder with the lipstick-stained tissue, her eyes wide and sparkly, a guileless pink grin spanning her face.

'Yes . . . that's right,' I reply, thankful that someone has, after all, told her I'm here.

Marguerite's mouth falls open in faux shock. 'Oh! Is it *really?*' She spins to Fiona for confirmation. Fiona nods wearily. Marguerite spins back to me. 'Oh my, I *am* clever sometimes, aren't I!?' She hoots with laughter so hard I jump. 'And where's my darling Walt? And young Alice! Tell me – is she liking Keen-ya?'

'They've gone down to the Club for morning tea, but they'll be back any minute,' Fiona says, speaking to her stepmother as though she's addressing a hyperactive five-year-old. 'Now, Marguerite, can we please put all these bags away so they don't confuse Dad? He'll think he's about to go on a holiday if he sees them.'

'Ohhhh, the *Club!*' Marguerite shrieks again – startling Esther, who's come through with a tray of tea for us; the teaspoons jitter against the saucers as she makes her way to the patio. 'Shall we meet there for lunch?' Marguerite asks. 'Is it curry day!?'

'No, Marguerite. Khamisi is making us lunch. We're having roast beef. It'll be ready at half-twelve.'

'Who's "Kasimi" then?' asks Marguerite, sitting on the edge of the settee to peel her flight socks off.

'Khamisi. He's your new cook,' says Fiona. The Smyths' old cook had retired several months ago, and Marguerite had no intention of hiring a replacement.

'Do we really need a cook? Surely with all these young helpers around there are enough of us to take care of the kitchen.'

'You'll need a cook to make it easier to cater for Dad,' says Fiona. 'Khamisi is very good. I'm sure you'll be happy with him.'

'Oh, how *lovely*! Alright then. We'll do the Club tomorrow. I say, the weather really is *much* nicer here than in England. Do you know they've closed Heathrow for the snow? I must have only *just* escaped it. Oh, I *do* have such wonderful luck sometimes . . .'

On and on it goes, this soprano flurry of noise and movement, whirling around the house. Marguerite asks me to help set up her new laptop, and her shoe rack, and to sort out the SIM card for her Kenyan mobile phone. I can see where this is going. I won't just be Walt's 'carer' here – I'll also be her personal assistant.

Discrete piles of belongings start forming in various corners of the living room: soaps and shortbreads, scarves and shirts and socks. Marguerite hands them out as though they're gift bags. 'Alright now, David, *you* take this stack of goodies through to the bathroom for me, won't you? And James, *you* take this lot through to the pantry, there we are. And *you*, Esther, can take *this* lot through to my bedroom.'

Marguerite has brought a whole pile of things for Walt with her from the UK. But as Fiona points out, they're all wrong. The Harrods socks are too thick: they'll make Walt's feet sweat – no good. The lavender-scented hand soap will be too harsh for his skin. He can only use soap-free products from the chemist; Marguerite should have known that. The polo shirt is too bright; he'll never wear that colour. And in any case, short sleeves are no good.

'Dad bleeds very easily, Marguerite. His skin is very fragile.'

'Yes, Fiona. Mine is too. That's what happens when you get old.'

'Yes, Marguerite. But the thing is, Dad's skin is thinner than most.'

'What a pity. I'll have to give the soap and socks to the staff, I suppose. Perhaps you could exchange the shirt when you go back to England?'

'Actually, I can imagine Jonathan pulling this off. He'd quite like it!'

Jonathan is Fiona's husband. He's 'minding the fort' for her back in England. I suspect he does and wears whatever she tells him to.

'Oh well, by all means, give it to him then! Better to have it go to good use.'

This patina of impeccable manners between two women who hate each other baffles me. Perhaps they've patched things up on the phone? Is it just because they're so English? I can't figure it out. If it was my family, we'd be screaming and shouting and throwing things at each other. I've always felt open hostility is a healthier option than passive-aggressive antagonism. The unspoken tension makes me uncomfortable, so I excuse myself to my bedroom to catch up on some emails. *God*, I think. *We've got to get through a week of these two in the house together.* I'm interrupted moments later by Fiona bursting through the door.

She dashes across the room to stand flat against the wall between the two windows that open onto the garden.

'Is she out there?' Fiona whispers to me, glancing out the window.

I stand up from my desk to lean out for a better look.

'No! Get down!' she hisses. 'Don't let her see you – draw the curtains. See what you can hear.'

Marguerite is in the garden on the phone. She's pacing up and down the lawn, the dogs trotting along behind her, stopping now and then to scratch around in one of the freshly planted flowerbeds. Small plumes of smoke grey the sky in the distance; squirrels tickle the branches of an acacia tree just behind the back fence. I spot Patrick stalking through the fig trees, collecting pebbles for his slingshot and squinting as he scans the canopy for monkeys. I wonder what he goes home and tells his wife and kids about the mad family he works for – whether he thinks about the Smyths at all once he's clocked off for the week.

Marguerite is talking with one hand cupped around the mouthpiece and glancing back towards the house. Out there, she seems a much more devious figure than she seemed inside – like the person I'd first imagined her to be. Snatches of her conversation float through the window each time she turns to walk towards us.

'She says I'm to sleep in the study! So as not to distract him in the night. Well, really – if she knew anything she'd know it's the other way around! And he loves having me there beside him when . . .'

'Who's she talking to?' I ask Fiona.

'One of her horrid lawyer cousins, I imagine,' she says. 'There are a whole lot of them she's always running off to visit.'

Marguerite comes our way again.

'. . . There's another Australian girl here. "Kirsty" someone or other. I don't know where I'm supposed to put them all! Or what sort of arrangement Fiona's made for them to be paid . . .'

Ummm . . . hold on. *What's this about not knowing how we're meant to be paid? Shouldn't they have figured all this stuff out before flying us over? Alice said it was all sorted.* I look at Fiona for a response, for some sort of reassurance, but she's intently focused on Marguerite.

I hear my mother's voice in my head: 'Stop picking up *stompies*!' This is one of the many sayings my parents brought with them from Zimbabwe. *Stompies* is an Afrikaans word for cigarette butts; to 'pick up *stompies*' – and smoke them, as the poor do – means to overhear only bits and pieces of a conversation and get the wrong idea of what is being discussed. When we were children, my parents invoked the phrase as a reprimand if we tried to eavesdrop. But here, it's clear that Fiona expects me to pick up as many *stompies* as I can.

Millicent pulls into the driveway in her old Datsun at the same time as Alice gets back from the Club with Walt. He climbs out of the Mazda and marches over to Millicent's car. 'Who are you?' he demands. 'Where is your driver?'

We watch from the kitchen window as she winds down her window to talk to him, and Fiona races out to calm him down. Millicent isn't actually needed today, but Fiona wanted her here for lunch. 'It's important that we all put on a united front for Marguerite when she gets back,' she'd said. 'To show her how things are going to be.'

A flicker of irritation crosses Marguerite's face when she sees how things are going to be. 'Good lord, how many people does she think we need!?' she mutters, before heading out to the driveway herself. 'Hellooooo, *Millie!*' she coos, arms stretched wide for a hug. 'How *maaahhhrvellous* to see you! How is your dear old mum?'

Before Alice and I go through to the dining room for lunch, I snatch a moment with her in our room. 'Oi,' I hiss. 'Do you know anything about how we're getting paid?'

'Ummm, Fiona mentioned something about that. I was getting paid through the agency while I was in England, but I think here it will be through the family trust or something? I'm sure they'll sort it out.'

Awesome: she's as vague about it all as I am. This is what happens when you're brought up having things too easy – you just figure everything will fall into place, because it always has.

We hear a bell ringing from the dining room. *Oh Christ, the bell. Not the bell.*

'Yoo-hoooooo! *Yooooo-hooooooo!* Girls! *Aussie* girls! Lunch is on!' Marguerite calls.

We get to the dining room just as Khamisi proudly delivers the meal. 'Roast. Beef.' He announces, revealing a sumptuous lump of meat on a tray in the middle of the table, then points to the golden batter cakes and peas and carrots scattered around it. 'Yorkshire. Puddings. Ve-ge-ta-bles.'

'Well, I say, this all looks *splendid!* Thank you *very* much . . . What did you say your name was?' Marguerite asks her new cook.

'Khamisi, *memsahib*,' he says, grinning.

'Well *very good*, Kisumu!' she says.

'Khamisi,' Fiona corrects her.

'Yes, Khamisi!' says Marguerite, as though that's what she'd said the first time.

'Okay, thank you, thank you. I hope you enjoy,' Khamisi says, bowing as he backs out of the room.

'Let's tuck in, shall we!' orders Walt impatiently from the head of the table, so we all pick up our polished silverware and begin to eat. Except for Millicent, who shuts her eyes and quietly says grace. Marguerite catches me elbowing Alice to point it out, and for a moment I worry she'll scold us for being so rude. But instead, she winks and makes an elaborate sign of the cross before swigging a big sip of wine.

After lunch, I learn how to spy. Walt and Marguerite take an afternoon 'zizz', and Fiona shows me and Alice how to use the baby monitor to listen in while they're in their bedroom. 'Millicent doesn't need to know all this,' Fiona says. So Millicent sits quietly in the living room, reading a magazine, while we have our clandestine meeting.

Marguerite knows about the baby monitor – but doesn't know that it has sound. Fiona wants us to make sure it stays that way. She says to make sure we have the receiver muted whenever Marguerite might see it, and insists that anything and everything we can intercept will be valuable. She'll be going back to England in a few days' time, leaving us to look after Walt; she wants us to report back with regular updates. No piece of intelligence is too trivial to matter, apparently. Not even the conversation we're listening in on right now.

Marguerite: 'I saw Nancy and Ted in Dover; they send their regards.'

Walt: 'Oh how lovely.'

Marguerite: 'We had a marvellous round of golf. A full eighteen holes! Ooooh, I was tired that night. I won, though, of course. Now there's an idea! Shall we go for some golf tomorrow?'

Walt: 'If the sun's out that should be splendid. It's years since I've been down to the course.'

Marguerite: 'Don't be silly, darling – you went just this morning with Alice!'

Walt: 'Who?'

Marguerite: 'Alice! One of your young Australian fillies!'

Walt: 'Oh . . . we did, did we?'

'You see!' Fiona says. 'You see what she's like with him? Why does she try to make him remember things that he can't?'

Because she hasn't come to terms with the fact that her husband's mind is disintegrating? Or am I missing something? I look at Alice for a clue as to what Fiona's getting at. She shrugs back at me.

On the monitor, we watch Marguerite hunch over the side of the bed, taking her shoes off.

Marguerite: 'How we go about paying them is going to be a bit tricky. I don't know what Fiona's promised but you can be sure it will be coming out of our accounts.'

Walt: 'Oh dear – do we need to withdraw some money?'

Walt starts feeling around for his wallet.

Fiona throws her hands up. 'And money! I've *told* her not to talk about money with him! It's a trigger! He doesn't need to be worried with those sorts of things.'

Maybe Walt doesn't need to be worried about the logistics of our pay, but I am.

'How *are* we going to be paid, by the way?' I ask Fiona, another question I should have asked before getting on the plane. I guess I figured rich people would have all that stuff worked out. I had a small reserve of savings to rely on, and a credit card for emergencies, but certainly not enough to see me through the months I'd be away.

'Don't worry, we'll sort that all out later,' Fiona says. 'Just keep listening – she's up to something. I just know it.'

But all we see is Marguerite swinging her feet up onto the bed beside Walt, and the pair of them holding hands as they drift off to sleep. An old married couple lying beside each other, having an afternoon nap.

6
THE CLUB

The next day, I have the most fitting possible introduction to the Club anyone could hope for: a Sunday lunch with two of its oldest life members, Marguerite and Walt.

It's Fiona's idea. Over breakfast that morning, she tells Marguerite to arrange for me and Alice to be signed up as guest members and issued with our very own membership cards. 'The girls need to be able to take Dad there at any time,' she says. 'And it'll be a good place for them to go to unwind in their time off. They can join the gym. And swim in the pool.' Millicent has gone home for the day to check on her mother, but she's already a member.

'Why yes, of course,' says Marguerite, as though it's already occurred to her – maybe it has. 'I'll get the forms and sort it out today.'

'Forms?' says Walt, suddenly looking up from his toast anxiously. 'Do I need to fill in some forms?'

Marguerite and Fiona both move to reassure him.

'Nothing to worry about, dear – I'm just going to join these lovely girls of ours up to the Club,' says Marguerite, patting his hand.

'Here we are, Dad — how about we take your pills?' says Fiona, distracting him from the other side of the table with his tablets and a glass of juice.

Walt looks around at the four of us staring back at him. It's touch-and-go for a moment. Does he know who any of us are, I wonder.

He softens, breaks into a smile. 'What hope does a man have with so many women telling him what to do!?' He laughs, wagging his finger at us, then swallows his pills. Phew.

'Don't you think it's weird how Marguerite is with Fiona?' I say to Alice, as we get ready in our room. 'I mean, Fiona is basically bossing her around in her own house, and she's just copping it.'

'Yeah, to her face,' says Alice, 'but she's sneakier than you think — you haven't seen it yet. Just wait.' Alice screws her face up looking at my outfit. 'Mm . . . you better not wear that.'

I glance down at myself. 'Really?' Fiona has already warned us about the dress code at the Club: no bare arms, no exposed midriff, nothing too tight or short. I'm wearing a collared, button-up blouse and a knee-length denim skirt. I don't see what the problem is. 'This is pretty fucking tame. It's the most boring shit I own.'

'Yeah, it's just —'

'This is like, Country Road spring casual, circa 2002. It's Grade Five teacher at St Francis. It's private-school piano recital chic. I know what I'm doing. I've been to a Country Club before!' I haven't. 'Look at you! You're wearing Thai fisherman pants and a tunic.'

'What's wrong with my fisherman pants?' says Alice.

'I just don't see why that outfit is okay and mine's not!'

'It's the denim,' Alice says. 'They've got a real thing about it. No denim — it's in the rules.'

'Ah. Right. *Posh cunts.*' I lean on my North Queensland drawl for effect, as I change into a navy-blue skirt.

'Exactly,' says Alice. 'Posh cunts.'

As we pass beneath the boom gate and pull into the driveway, I realise my membership card will be much more than a way to keep Walt entertained — it will be an all-access pass to a fully immersive time-travel adventure. The Club is a flashback shrouded in thick ficus trees. It's a sprawling stone complex with white colonnades and a slate-shingled roof, home to hundred-year-old hospitality. Access is granted only to members, their guests, and pre-approved members of reciprocal clubs. No exceptions — sticky-beaking tourists are certainly not welcome.

From the moment we enter the foyer, we're surrounded by waiters in green blazers asking how '*Bwana* Smyth' and '*Memsahib* Marguerite' are.

'Splendid!' Marguerite beams, relishing the VIP treatment. 'And how are *you*?'

'Very well, thank you, madam,' says Moses, the head butler. 'We have missed you!'

'Ah yes, well, we've missed you too,' says Marguerite. 'Haven't we, darling?' She elbows Walt.

'Oh yes, yes indeed,' he says, smiling and shaking Moses' hand.

We're ushered through to the garden room. Walt nods and smiles at everyone we pass, as Fiona firmly guides him to a chair against the window. A waitress brings us a tray of drinks, carefully placing it on the table with Walt's 'special shandy' in front of him.

Alice knows the drill. 'The staff are so great,' she whispers to me. 'They all know to make Walt's on that alcohol-free beer. Fiona brought a crate of it in. They even think to put an empty bottle of Tusker beside it!'

That's not all. Fiona has also made sure the staff know to fill an empty bottle of red wine with Ribena for our table in the dining room, and to put *two* straws into Walt's glass when we get a round of Club Pimm's Specials (so that we know which one is alcohol-free), and to take the salt shakers off the table so that Fiona can replace them with dummy ones brought from home, and to make sure his decaf coffee comes in a separate plunger with a *green* handle.

It's all French-polished furniture and white wicker chairs, parquetry floors and uniformed waiters, pots of strong tea and stronger pink gins, lacy tiers of cake and cucumber sandwiches. The latest British newspapers and magazines are flown in from London, left to lounge in leather dust jackets by the fire. A squash court, a croquet lawn and a library are available for our leisure.

Fiona grabs me and Alice just as we instinctively reach for our phones to digitally document the moment. 'Girls, meant to tell you, they're strict here – absolutely no mobile phones, no cameras. Use the computer room if you've got to take a call.'

Marguerite wags her finger at us. 'Naughty, naughty girls!' she scolds, while responding to a text message under the table.

So, modern technology is out – but old-fashioned decadence is in. Poolside gin and tonic? *Let me bring you a cushion for your sun lounger, madam, and fresh towels are by the bar.*

The walls are lined with fading sepia photographs of hunting parties fresh back from safari; one of their kills, a scrappy old lion, sits defeated in a glass box at the end of the hallway. Marguerite tells me it's taken more live rounds since it left the taxidermist than it did alive. 'Cheap pot shots from drunk hooligans!' she hoots, then leans forward with a stage whisper and knowing nod. 'That's why they had to put him in the case. For his own protection.'

Walt, Alice and I all laugh at Marguerite's dramatic flair. Fiona rolls her eyes.

'Why don't we go and get these guest member forms sorted out for the girls, Marguerite?' says Fiona, getting back to business.

'You stay here with Walt,' Alice says to me. 'I can sort yours if you like, Pig?'

'Pig! Did you just call her "Pig"!?' shrieks Marguerite, bringing all the conversations in the room to a standstill. One of the waiters shoots us a dirty look, but even Fiona looks mildly amused this time – a smile cracks open on her face.

I'm slightly embarrassed by the scene we're creating, but in typical Alice style, she doesn't seem to see what the big deal is. 'Yeah . . . what? That's her nickname,' she says indignantly.

(I picked it up from my hockey teammates when I was about thirteen, thanks to my healthy appetite. The name stuck – all the way through school and uni, and even into my professional life. Some people find it a bit confronting, but I like it. What can I say? I'm a fan of robust displays of affection.)

'How horrid!' Marguerite snorts. 'What a beastly name!'

'"Pig", did you say?' says Walt, baffled, and then suddenly he gets all sweetly gallant in my defence. 'Someone called you a "pig"?'

'It's okay, Dad,' says Fiona, settling him. 'It's a joke.'

They're all staring at me now, waiting for a response.

'It's okay – really, I don't mind!' I say. 'Actually, I quite like it. All my friends call me "Pig", or "Piggy". Or "Piggus".'

'"Piggus"?' says Walt.

'Or "Piglet",' says Alice.

'"Piglet" is much nicer,' says Fiona.

'Yes, I actually think "Piglet" is quite cute!' says Alice.

I notice a group of Kenyan women sitting at the next table are listening in on our debate, laughing. I smile and shrug back at them.

It probably goes without saying that until the late sixties, the Club was for whites only. Whether that was primarily to 'maintain standards' or to protect reputations is debatable. The Club is notorious for the raucous shenanigans that have taken place within its walls – some so ripe they are 'purposely avoided' in the First Volume of its history, a heavy tome lovingly compiled by members and for sale at the reception desk. One story that *is* reliably reported is that of Prince Edward's visit in 1928, when a guest was physically removed from the dining room: 'There is a limit, even in Kenya, and when someone offers cocaine to the Heir of the Throne, something has to be done about it, particularly when it is between courses at the dinner table.'

I bear that all in mind when I look around the room at all these people with their heads stuck up their arses. It's too bad they've forgotten how to have fun.

No cash changes hands on the premises – that would be uncouth. Instead, all orders are signed to handwritten chits, with accounts settled monthly by cheque. When I ask Fiona how I'm supposed to settle my own bills, she says not to worry: Marguerite will have it covered. 'It's part of the cost of looking after Dad.' If there's something I feel I ought to pay for, I should take a note of the amount and sort it out with her later – otherwise, all my chits are just magicked away in a green leather folder and added to the Smyths' tab. But it's not really Fiona's place to be generous, given Marguerite will be the one settling the bills, and I can't help but wonder how much of Fiona's gesture is motivated by spite. I decide I'll keep track of all my bills and at the very least offer to pay those that aren't incurred as part of my duties with Walt.

Moses reappears to show us through to the dining room. As we enter, Walt makes an observation that will become his standard remark every time we visit. He turns to me, eyebrows raised, 'I say, there are a lot of blacks, coloureds and Asians here today!'

Oh god, I think, mortified. *Oh god, oh god. Please don't let anyone have heard that.* But also: *Christ, Walt, you're a horrible racist prick.* Immediately followed by: *Eugh, it's not his fault. He's a product of his time. And totally senile!* I mean – what am I going to do? Shit on an octogenarian who doesn't know what year it is and has diminished impulse control? I'm reminded of the time my demented grandmother told the lovely Blue Care nurse who was taking care of her that he looked like 'that horrible fat man off TV – Kim Beazley!' and couldn't understand why my mother was so embarrassed.

As we take our seats at the table, Walt looks disapprovingly around the room, leans forward and whispers across the table, 'They really have let the standards drop here!'

'Dad,' Fiona says in a low voice, taking his hand, 'Keen-ya's been independent fifty years now. *Harambee!* Remember?' ('*Harambee*', meaning 'working or pulling together', was the slogan of the country's first independent government. Fiona has also co-opted it as a catchphrase for us to use when helping Walt in and out of chairs.)

Walt sulks for a bit, then comes around. 'They have dressed the part, I'll grant them that.'

'And they wear such shiny watches!' adds Marguerite, making eyes at the thick gold Rolex on the wrist of a businessman at the next table.

I glance at Alice. She's holding her head in her hands and staring straight down at the table. I force myself to look at the shiny watch man – he either didn't hear or is pretending not to. Maybe he's used to this sort of shit.

I can see why Fiona is so keen on us making good use of the Club. It's one of the few places Walt still finds familiar – a small corner of the real world that aligns with the ghost world of his mind, confused only by a display of racial equality that didn't exist in his day. We make our way along the mouth-watering curry buffet, piling our plates with sambals and samosas, coconut rice and pappadums. Fiona deftly removes the tandoori chicken pieces that Marguerite puts on Walt's plate as quickly as she puts them on.

'They're his favourite!' Marguerite says.

'They're a choking hazard,' Fiona replies. 'We can't trust him with the bones. You must be careful about what he orders here – try to guide him towards the white meats and salads, and don't let him loose with the salt.'

Fiona suggests we use the Club as a change of scenery when Walt's feeling cooped up at the house. 'It's a great place to bring Dad. He'll always have old friends here. He won't always remember exactly who they are, but he's polite enough to at least pretend to! I've managed to get hold of most people and make them aware of his condition – they know to play along.'

We bump into a few people who do indeed say their 'hellos' with a knowing wink and politely pretend not to notice that Walt doesn't quite know how to place them. But towards the end of the meal, a cheery man in a bow tie stops by our table. 'Walter Smyth! Well, I'll be blowed. Haven't seen you in years! How are you doing, old chap?'

'Oh, hello . . . Do I know you?' Walt says, looking to the rest of us for guidance.

'Hahaha, are you playing around? It's me! John Sterling!' John looks to the rest of us too, now. As though asking if there's a joke he doesn't get.

'Of course! You remember John, darling, don't you?' says Marguerite.

Walt looks at her with uncertainty, then resolves to play along. I realise I'm already starting to notice the subtleties in his facial expressions – the tells that reveal which way his mind is about to wobble. 'Ohhhh, yes,' he says, 'of course. John . . . Sterling . . .'

'And who are all these lovely young ladies you've got with you?' John says, beaming at Fiona, Alice and me.

Fiona jumps in, holding out her hand. 'Hi John, Fiona. It's been a while.'

'Fiona! My word – a bloody long while. You were barely out of school last I saw you! And these two young lasses?' John Sterling gestures at me and Alice. 'Granddaughters?'

'Errrr . . . yes, sort of,' Fiona says.

'*Nurses,*' Marguerite whispers. 'For the *bwana.*'

We should really get our story straight, I think.

'Not quite nurses,' Fiona explains. 'Carers. For Dad. He's a little forgetful these days.'

'Hi!' I say. 'I'm Kirsten.'

'And I'm Alice.'

'Oh, I see!' says John, shaking both our hands, clearly amused by our antipodean accents. 'And you're both *Or-stray-lyans*, I take it?'

'Yes, yes, we're *Or-stray-lyan*,' says Alice, wearily. We're both getting a bit over our nationality being a joke to everyone here; I don't understand what's so funny about it.

'*Are* you?' says Walt, rejoining the conversation.

'Right,' says John, nodding slowly. 'So, how long are you in town for, old boy?'

There's a sudden commotion at the edge of the dining patio – a Sykes' monkey has jumped onto the empty table beside us and is scooping up half-eaten dinner rolls from the side plates.

'Shoo!' Marguerite shrieks. Diners at nearby tables squeal and scramble to protect their lunch.

'Oh dear, sod off!' says Walt, standing and waving his napkin at the monkey until Fiona pulls him back down into his chair.

Two waiters chase it into the garden, knocking over a chair in the process and spilling a glass of wine. They shout and hiss at the monkey, which stares back insolently, enjoying its stolen meal from the safety of a fig tree. Alice and I are in stitches, and for all the pantomime irritation I can tell no one here really minds these cheeky primates disturbing the peace.

Fiona steers us all back to the conversation at hand. 'Dad's staying here for good,' she says, looking pointedly at Marguerite, 'away from the horrid cold of England.' Marguerite ignores the provocation, though John Sterling seems to notice it.

'Do send our love to Cindy,' says Marguerite. 'Ooooh! Do you think she'd like to play golf with me sometime?'

'No doubt she would!' John says. 'I'll tell her to get in touch.'

'Who's Cindy?' says Walt.

'You know Cindy!' says Marguerite impatiently. Fiona rolls her eyes.

A young couple walk in – a black woman with a white man – and take a table near the window. They look happy, relaxed. No one else in the place seems to find it noteworthy, but Walt looks mildly scandalised. Part of me wants to say to him, *Yeah, that's right, Walt! You can shack up with anyone you want to these days! It's great!* The more compassionate part wants to say, *Oh, mate, so much has changed since you've been away.* But my more immediate concern is that I need to intervene before *he* can say anything to them. They don't need to be insulted by some bigot from the past.

'More wine, Walt?' I ask, topping up his glass with Ribena and bringing his attention back to the chat about Cindy.

'Marguerite, of course he doesn't know Cindy,' says Fiona.

'Cindy who?' says Walt.

'John's Cindy!' says Marguerite, exasperated. 'Cindy Sterling!'

'Sterling?' says Walt.

'An old friend from your farming days, Dad,' says Fiona.

'Are you Cindy?' Walt asks, peering at me intently. He doesn't seem to notice John standing beside him anymore.

John takes this as his cue to leave, finally clicking that his old friend Walt isn't the man he used to be. 'Okay, well, I'd best be off. No doubt we'll see you around.' He walks away.

'I'll catch him later and explain the situation,' Fiona says to us, while Walt's distracted by a faux salt shaker. 'It's best that everyone knows what's going on – Dad's so good at hiding it in public, a lot of people don't pick it up themselves. They just think he's being rude, or a bit odd.'

But what, I wonder, do they think of us, his harem of devoted carers? Of his special drinks, and favourite chairs, and the cold war between his eccentric wife and overbearing daughter – what's their take on the whole elaborate charade?

Later that day, while Walt is having a nap and Marguerite is out at the hairdresser, Fiona breaks into Marguerite's desk. She rifles through the messy paper strata of Christmas cards and bank statements and instruction manuals and finds buried at the bottom – aha! – a printed copy of an email from Marguerite to Dr Andrews, the Smyth family's GP in Kenya. It was sent just before she came back from England.

Alice is still down at the Club when Fiona bursts into our room, breathless. She thrusts a piece of paper at me. Demands I read it.

Subject: *HIGHLY confidential!*

I scan the page. I can't quite work out who it's to or from at first: it's a stream-of-consciousness ramble, riddled with typos, random capital letters, exclamation marks and ellipses. It claims Fiona has turned into 'a control-freak nurse'. That despite having had 'little interest in her father until now', she's taken over his life and completely changed all the medication he was put on by Dr Bridges, Marguerite's doctor in England.

It's also addressed to one of the trustees, the one Fiona says is Marguerite's ally. I'm not entirely sure what this is meant to prove, other than that Marguerite is pissed off at having control over her husband's healthcare taken away, which is hardly surprising.

Then Fiona hands me Exhibit B – a letter from a solicitors' firm in the UK, confirming a December appointment with Marguerite. There's a map enclosed, and a reminder for her to bring her passport 'to comply with money-laundering checks'.

'That *proves* she plans on going back to the UK!' Fiona declares triumphantly.

'Yeah...' I say, confused. I didn't think this was a secret. 'Didn't she say she has to go back for a follow-up after that operation she had, and to check up on the repairs to their house?'

It doesn't matter. Fiona found lots of smoking guns in the drawer: prescriptions, blood-test results, airfare receipts. She hands them to me in a pile. A dossier of evidence of... I'm not quite sure what.

'I want you to take these down to the MiniMart – there's a little stationery *duka* there, do you know it? Down the bottom, next to the Barclays Bank.'

I hesitate. I'm not actually on duty. Do I have to get involved?

'Quickly! Before she gets back. Get two copies of everything. I want one for the medical file, and one for me. Peter will take you.' Fiona drags me out the door.

Peter's sitting on the stump in the garden, reading a newspaper. He jumps up when he sees us, throwing on his cap as he jogs over to the Peugeot. He can see that this is urgent.

'Take Kirsten down to the MiniMart, please, Peter.' Fiona shoves me into the passenger seat, then buckles me up like I can't do it myself.

Peter starts the engine; Patrick opens the gates.

'Wait!' Fiona slaps my window. I wind it down and she hands me a blue folder. 'Put the copies in this. And watch out for Marguerite – she's got eyes everywhere!'

Peter doesn't ask any questions but surely he must have some. We look at each other as we pull out of the driveway, silent, both a little unsure of how we've been roped into a special operation we don't understand.

'You know, not all *mzungus* are this crazy,' I eventually offer, lurching into the dashboard as the Peugeot bounces over an unmarked speed bump.

He laughs. 'Ahhh, it's okay. Everybody has problems.'

'Yeah, but these guys, they're an extreme case.'

'Ay, yes – they have many-many problems. Because of the *bwana*,' Peter concedes. 'You see, they are all wanting to be helping the *bwana*. But they are fighting, always fighting, Marguerite and Fiona. And this is not good for the *bwana*.'

'I wish they'd leave us out of it,' I grumble. 'I'm only supposed to be here to look after Walt.'

'Ach, *pole*, Kirsten, *pole sana*,' he says, with mock sincerity. ('*Pole sana*' is a Swahili expression of sorrow or sympathy, usually used in more tragic situations.) His sarcasm takes me by surprise and I laugh as he looks sideways at me, grinning, slapping his thigh.

The young guy manning the kiosk doesn't ask any questions either. I hand him the file and ask him for two copies of each page. He slowly feeds the paper through the photocopier, thumbing his mobile phone with his spare hand. 'Two hundred bob,' he mumbles once it's all done, then spends an age handwriting a receipt after I pass him the cash. *Come on, come on . . .* I think. *I want to get this over with*. Finally, I tuck the warm sheaf into the back of the folder and race up towards the car park.

Halfway there, I freeze.

'Yoo-hoo! Is that you!?'

The voice is coming from somewhere above me. I look up.

'Ohhhh, it *is* Kirsten! It's *youuuuu*! I thought it was!' Marguerite's pink face is gawping down at me from the balcony outside the beauty salon – stripped raw of make-up, flushed and dewy, framed by a silver bouffant that's gone flat at the back. She looks like a galah.

Her squawking has now got the attention of everyone seated at the tables in the courtyard café.

'I've just had a *woooooonderful* facial. The girls at the hairdresser talked me into it. Have you had one before? Oh, you must!' Then in a stage whisper that still manages to echo around the atrium – 'I even fell asleep for a bit!' – followed by a cackle so merry I can't help but smile at it.

I walk up the ramp to meet her outside the curio shop.

'Have you come to do groceries?' she asks, glancing down at the blue folder tucked under my arm.

Oh Lord. I must look guilty as hell.

'Um, no – I'm . . .' I find a lie just in time. 'I just wanted to get some money changed at the forex . . .'

Marguerite's eyes light up. 'I say, would you mind checking whether we've had any mail down at the Club?' She pulls an exaggerated face, puts on a tone of extreme self-deprecation. 'I forgot to when we left after lunch today. Silly, silly me!'

In an instant she's back to her sparky self. 'Ask the nice chap behind the desk, would you? He'll look in the pigeonhole. And see about the papers, too? Thank you ever so much. We didn't get the *Tele* yesterday. Sometimes there's a hold-up and a whole week's worth comes at once in a jolly big wad. Well, they're no good to us by that stage, are they? Although Walt doesn't mind reading them. It's all the same to him!'

She laughs. It's not a cruel laugh – it's almost a sad one. It's the laugh of a woman coming to terms with the absence of her husband of four decades, even while he's physically present. But she's not sad for long: she's spotted a pink striped *kikoy* hanging on the door to the curio shop.

'Would you look at that! Isn't it pretty? Yoo-hoo! Excuse me – yoo-hoo!' She waves madly at the Kenyan shop assistant – interrupting her while she's midway through serving another woman at the counter – and beckons her over, holding the *kikoy* up in the air and over-enunciating, 'How-much-is-it?'

'See you at home then!' I say, slipping away.

I find Peter having a cigarette in the car park with one of the yellow-coated parking attendants. He rushes to stub it out.

'It's alright,' I say, 'finish it, Peter. Actually – if you don't mind, I'll have a drag.'

'You smoke!?' he says, passing it to me.

'Only when I want a head spin,' I say.

We share the rest of the cigarette leaning on the bonnet of the Peugeot, and I start to worry about what I've got myself into.

As we pull in to the driveway, I see Walt staring at us through the dining-room window. Before we've even come to a stop, he's rapping on Peter's door, Fiona chasing behind him.

'*Jambo, bwana,*' says Peter, careful to keep the keys out of sight as he gets out of the Peugeot.

'What are you doing in my car?' Walt says.

'He knows the sound of this engine a mile away,' Fiona says. Peter, evidently, knows to play it cool, keep a cheery tone – to de-escalate the situation.

'It's okay, *bwana,*' he says, casually. 'I was just taking Kirsten down to the MiniMart.' Peter discreetly hands Fiona the keys behind his back.

'Come on Dad, let's go and see what James is up to,' Fiona says, trying to turn Walt away from the Peugeot to face the garden, where James is watering in some freshly planted flowers.

I find Alice in our room and fill her in on my little assignment.

She doesn't find it all that intriguing. She's more interested in the article she's reading about the Samburu warriors of north Kenya. They probably are more interesting than the Smyths, to be fair.

So I email Sarah and Jack, my friends at the High Commission, to see if they want to catch up the next day. Surely they'll find this all as outrageous as I do.

We meet at their local bar, which has a shady beer garden and is a short walk from their place. It's on the other side of town, and a bit of a mission to get to, especially in Nairobi traffic. Peter gives me a ride – Alice and Fiona have taken Walt to a doctor's appointment, and Marguerite has arranged to play bridge with a friend nearby, so nobody needs a driver for the morning.

Apart from the drive from the airport, this is my first time venturing much further than the Smyths' environs. Beyond the high walls and security fences of the top end of town, I'm reminded that Nairobi is a modern and vibrant city, suffused with optimism despite being weighed down by poverty. It's a place of traffic jams and beggars and celebrity gossip, of stand-up comedy and fashion shows and shoe-shiners. Street hawkers from the slums flog phone chargers and counterfeit DVDs to commuters in air-conditioned luxury cars. Kenya's capital is full of banal and beautiful scenes that will never be on the cover of *Lonely Planet*.

Peter narrates the route for me as we go, seemingly keen to help me find my bearings. 'This is Limuru Road. *Limuru*. That's the Aga Khan Hospital, where Bwana Smyth sees the doctor. That's City Park, where we go to the markets for fruit.'

We pass a rugby union team training on a well-kept field, while families picnic at the sidelines. The radio plays a news bulletin telling of raids on suspected Al-Shabaab militants in Eastleigh, of police shooting 'thugs' dead in the midst of a robbery in Nakuru, of the Wheat Farmers Association urging the government to raise the price of their crop, and of Kenyan runners winning gold medals in international marathons.

'Do you know Eastleigh?' Peter asks me.

'No, where's that?'

'It is the suburb where all the Somalis live, next to downtown. It is very-very dangerous! You must never go there,' he wags a finger at me. 'They have AK-47s everywhere – I have seen them! It is not safe.' Then shaking his head in disapproval. 'Mm-mmm.'

Later, I read up on Eastleigh – or 'Little Mogadishu', as it's sometimes known. It's where most Somali immigrants end up settling in Nairobi, including a great number of the undocumented refugees who spill over from the border to the north. This entrepreneurial community supports its own thriving economy, and I get the sense that this, combined with ethnic divisions, is a source of tension and envy for less-fortunate Kenyans. In more recent years, the Kenyan police have taken to harassing Eastleigh residents they suspect of harbouring terrorists, but so far no convincing cases have been made.

We nose our way through the congestion around Westlands and turn onto Waiyaki Way, one of the city's main arterial roads. Casinos and hotels and corporate head offices fly by, as Peter expertly avoids the *matatus* that pull on and off the road without warning. *Matatus* – Kenya's infuriating and indispensable minivans – are ubiquitous throughout the country and especially within Nairobi, operating as a semi-formal public transport system relied upon by 70 per cent of the population. Peter explains to me how the fourteen-seater Toyotas are privately owned but follow set routes determined by the government, with drivers paid by the number of trips they make – an incentive for reckless driving. *Matatus* don't so much own the road as indecently assault it and everyone else on it. They ignore lane markings and traffic lights, mount kerbs and drive along footpaths and veer into oncoming traffic to push ahead in traffic jams. They're a menace, but without them the city would shut down. (The word *matatu*, originating from the Kikuyu language's word for the original thirty-cent fare, *mĩrongo ĩtatũ*, is fittingly close to the Swahili word for 'problem', *matata*.)

Peter weaves his way through the roadworks and Chinese labourers who have recently come to Nairobi – thousands of men in silver conical hats building super highways and flyovers, climbing the scaffolding of the new hotels and office towers that are flapping with wraps of green shade-cloth and fronted with project signs bearing the name of Chinese developers in English and *hànzì* characters. The newspapers and TV news programs show pictures of politicians and Asian businessmen shaking hands with wide smiles and captions full of dollar signs, but ordinary Kenyans seem less sure about their new business partners.

We drive past a building site where three Chinese men are shovelling hot mix and gravel in the sun, dressed in business suits and ties. 'They are very strange, these people,' Peter says, pointing them out. I must admit, I'm as perplexed by their choice of attire as he is.

On the radio, a talkback program is discussing the social tension caused by the growing Chinese presence. Many callers are aggrieved that contracts and jobs are being awarded to foreigners when so many unemployed Kenyans could do with the work. Others argue that the expediency is justified, saying the country desperately needs to have infrastructure built quickly if it is to lift itself out of poverty and can't do it without outside help. The hosts start ranting about local businesses that aren't up to scratch – Peter leans forward to turn the volume down. 'Ach, they have the same fight every day!' he says. 'Is the radio in Australia like this too?'

'Yeah, pretty much!' I laugh, thinking of the radio shock jocks back home, and the similar anxieties people have there over the next wave of immigration. I feel sorry for the Chinese men we drive past. Like the convicts sent from England to Australia, they aren't really here by choice. Many are rumoured to be prisoners on forced labour programs – at the very least, they're an impoverished underclass who have moved here out of pure economic necessity. Imagine being a dirt-poor Chinese villager, flown to the other side of the world to build roads for people who are openly hostile to your presence and speak no common language. Will these people even *want* to stay once their contracts are up, I wonder. And if so, where will they fit into the melting pot of modern-day Kenya – a country of over forty different ethnic groups, each with its own language, beliefs and customs – where the daily fight for existence is already tough enough?

Peter drops me in the car park outside the bar and shows me where to find a private taxi to get home again. 'Don't get one from the street,' he says. 'They are not safe.'

I make my way through the friendly crowd of middle-class professionals filling the place with laughter and good cheer. Younger and older people of all races mix readily – the only hint of colonialism is the cricket and rugby playing on TV screens at the sports bar. It's a world away from the Club.

Sarah and Jack are waiting for me at a table in the courtyard, with a round of icy-cold Tusker beers. God, it's good to see familiar faces from home.

Sarah grins. 'Hey, bitch.'

'What's up, Pig?' says Jack, giving me a big hug.

'Lots,' I say, taking a seat and a big swig of beer. 'What a crazy way to meet up, hey? Let's eat, I'm starving.'

The menu offers hearty barbecue pub grub with an East African bent: *nyama choma*, *masala* fries, tilapia with a side of *ugali*.

'You gotta get the *nyama choma*,' Jack says. 'It's basically the Kenyan equivalent of a chicken schnitty.'

'It's not crumbed chicken, it's roast meat,' Sarah clarifies. 'All kinds – beef and lamb, but usually goat.'

'And get the *masala* fries 'cos they're the bomb,' Jack adds, 'but also you should get some *ugali*, just to try it.'

'What's that?' I ask.

'It's this stodgy dough stuff, kind of like thick mashed potato. But made of maize flour.'

'It's the staple diet here,' Sarah explains. 'Like rice is in Asia. Kenyans eat it with pretty much everything.'

I remember my parents talking about the equivalent in Rhodesia, but there they called it *sadza*. Mum and Dad always thought it was horribly bland, but my sisters and I loved it when we tried it on our family trip to Zimbabwe. I'm keen to see how it is here, and to try some authentic Kenyan food. So I take Jack's advice on what to order. I don't regret it. The meat is delicious.

Over the rest of the afternoon, I fill my friends in on the old man and his wife and daughter, the dead lion and the Club, the cameras and the bed alarm and the pills. They both – quite rightly – think it's all ludicrous.

'Piggy, what the fuck?' says Sarah. 'How did you get into this?'

'Alice . . . She got me the job.'

Sarah knows Alice from school. 'Of course she did. Well, you are totally fucking insane for agreeing to any of it.'

'Look, yes, having heard myself say it all out loud, it does sound a bit mental, I'll admit.'

'Hey,' says Sarah, 'if you ever need to get away from the asylum, you can come and stay at ours. We've got plenty of room. Stay tonight, if you like?'

I'd love to, but I can't. I have to get back to take over from Millicent for the night shift. Instead, I make a plan to spend a night at Sarah and Jack's apartment next time I have a weekend evening off.

I spend the taxi ride home staring out the window giggling to myself, thanks to the tipsy haze that brings the absurdity of this whole scenario into sharp relief. Though maybe I'm more than tipsy . . . Millicent brings me a Nescafé but says nothing when I get back. I appreciate her discretion.

At bedtime, as I walk Walt down the hallway to his room, we pass her kneeling on the floor beside her bed, saying an evening prayer. He stops and gawks, incredulous. I drag him onward before he can interrupt her.

'We've got a very pious houseguest, I see,' he says, closing his eyes and holding his hands together in a pretend prayer as I close the door behind us.

'Yes, Walt, that's Millicent – she's very devout,' I whisper. Then in the cheery way Fiona has shown us, 'Now come on, let's clean those chompers of yours!'

'As long as she's atoning for *all* our sins!' he says back, with a camp air-slap and guilty giggle. He thinks we're being *very naughty*. I'm glad he's in a good mood – that makes it easier for me to convince him to brush his teeth.

Then I'm not so glad. It also, evidently, makes him randy. He begs me for a goodnight kiss and tries to drag me into bed with him when I tuck him in. I manage to escape with just a pinched arse.

On the upside, having him go to sleep laughing means there are no major interruptions in the night – the bed alarm only goes off once, around two o'clock. On the night-vision screen, I groggily watch him do a wee, then wander around the room aimlessly for a few minutes before he puts himself back to bed. A pinched arse, I figure, is a small price to pay for a good night's sleep.

By morning it's overcast, and Walt is grizzly. Fiona says the weather can have a huge influence on his mood, that grey sky makes him sulk. I'm not sure what any of us can ever hope to do about that, but I wouldn't be surprised if she has some kind of strategy for keeping the clouds out of his sight.

We've only just sat down to breakfast when the phone rings. I'm sitting closest so I answer, but before I have a chance to say 'hello' a frantic voice is warbling at me through the handset. It's a woman with a strong German accent. 'Yes, I was thinking, how is it if I come around this morning for tea? You will be home, yes?'

'Sorry, hello?' I say.

'Oh yes, hello, hello, yes hello. It is I, Magda. *Magda.*'

It's Magda, I mouth to the table.

'Ooooh! Magda!' Marguerite squeals, causing Walt to jump. Fiona sighs and folds her arms.

Magda continues monologuing in my ear, leaving no space for me to respond to any of her queries. 'You are one of the Australian girls? Yes, yes, I can hear it in your accent. Which one are you? Never mind, we will meet today I suppose. Juma has made some wonderful cakes, I will bring them for us to eat with tea. Is Marguerite there? I heard she was back from UK. John Sterling said he saw them at the Club. And Walt?'

'Ah, yes, they're both here –' I manage to squeeze in.

'Oh, hello, Marguerite – yes, it's me!' Magda is now hollering from the other side of the table.

I hold the receiver up so the women can talk across the room.

'Yes, do come around, Magda, that will be lovely,' Marguerite bellows. 'Won't that be lovely, darling?' she asks her husband.

'Who's that?' asks Walt.

'It's Magda!' says Marguerite.

'Helllooooo!' Magda shouts into the phone. 'It's me, Walt! Hellllooooooo!'

'Oh *Magda*,' he says. 'Yes, super.'

'Very good, I will come at ten.' *Click*. Flat tone. Fiona, noting my bewilderment, says, 'Magda's a bit different.' *Everyone here's a bit 'different'*, I think.

We've only just managed to get Walt's teeth brushed and have him settled into his patio chair for morning tea when we hear Magda's car pull into the drive. The sound of the engine brings him straight back to his feet. 'Now, whose car is that?' he mutters, heading off for the driveway with Fiona chasing after him.

'Bugger,' she says on her way past. 'We should have told Magda to park down the road a bit. Cars always set him off.'

'Well, that's just ridiculous,' says Marguerite, as soon as Fiona's out of earshot. 'We can't ask visitors to park down the bloody road and walk to the house. And what about *our* cars? There are three between us, and we'll all have to be coming and going if we want to do our own thing, won't we?'

Magda, I soon learn, was a journalist. She came to Kenya in the 1960s on a short-term assignment and never left. She's a decades-long friend of both Walt and Marguerite, and as she lives in the next suburb over is one of their more regular visitors. Magda wears only purple and green, loves books and art, and doesn't seem to understand jokes but laughs at them all the same.

I quickly come to love her — she isn't a typical colonial. She's interested in the world around her in a way that most whites her age in Nairobi don't seem to be, and is excited when she discovers I'm a journalist too.

'And will you do some writing while you are here?' Magda asks, as Esther brings our morning tea out to the patio.

'Oh maybe,' I say. 'Yes, I hope so, if there's time.' Although, when I think about it, I'm not sure I want to do much more than just take things in for the time being.

'Oh, you must!' she exclaims with a mouthful of cake. 'There are so many wonderful stories here! Not these stories,' she waves dismissively at the newspapers laid out on the table, '*good* stories! Stories people don't expect from Africa.'

'Are you trying to convince foreigners of the natives' hidden talents again, Magda?' Walt teases.

'But what do you mean, Walt?' Magda says, missing the goading in his question. 'Why would they hide their talents?' Magda, I take it, doesn't conceive of herself as a superior being.

'Our European friend here has always been a do-gooder,' he says to me.

Magda ignores him. 'Anyway, I do think you should do some stories. And you must travel, too.'

'Oh yes!' says Marguerite. 'You really must see more of Keen-ya while you're here. We'll make sure you go to the coast, and do a safari, of course.' As long as they make sure I'm paid and we can arrange the time off, that shouldn't be a problem.

'I'm really hoping to do an overland trip at some point,' I say. 'To Rwanda, to see the mountain gorillas.'

'Ohhhh the gorillas, yes, yes yes!' says Magda. 'They are magical. I went many years ago. But have you applied for your visa yet? Because you know I hear they can take a long time to approve. You have to take your passport into the embassy. I will take you now, if you like? It is not far. And I am wanting to see the flower man on that road anyway. They have some lovely tulips at the moment.'

'Ummm . . . . Sure?' I say, looking at Fiona to get the okay. She nods. I race inside to grab my passport, leaving Alice to distract Walt from the sound of the car engine starting up again as we leave.

Magda interrogates me as she drives. 'And how is Walt, as you see it?' she asks, peering at me intently instead of watching the road. Magda blinks a lot, chews her bottom lip and twitches her nose. She makes me think of a concerned squirrel.

'He's doing okay,' I say. 'He's obviously very forgetful, but I think his physical health is actually improving.' I suddenly realise that part of my responsibility as Walt's carer is to make judgements and assessments about his condition: whether he's getting better or worse, how 'happy' or otherwise he seems. I stress to Magda that I have no nursing or medical qualifications whatsoever – that I've not even been here two weeks yet.

'Yes, yes,' says Magda, 'but we all could see, he has been like this for a long time! It is strange that only now Fiona seems to notice. She has really not had anything to do with Walt for twenty years. And now she just comes here and takes over! We all here think she is being very unfair to Marguerite.'

'Oh?' *Who's 'we all'?* I think. *Does the whole of Nairobi know what's going on in this house?*

'Yes, well, we are all — Walt's friends, that is — wanting to be what is best for him, of course,' says Magda. 'And we must remember — Marguerite, she is old too! She can be forgetful also — yes, I know this, she does need help too, but she is very good to Walt. I have known them for so many years. He would not want to be without her. Fiona shouldn't tell her to leave!'

'She's telling her to leave?' That's news to me.

'Yes! Marguerite tells me Fiona says she is to go back to England and leave Walt here with his carers.'

Well, this is not quite how Fiona has put it to me. I stand in line at the Rwandan High Commission feeling very confused, as though I can't fully trust Marguerite *or* Fiona. Or what they tell me about each other. But what Magda's told me about Fiona's previous lack of interest in her father has sparked a theory in my own mind about what's going on here: I reckon Fiona saw Walt lying in that London hospital bed, knocking at death's door, and got the guilts. Confronted with his mortality she's now pulling out all the stops to make up for the years she'd neglected him and blaming Marguerite for not doing more to halt his decline — or worse, for causing it. And hearing an outsider like Magda tell me that Marguerite and Walt had a good relationship makes Fiona's allegations of neglect seem more dubious. But then . . . even Magda thinks Marguerite needs help looking after Walt.

Finally, I reach the counter and hand over my passport and application form to the woman behind the glass. As she begins to process my documents, her demeanour changes. She becomes surly. She glares at me. 'You are Australian?'

'Yes . . .' I say.

'Where is your letter of invitation?'

'. . . what's that?'

'You must include a letter of invitation stating *why* you wish to visit our country.'

She hands me a blank piece of paper. It seems I must invite myself.

'Oh, okay,' I say, wondering if this is standard protocol for all Australians, or just for me.

'Over there,' she says, directing me to a counter across the room. I take my blank page and write what I hope reads as a flattering request to visit Rwanda to see their world-famous mountain gorillas, and rejoin the queue.

'One hundred US dollars,' the woman says when I finally reach her window again.

'How long will this take?' I ask, handing her the cash, and watching my passport disappear into a drawer.

'I cannot say.'

'Okay, but . . . are we talking days? Weeks?'

'You will have to call to check. Next!'

Whatever Australia did to Rwanda, they haven't forgotten about it.

I ask Magda to pull up outside the gates when we return to the house, to avoid distracting Walt with the sound of the car engine. It's daylight, Patrick is right there, ready with the keys, so I figure it's fine to take the risk.

'You girls here will be very good. You will be a help to him and Marguerite, I am sure,' Magda says, as I climb out of the car. She purses her lips together, frowns, then breaks into a grin. 'Okey-dokey, then. Bye now, bye!'

With that, she hits the gas.

That evening, while Alice is taking Walt through his evening routine, Fiona comes into my room with more reading material: a letter she's written to 'the Keen-ya crowd'.

It's to be attached to a printout of the Wikipedia page on Citalopram, then delivered to all and sundry tomorrow, before she flies out the following day.

The letter is nuclear.

It accuses Marguerite of convincing her doctor in the UK to put Walt on sleeping pills and antidepressants because she felt he had become 'unmanageable'. Fiona writes that this was an underhand way of resolving marital problems, and unethical given Walt wasn't properly consulted or able to understand what he was being given.

She reiterates the points she has highlighted on the Wikipedia Citalopram article: about apathy and emotional flattening, weight loss, insomnia, blood-pressure changes and heart palpitations, about interactions with other drugs.

Fiona writes that when Walt came to stay with her after a trip to hospital, *her* doctor made him immediately stop taking the antidepressants, which made Marguerite very angry.

She writes that she hopes people will consider this information when they wonder why Walt seems so much better from when they last saw him, and when Marguerite tells them her version of events. She finishes by writing that she feels it's best for Walt that he spends his final years here in the 'warmth and sunshine' of the country that he loves, with his dearest friends, and where his health problems can be managed correctly.

And then she asks me what I think.

I'm not sure what to say. So I ask her – as gently as I can – whether she's sure it's a good idea to put all that down on paper and hand it to people who will almost certainly tell Marguerite they've received it.

'Absolutely!' she says. 'People here need to know what's been going on. I know Marguerite's poisoned them all against me – they think I'm a horrible bitch. And some of them will still think that regardless.'

She's probably got that much right. No one has explicitly said it, but I get the sense that most people around here are on Marguerite's side and think Fiona is kind of bonkers. Then again, not many of them realise just how bad Walt's mental state is – he's surprisingly adept at masking it in public. With, of course, our assistance.

'But I don't care,' Fiona adds. 'I have to have my say.'

'Okay.' It's none of my business, really.

Except that the next morning it becomes my business.

First thing after breakfast, I'm back at the copy kiosk. Fiona has requested twenty-five copies of the letter, to be inserted into twenty-five envelopes in a variety of colours and shapes and sizes. She insists this isn't overkill. 'You don't know who you're dealing with.'

She wants each one to be addressed in different handwriting and with a different pen so that if Marguerite twigs to what we're doing and tries to get the letters back after they've been delivered, she won't know which ones to take out of people's mailboxes.

The same young man who served me the first time I came in knows something is up. He locks the door and turns the sign to 'Closed' when he notices me poking my head around the corner to see if anyone is coming my way. He hands me my rainbow assortment of envelopes, and I can see he wonders what he's a part of, but I leave without telling him – there's no time to get into it. I've got miles to cover by lunchtime.

Peter and I spend nearly two hours driving around town in the Peugeot: pulling up at the gates of old houses, asking the *askaris* to put this envelope in with the rest of the day's mail.

The whole time, I'm vaguely mulling over the ethics of this situation. I figure it all depends on whether Fiona's right about Marguerite's intentions. And given I don't fully trust Marguerite, I can't be certain either way. Fiona has known her much longer than I have, after all. So I decide, since the stakes are so high – a man's life in the balance – it's best to err on the side of caution. That it's fine for her to be letting people know they should keep an eye out for him. And I convince myself that what I'm doing is okay because I'm just following orders. Then I realise that's the Nuremberg defence – that I'm basically a Nazi courier, delivering other people's dirty laundry. Bugger.

Fiona leaves for England at the crack of dawn. We promise to keep her in the loop, and to call her any time, day or night, if Walt gets worked up and we can't calm him down.

With her gone, the end room is freed up for Alice to move into, giving us both a bit more space.

Finally master of her own domain, Marguerite decides we should go down to the golf club after breakfast and do some putting. 'Walt loves it. Especially when the weather's as lovely as this.'

It's my morning on duty, so I tag along. One advantage of the outing is that I get an insight into the dynamic between Marguerite and Walt without Fiona around, and a sense of the patter of an ordinary day. A disadvantage is being a passenger while Marguerite drives.

To reach the golf club we've got to get through one of the main highway interchanges, which – like so many crucial intersections in Nairobi – is currently being upgraded.

'Look at this mess at ten o'clock in the morning!' Marguerite exclaims, swerving as she points at the road workers in their conical aluminium hats. 'Oh, it's the Chinese.'

'What in heaven's name are they doing digging everything up?' says Walt.

'They're building a new road, Walt,' I say, my stomach lurching as Marguerite overcorrects her steering. This is the woman who scolds Peter for a bumpy ride, as though he can do anything to avoid roads littered with potholes.

'Oh well, fair enough I suppose,' Walt mutters. 'The Europeans have given up. Might as well let someone else have a turn.'

'These two are going right around there!' Marguerite points at a couple of *matatus* mounting the kerb to get past. 'Oh, that *is* clever. Shall I do that too?'

'Please don't!' I say, clinging to my seatbelt.

'I imagine they've no idea what they're doing themselves,' says Walt. I'm not sure whether he's talking about the Chinese workers or the *matatu* drivers.

'Now you can see why we don't go driving anywhere. And it's not even the rush hour! Oh look, the man behind me is overtaking. No!' Marguerite waves madly into her mirror, wagging her finger at the driver trying to pass. 'No! You just go back, you naughty boy!'

'He just fingered back!' says Walt.

'Did he!?' Marguerite briefly hits the brakes in a fit of indignation. I brace myself against the front seats.

'Deary, deary me.'

By the time we pull into the golf club car park I'm nauseous. A mob of caddies swarm the car. 'Now, they're all going to come up and say to you, "*Jambo, bwana*,"' Marguerite tells Walt, leaning across the centre console to whisper in his ear. 'So, all you do is pretend you know them all and stick your hand out.'

It's obvious this is how he's made it through all these years without his mental decline being clear to everyone around them – she's been helping him muck along, his personal guide to everyday life. Like one of those assistants who whispers into a president's ear, reminding them of the name of every person whose hand they're about to shake.

'Oh blast, I haven't got my clubs with me, have I?' says Walt.

'No, you've only got a putter. But that's alright because we're only putting today!' Marguerite shoos a caddy away through the window – 'No! No!' – then says to Walt, 'They're all coming to see you. Let's go and pick one, shall we? How about that nice chap,

Ernest. He was good last time, wasn't he? And doesn't he look smart in his cap and vest.'

Ernest carries the clubs down to the practice green and I hover nearby, staying out of the way but close enough to observe Walt and Marguerite together. Small groups of other grey-haired golfers in knits — Indian and African and European men and women — wave familiar hellos as they pass by on their way to the first hole. Every now and then I wander over to tie Walt's laces when they come undone, or to help Marguerite chase Egyptian geese back down to the water. I watch closely for any signs of tension between them. But all I see, all I overhear, is a sweet old couple tapping some golf balls around: 'Splendid shot, darling!' 'Jolly good show!' 'Oooof, you only missed that one by a whisker!' They laugh, they tease, they enjoy the morning sun. You wouldn't know there was anything wrong with Walt. There's nothing for him to remember or forget: he just has to live in the moment. This is surely as good as things can be for anyone in his condition.

Eventually, they've had enough. Ernest collects the balls and takes the clubs back to the car while we head inside for tea and warm *mandazis* — East African doughnuts — in the clubhouse. Walt shakes the hands of a dozen people he doesn't remember and Marguerite tells a seven-year-old Kenyan boy, dressed head to toe in Callaway apparel, that he looks 'just like a baby Tiger Woods!' His father doesn't seem to mind. He and Marguerite arrange to play the following week.

'You know, my handicap is still just thirteen!' Marguerite brags.

'Oh, I know, Mrs Smyth,' the Kenyan boy's father says, laughing. 'You are the star of this course!'

Marguerite is beaming by the time we're back in the car to drive home, and Walt is in a wonderful mood too.

'That was great fun, I thought,' Marguerite says, blindly reversing out of the parking spot. 'We all enjoyed it, didn't we? And your new granddaughter — she enjoyed it.'

'Who?' Walt says.

'Me, Walt!' I say from the back seat. 'I'm sitting here behind you!'

'Kirsten – your new granddaughter!' Marguerite says.

Walt spins to see me, as though for the first time, even though only moments earlier I had helped him into the car and done his seatbelt up for him. 'Oh, yes – hello there . . .'

We take the backstreets to get home. It makes for no smoother a ride, though it does mean we pass by the British High Commissioner's house where a TV crew are setting up cameras out the front.

'Aha! I'll tell you who they're waiting for,' Marguerite says, drifting off the road briefly as she turns to tell me. 'They're waiting for "the couple".'

She's talking about the Chandlers, a British couple who were kidnapped from their yacht by Somali pirates and held hostage for over a year. I'm well across this story – Dad forwarded it from the BBC News site in an email that just said, 'Piglet – watch out for bloody *nyamazanes*.'

'They've been found,' Marguerite says. 'Well, they were released. Very lucky. They were very stupid. They were told not to do it, and they did it. *Stupid!* Went on a boat from the Seychelles to Kenya. Now they're with the Commissioner having special tea. I know, you see, because I met a girl from the High Commission yesterday at the Club and well, you know, I do like to find things out, so I made her tell me!'

'They were on a cruise?' Walt says.

'No,' says Marguerite. 'In their own sailing boat. And they were told not to. Husband and wife. And they were captured.'

'By whom!?' Walt is outraged.

'The Somalis,' she says.

'Somalis?'

'Yes, pirates!' Marguerite says. 'You're really not following, are you darling? And they wanted an enormous ransom. Well, the people did not have the money. And you know, the British government won't pay it, nor any government. But somebody got half a million from family, and somebody paid the next half – you know, kindly. And they were released.'

'Thank heavens!' says Walt, as we fly over an unmarked speed bump.

'But they were in a terrible state!' she says. 'Lost all their teeth. Can you imagine!? They were thirteen months in the jungle. Separated, too. Him in one compound, her in another.'

'Jungle or sea?' asks Walt.

'Jungle,' says Marguerite. 'In Somalia.'

I say, 'I don't think there is a jungle in Somalia . . .'

'Oh, you know, the desert-jungle. Mud huts and all that lot.'

'Well I think it's a very good thing,' says Walt. 'All these foolish people who come out and don't do as they're told. But off they go because they think they're being big bright safari people. But they don't know Africa! I think it's bloody good if they're put in jail for six months or so. They cost the British government thousands of pounds.'

Marguerite pulls up out the front of the Club, just as fat raindrops start splatting on the windscreen. 'Now you wait here. I'll run in to see if there's any mail. Won't this rain be good for the country?!'

She races inside, and we sit quietly for a few seconds, as the percussion of the sun shower picks up pace. Walt taps the dashboard, mutters to himself, 'I have no idea what's going on. No idea at all.'

'We're just at the Club, Walt,' I say, 'checking the mail, then we'll head home.'

He spins around to look at me, startled. I realise he thought he was alone in the car. Then he offers his hand and smiles. 'Oh, hello there! I don't think we've met . . .'

'Hi Walt, I'm Kirsten,' I say, for what must be upwards of the hundredth time.

'And you're here with the Foreign Service?'

'Um, yeah – that's right . . .' Sure. Whatever. It doesn't matter, does it?

'Oh, splendid. Well, I'm sure they'll make sure you have a marvellous time here. They don't like to work you lot too hard.'

~

Walt remains in a good mood for the rest of the day and is still chipper when Alice puts him to bed around nine o'clock.

But around half an hour later, when Marguerite joins him, things turn sour. Their voices grow louder. Alice brings the monitor into my room. We watch Marguerite sitting on the end of her bed, Walt pacing up and down past her, waving something we can't quite make out in her face.

'Darling, I told you,' she says, 'there's plenty more cash in the safe!'

'Don't "darling" me!' he snarls.

'And we have our chequebooks too, of course. And we can go to the bank tomorrow and get you more cash, if you like.'

'I know what you're up to – you're all up to your elbows in it!'

'What are you talking about?'

'If you swallowed a nail you'd pass a screw! The lot of you!'

'Walt, you're being very silly now.'

'Get out!' he shouts. 'Get out of my house!'

'It's *my* house too, you know.'

'No, it bloody well isn't!'

'Okay, darling. I'll sleep in the study, shall I? Just let me get my night things then.'

Marguerite gathers her robe and some items from her bedside table. She pokes her head into our room as she comes down the hall.

'I think I'd best sleep in the study,' she says. 'My friend through there is quite cross with me tonight.'

Walt follows her down the hallway. 'If I see you in here again I'll knock your bloody block off!'

'Alright then,' says Marguerite, starting to sound a bit shaken.

He stops at my doorway on his way back to his room. 'And you too! I want all of you out of my house in the morning.'

Behind him, Millicent sticks her head out of the sunroom and pulls an alarmed face. She's on duty in the morning. If we make it that far.

'Okay, Walt — we'll leave tomorrow,' Alice says, taking him back to bed. 'Promise.'

'That was hectic,' I say to her when she returns. *No wonder she wanted him sedated*, I think.

'Yeah. Pretty standard, though. He'd have episodes like that fairly often when we were in England.'

'But he was in such a good mood today! They were getting along so well.'

'Yep. It can turn just like that. It's so hard to predict. Usually something has triggered it, though. Probably Marguerite said something to make him start thinking about money. He's always on about having enough cash — that's why we need to make sure his dummy wallet is always full. It's actually good having the shillings here because they're all in hundreds, so it makes him feel like he's got heaps. When really it's just a few dollars.'

By morning all is forgotten. Walt is fawning over Marguerite at breakfast, flirting with me and Alice, cooing at the dogs and the birds. He's even being nice to Millicent — takes his pills when she asks him to, brushes his teeth without complaint.

Marguerite goes out to get a blow-dry. While Walt sits reading the papers on the patio with Millicent, I take a Skype call from Fiona who wants an update on the situation. I tell her about his little rampage last night — and she immediately blames it on Marguerite. 'I think we just need to say "no" to golf from now on.'

'I don't think it had anything to do with the golf,' I say, confused. 'I mean — golf was in the morning. This was late last night. He wouldn't have remembered by then that we'd gone at all.'

'No, you see, it stirs him up too much. Too much excitement. He may not even realise — it's all about routine.'

'But he really enjoyed it!' I say, horrified that she would want to ban the one activity that I've seen put him at total ease.

'No. It's too much for him to handle. Physically, as well as mentally. His heart can't cope — it increases the chance he'll have a heart attack or a stroke. Marguerite should know better.'

'But it's just putting on the practice green. It's not like they're going for big walks around the course or anything.'

'The problem is trying to stop Dad from doing too much once he's out there. I think it's safest if we just don't take him at all. I don't trust her not to let him overdo it.'

'Okay,' I say reluctantly. 'No more golf.' But I don't really mean it. I'm not going to tell his wife what she can and can't do with her husband of forty years. They've come this far already — surely they deserve to see out the end together too.

Apart from Walt's unpredictable upsets, we settle into a comfortable routine — Alice, Millicent and I sharing the load with Walt, while also doing what we can to help Marguerite keep the household ticking over and organise her busy social life. There are hair appointments to book, and bridge games to attend, and printer cartridges to be replaced in the printer that always needs unjamming. Alice and I often volunteer to do a run with Peter or James to pick up groceries, or fuel for the generator, or to collect the newspapers from the Club — even if we're technically off duty, it's a pleasant escape from the house, an encounter with the outside world and a reminder that the Smyths really are an aberration.

One of my favourite errands to run is the Thursday morning trip to the City Park market, to buy fresh fruit and vegetables for the week. Peter leads me through the stalls, helps me barter for pawpaws and mangoes, tells the women off in Swahili if they try to rip us off, the place erupting in theatrics and laughter when they're caught. He's scrupulous with the Smyths' money, refusing to pay more than we should for anything, keeping careful track of how much we've spent on a scrap of paper, down to the last shilling. Sometimes, if we have time, we go to the open green park behind the market, where we buy ten-bob bags of peanuts to feed the monkeys. Peter and I load up our pockets and hair with nuts, then sit still on the edge of a park bench and wait for the monkeys to climb all over us. They balance on our heads, our shoulders, our laps, nimble fingers tickling all over in the hunt for their favourite treats.

Fiona calls every day – sometimes twice a day. She sends text messages and emails, asking what Walt had for lunch, who Marguerite's been talking to on the phone, whether there've been any visitors to the house, making sure we've remembered to keep the pills well stocked, checking if there's anything we need sent over from England. At first, I indulge her with tedious detail, thinking that overwhelming her with transparency might help put her mind at ease. But this does little to placate her – in fact, it often leads to more demands, more questions. So I limit myself to responding only once per day, with a summary of that day's events and Walt's mood and condition.

Meanwhile, the more time I spend with Walt, the more I learn to pick up on his idiosyncrasies, and the better I get at reading his mind. It's like being immersed in a new language – one made up of fidgets and sighs and tics and pursed lips, and patterns of behaviour that eventually reveal meaning.

A sharply exhaled breath on its own doesn't mean much, but if it's closely followed by another I know his mood is about to turn dark. It's a cue to intervene with some upbeat chitchat, or to call one of the dogs over for a scratch – although I soon learn that Jua, the golden retriever doppelgänger of Walt's dog in England, can cause her own problems.

'Oh come here, Bella, you lovely mutt,' he'll say.

'No, Walt – that's not Bella, that's Jua,' I'll gently explain.

'How absurd. A dog can't be Jewish.'

'No, Ju-*a*. That's its name.'

'Its name is Bella!'

'No, Bella is your dog in England.'

'We are in England!'

Unprovoked nervous laughter means I've got about five minutes to help him find his bearings before he descends into a dizzy spiral of anxiety and repetition that can go on for hours.

Opening and closing drawers means he's lost his wallet and is fretting about money.

Eyebrows at a plaintive angle means he's worrying about his mother and will soon ask if he can speak to her on the phone. A bouncing right knee means he's about to start looking for the car keys – a sign that he's feeling cooped up and needs to get out of the house.

Millicent, Alice and I gradually learn how to arrange the small details of the world around him just so: he doesn't like the foot of his sun chair to touch the grout between the tiles on the patio. He insists the concertina doors that lead through to the living room should be folded flat at the hinges when they're open. His sunglasses should always be left in their case on top of the writing cabinet, so that each time he goes past he can pick them up to give them a polish and put them back again. He likes to sit with his back to the window in the tearoom at the Club, for the car to be parked with plenty of space for him to get out of the passenger side, for the butter to have been out of the fridge long enough to soften, and for his plate to be warm for meals.

Whatever it is that Walter Smyth likes, we go out of our way to make sure he gets.

Swahili is the other language I start to learn. It's got a beautiful sound, fluid like French and rhythmic like Spanish, but unspoiled by guttural harshness. A Bantu language that evolved on the eastern stretch of Africa from Lake Victoria to Lake Malawi, the Swahili (sometimes known as Kiswahili) vocabulary is heavily influenced by a number of Arabic, Persian and Indian words brought by the traders who first visited the coast. It soon became a lingua franca across much of East Africa, especially Kenya, Uganda, Tanzania and Rwanda. Most Kenyans also speak English, along with the mother tongue of their tribe.

I love hearing the Kenyan staff speak it – among each other, and with Walt. And I'm desperate to learn some, so one rainy afternoon, while the two of us are stuck inside by the fireplace, I ask him to teach me the basics.

'You want to know some "kitchen" Swahili?' he says, teasing, describing the bare minimum attempts most colonials made to communicate with their staff. 'Or real Swahili?' People like Walt, who lived on the land, tend to speak it far more fluently.

'Well, ideally more than just "kitchen" Swahili,' I say. 'But sure, that sounds like a start.'

Walt seems to spark up – maybe it's with relief, or perhaps pride, at being tasked with an intellectual challenge he can cope with. For all his faltering faculties, he hasn't yet lost his grasp on the language.

He starts by teaching me how to count to ten: *moja, mbili, tatu, nne, tano, sita, saba, nane, tisa, kumi.*

Then the most important day-to-day words: *ndiyo* – yes, *hapana* – no, *asante* – thank you, *tafadhali* – please, *najua* – I know, *sijui* – I don't know, *kitu* – thing.

Then the important phrases: *kuja* – come, *hapa* – here, *leta* – bring, *moji* – water.

But Walt's brand of Swahili is becoming a little too focused on issuing instructions *to* staff, so I decide to source more practical lessons *from* the Kenyan staff.

In the kitchen, I help Khamisi prepare dinner, and he teaches me that *sukuma wiki* — the name for the spinach greens that, served with *ugali*, are a staple meal here — literally means 'push' or 'stretch' the week, reflecting the fact that most Kenyans can only afford meat on weekends.

Peter teaches me that the standard greeting for 'Hello, how are you?' — *Jambo! Habari ako?* — literally translates as 'What news do you have?', and that the answer should always be *mzuri sana* — 'very good' — even if you aren't feeling *mzuri sana*. In the car on the way to City Market to buy more fruit, he explains that changing from singular to plural for nouns describing people is simply a matter of replacing the pre-fix 'm' with 'wa'. *Mtu* is person and *watu* is people, while *Mtoto* is child and *watoto* is children. Even better, *mbenzi* is a rich person and *wabenzi* is rich people, so named because of their taste for Mercedes-Benz cars.

I especially love the etymology of the word for white person, *mzungu* (or *wazungu* for the collective) — and so does Peter, when I tell him what I've read about it online.

'So, apparently it comes from the Swahili word for "dizzy",' I say. '*Kizunguzungu?*'

'*Kizunguzungu*, yes, that is where you are dizzy,' he says. 'And that means *mzungu?*'

'Well it says here that "East Africans thought this best described the expressions of the first white people to arrive on their shores, looking lost and disorientated".'

Peter laughs, slaps his thighs. 'Ohhhh, that is *very*-very funny,' he says.

Over the next few days, I find myself making notes of other words and phrases that tickle me. *Kuku* for 'chicken', and *wasiwasi* for 'anxiety'. *Sawa-sawa* — an all-purpose phrase like the Australian 'no worries', which literally translates as 'the same' or 'equal'.

I bump into Esther in the laundry and she says, 'Oh, *pole!*' (pronounced 'poh-lee'), which leads to an explanation of the many uses of that word. '*Pole* means "sorry",' she says. 'And *pole-sana* means "very sorry", because *sana* means "very".'

'But *pole-pole* means to go slowly?' I ask. I know this because Fiona says we're to always say it to Walt if he's walking too fast.

'Yes.' She laughs. 'I don't know why.'

I love it when Marguerite tells the staff they look 'very *maridadi*' (stylish) when they dress up on Sundays for church, or when Walt teases me for being *kidogo* (small), or when we all call him 'the *mzee*', an honorific term for 'old man'.

I never become anywhere close to fluent in Swahili, but I'm picking up enough to feel like more than a tourist.

7

THE GREAT ESCAPE

I realise I'm starting to go stir-crazy when I have a fight with Millicent about whether it's acceptable for a woman to wear trousers to meet the Queen. (I argued the affirmative, she argued the negative, and then told me she wasn't going to 'sit here and listen to some *Australian* girl be disrespectful about the Royal Family'.)

It's understandable. It's been weeks and weeks of nothing but the house, the local shops and the Club.

'I can't do any more small talk about opera, or the 1970s tea trade, or the Gospel,' I say to Alice. 'Please! Let's go out or something. Let's see if the staff want to go for a drink somewhere.'

'Leave it with me,' says Alice. 'I'll tee something up.' That she does.

We tell Marguerite we're going to dinner with Sarah and Jack, then sneak down the driveway to meet Peter and James at the *matatu* stage up the road. They're going to show us the *real* Nairobi — take us to a local bar, get some authentic *nyama choma*.

A *matatu* pulls up thumping with the syncopated beat of Swahili pop, and for a fleeting moment I hesitate. Two young Western women heading into downtown Nairobi? At night? This is not following DFAT travel advice or heeding the warnings of my parents. If the Smyths find out they'll have a fit. But the moment passes, leaving me all the more determined to go. I've travelled enough to know these things are never as dangerous as people make out, as long as you keep your wits about you.

The 'moneyman' – a young guy in a backwards cap sitting behind the driver – takes our twenty-shilling fares. He directs Peter and James to the back seat, where the other passengers have squished up to make room for them, while Alice and I are encouraged to sit on the laps of two buxom women who are apparently delighted to oblige. One beams at me, slapping her ample thighs in welcome. 'Come, *toto* – come!' I don't have another option. The van is already carrying four more people than it has seats – though by *matatu* standards this is decidedly under-crowded.

Our *matatu* bounces on into town, collecting more and more travellers on the way. Soon everyone is seated on or under someone else, our limbs and necks bent awkwardly and our faces pressed against the glass in a game of human Tetris, but the moneyman doesn't stop hustling. Colourful disco lights flash on the ceiling, reggae rhythm blares through the speakers, glittering pictures of Barack Obama and Shakira adorn the walls. The ladies wrap their arms around me and Alice, holding us tight to their bosoms when the driver sails over speed humps or swerves around potholes. Alice and I scream in terror when he nearly careens into a bus. Everyone else laughs.

'Ohhhh, *pole-pole* [slowly]!' they roar.

But the driver isn't going to slow down for a couple of woozy *wazungu* women.

Finally, we reach our destination. The streets are busy and there are lots of stalls selling English soccer jerseys. Peter and James lead us through the bustle, fobbing off the hawkers trying to sell us mobile-phone cases and acrylic socks and hair cream. We wind our way through to a local butcher-cum-bar, where freshly slain goat and pig carcasses hang in a glass-fronted display and Justin Bieber bops on a screen in the corner of a neon-lit room.

Oh god, the beer is hot. Peter and James laugh as Alice and I grimace after taking a swig, struggling to swallow the mouthful of warm bubbles.

'*Baridi* – you have to ask for it *baridi!*' James explains. Only foreigners prefer their Tusker chilled; locals always have it *moto*, like their Coke.

It's such a relief to spend time together away from the rigid hierarchy in the house. They tell us about their families. Both men are married with children. Peter has two, a boy and a girl. James has six – three of each; they're all still at school and he hopes they'll go on to study at university. 'Rebecca, she is my eldest. She graduates next year and hopes to become a teacher,' he says, beaming with pride.

We discover Peter was once an apprentice mechanic – that's why he's so good at keeping the Peugeot going – but found it was too hard to get that sort of work. A job with the Smyths was a much safer option.

He and James want to know more about where we're from. *Are there many mechanic jobs in Australia? Is it hot? Have we seen kangaroos? Are there any black people there?* There are, we tell them, but not as many as in Africa. Some are from other parts of the world, some were in Australia *long long* before Europeans arrived. We explain that the colonisation of Australia was a sorry affair, that there are parts of the country even today where – to our great shame – Indigenous people live in poverty.

Still, they think our country sounds like a utopia.

'Life in Kenya is very, very hard,' Peter says. 'We have so much corruption. The government doesn't do good for the people – those politicians just do good for themselves. That is our biggest problem.'

'Do you like working for Marguerite and Walt?' Alice asks, direct as ever. I don't think it occurs to her that they might not feel they can be honest with us. But they both say they do and seem to sincerely mean it.

'Yes! It is a good job,' says James.

'Even though they can be so difficult?' I say.

'They are not so bad,' says Peter, waving the suggestion away. 'Many *bwanas* are difficult.' I have to admit, I'm surprised to hear this. A part of me had assumed they'd harbour some resentment over working for former colonials. Maybe they do, on some level. Or maybe the Smyths are actually pretty good employers in the scheme of things. (After hearing this, I start paying more attention to the stories in the newspapers of domestic worker abuse – the terrible cases of maids and nannies who are beaten and underpaid by their employers. Around two million households in Nairobi employ household help – mostly these are rural people from poorer, less educated backgrounds. There are only about sixty-seven thousand whites in the country, and these cases of exploitation appear to me to be class-based rather than racial. Even more of a problem seems to be the Kenyan workers – mostly women – who are sent to work in the United Arab Emirates, where they're treated as little more than slaves.)

A couple of *baridi* Tuskers later, we move on to a restaurant across the road. This too has skinned animals hanging in the window – only this time, they're ours to pick from for dinner. Peter and James point out a goat to the man at the door, then we head upstairs to an open-air restaurant decked out with plastic garden furniture.

The waiter brings a jug of soapy hot water around the table, ceremoniously pouring it over our hands as we wash them into a bowl. We order another round of beers – '*Pole*, we only have *moto* here,' the waiter apologises. That's fine, we'll cope. Halfway through the hot beers, it appears: half a goat, roasted, on a wooden board with salt piled in the corners, and side plates of *kachumbari* (a salad of finely diced tomato, onion and green chilli) and *ugali*. The cook comes out from the kitchen with a *panga*: a two-foot-long machete, the same kind famously used by Mau Mau fighters in the fifties – and hacks the meat into bite-sized pieces while we watch on, salivating. '*Karibu!*' He grins, leaving Peter and James to demonstrate how we are to eat the entire meal with our hands.

The four of us grab shamelessly at the pieces of tender flesh, roll them in salt and shove them down our throats, followed by chasers of zesty *kachumbari*, a cool crunch to freshen the palate. We mop up the juices with balls of *ugali*, suck on the slabs of fat, lick the grease from our fingers. We belch, groan, feast like vultures – there's nothing left but bones picked clean.

A few days after our night out, I'm sitting on the patio writing emails on my laptop, when James drags the hose around to water the garden. He waves hello, and I notice he keeps glancing back at me as though there's something more he wants to say. I close my computer, trying to appear more approachable. He sets the sprinkler up then comes over to the bottom of the steps.

'Excuse me, Kirsten,' he says, looking at the ground, nervous, 'you know I told you about my daughter, Rebecca? She is the eldest girl.'

'Yes,' I say, 'she's the one who's nearly finished school, right?'

'Yes. I was wondering ... Can you teach her how to use the computer?' He points at my laptop.

'Oh – yes, of course!' I say, not sure what else I was expecting.

'Because, you know, she will be studying to be a teacher soon. And I think it would be very good if she could learn computers. She will be visiting me next week. Maybe you can teach her then?'

'Of course, James. I'd be happy to. Just let me know when she's here. As soon as I'm not on duty with the *bwana*, I'll come around to see you.'

'Oh, thank you,' James says. '*Asante sana*, god bless!' He's far too grateful for such a small ask.

But the day Rebecca comes to stay, Alice is out, Millicent is on duty with Walt, and Marguerite is making life hard for everyone. At the very last minute she's decided to go for lunch with a friend instead of out to do the groceries, which she had absolutely insisted that morning was what she wanted to do because she just *loves* doing those sorts of things, don't you know? So now the shopping falls to me, and we're running low on a few crucial supplies – things Khamisi needs to make dinner, and Walt's blackcurrant juice 'wine' – and if I don't go to pick them up there's guaranteed to be a litany of tedious dramas tonight.

But I'm loath to break my promise to James. When he pokes his head through the kitchen door to let me know Rebecca is ready and waiting, I decide the Smyths' pantry can stay bare a little longer; fuck it, I'll deal with that bullshit later, and I sneak out through the side door.

'*Karibu! Karibu!*' James says, showing me into a room about ten square metres in size. It's the first time I've been inside the staff quarters, and if he didn't seem so proud to welcome me into his space I'd find it hard to disguise my shock. It's essentially a cement cube, windows on either side letting in a breeze and the sunlight. The only furniture is a bed, and a platform of pallet planks propped up on boxes and bricks, topped with a sheet of plywood to form a table in the corner. A radio and a phone charger are plugged into a powerboard in the corner, and a *jiko* – a small charcoal burner – sits against the wall near the door.

Rebecca is seventeen: a young woman born to illiterate parents in a village with no electricity, about to graduate into the world of the twenty-first century. She's sitting quietly in an olive-green

T-shirt with sparkly rhinestones that spell out 'Viva Nicole', her hands neatly folded in her lap, her feet resting gently together. Her voice is so soft I can barely hear it, causing me to slow my own movements, to lower my own voice.

William, James's six-year-old son, is also visiting. He's been practising his writing – scraps of paper scribbled with colourful alphabet and numbers are strewn across the table – but now he's hiding behind a sheet draped down from the ceiling as a screen, playing peekaboo then muffling giggles as he burrows into James's chest. They're going to watch the computer lesson, so James makes William promise to be quiet. They sit on the edge of the bed; Rebecca and I sit at the table on plastic crates.

I set my laptop down between us, and flip open the screen. Rebecca stares at it as the display lights up.

'Have you ever used a computer before?' I ask. She shakes her head. 'Have you ever seen one before?'

'Just one time at school,' she says, and I wonder where to begin.

'Okay,' I say, opening up Microsoft Word, 'let's start with typing.'

The blank white page appears, a thin black vertical line blinking at us from the upper left corner. In this room, my laptop is no longer a seamless extension of myself. I see it in a new light: a glowing machine waiting patiently for a human to tell it what to say, and not minding at all what that might be.

'See this flashing line?' I say. 'That's called the "cursor". It shows whereabouts on the page you are, where the words will go.'

I guide her hand to the keyboard, press her index finger onto the 'T'.

Ttttttttttttttttttttt

'That's it. Then you press this button – "enter" – to start a new line. Yup, exactly. Now, have a go. Type whatever you like.'

At careful five-second intervals, each new letter appears, nudging the cursor further across the screen.

rebecca

She hits enter and types her name again. Faster this time, though, her fingers growing more confident with every stroke.

rebecca

She types the names of her brothers and sisters:

william

emma

joshua

mary

daniel

And at the end of this list of the most important people in her world, the cursor just blinks back, impassive, as if to say, 'Yes, what else? A shopping list? A manifesto? It makes no difference to me.' I remember doing the very same thing when I was a kid: Dad would take me into the office with him on a Saturday morning and let me play on one of the typewriters. I'd just tap out my name, over and over again. When that got old, I would type a list – 'Mum', 'Dad', and the names of my sisters and then everyone else I knew, stamped in echoes of fading ink all over the back of scrap paper. There's something primal in that, I think: the fact that the self and family are the first things we feel an urge to express for the record.

I show Rebecca how to delete text. How to use the shift key and caps lock for capitals, how to use the arrow keys to move the cursor around the page. Then I explain how the trackpad works, how she can move the pointer on the screen by tracing her finger across it, how pressing down on the pad will select items. She can use it to make the text bigger or smaller. Make it underlined or bold or blue. Make it flow from the right-hand side of the page instead of the left.

All of it she picks up just like that, like it's obvious, and maybe it is. I hope that my astonishment is less about underestimating her than it is due to not appreciating how intuitive computer and software design must be, to allow someone who's never so much as seen a word processor before to learn in the space of five minutes how to type a letter.

She starts with a message for Emma, her youngest sister:

30/11/2010
TO EMMA
Despite being young you should start working hard early in advance as for the early bird catches the worm.
From Rebecca

Then there's Joshua:

30/11/2010
TO JOSHUA
I want to wish you all the best in your studies and remember that HARD WORK PAYS.
From Rebecca

And Mary:

30/11/2010
TO MARY
It's only ONE YEAR remaining 4 you in primary school so pull up your socks to get better grades to go to a good school.
From Rebecca

Just as she starts on her message to Daniel, Walt appears at the door. We all startle, but he comes in peace. 'Errr, um, hello,' he says, smiling. 'How d'you do? I wonder if you can help me? I think I've got myself a bit lost . . .' He looks around at this unfamiliar place a few dozen feet from his very own bedroom; he must think he's wandered onto one of the native reserves of the 1950s, and that I'm a European missionary. 'And I seem to have picked up a stray mutt along the way.' Shujaa — the brown mongrel — is with him, wagging her tail against his legs.

'Yes, of course, Walt,' I say, 'it's me, Kirsten — it's okay, we're here at your house, in Nairobi. You're in the staff quarters. This is James's room.'

'Hello, *bwana*,' James says, standing up as William ducks to hide behind him.

'Oh — yes — James, of course. *Jambo*.' Walt's forehead creases with relief as he recognises his gardener, though Rebecca and I are still very much strangers.

'This is Rebecca, Walt,' I say.

'She is my eldest daughter, *bwana*,' says James.

'Oh, yes, hello there,' says Walt, to which Rebecca gently replies, eyes downcast, 'Hello, sir.'

William peeks around from behind the edge of the cotton sheet. He seems frightened of the dog and of the *bwana*, but Walt lights up at the sight of the child's face, at the big brown eyes, so bashful. 'And who's that?' he says, in the gentlest tone I've ever heard him use, 'we've got a young chap back there, have we?'

James drags William out to shake the *bwana*'s hand, and now we're all of us acquainted. I know I should probably take Walt back to the house, that Millicent must be looking for him, but I want to see this unlikely moment play out a little longer. Part of the Smyths' arrangement with their staff is that in addition to paying them domestic salaries at twice the mandated minimum wage (still only about five hundred Kenyan shillings a day, or five Australian dollars), they pay for their children's education, too: school fees, uniforms and textbooks. They — like so many others — hand the money over but keep their distance, white guilt assuaged by the feeling they've done their bit — that it's up to the Africans to get on with it now. And I wonder if, on some level, Walt realises that the young Kenyans he's just been introduced to are the beneficiaries of his paternalism.

'I was just showing Rebecca how to use the computer, Walt,' I say. 'She's nearly finished school, and she's going to be a teacher.'

'Oh, well done you!' he says to her.

'Thank you, sir,' she replies, sounding proud.

Walt steps closer to the table, squinting as he stares curiously into the backlit future of the laptop screen. 'They do send you people over with the most marvellous contraptions these days, don't they?' he says, poking the liquid crystal display. James drags a chair in from Esther's room next door while I secure a nod from Rebecca that it's okay for Walt to watch her type her letters.

'She's writing to one of her brothers,' I tell Walt, as we watch size 36 font fill up the screen.

30/11/2010
TO DANIEL
I wish you all the best in your studies and just know that you are ALWAYS in my prayers.
From Rebecca

Walt thinks Rebecca's letters are great. He reads each one aloud as she types it, and he asks over and over again how the computer works, whether you can get paper out of the machine, how much the jolly thing costs. But eventually the spell is broken.

30/11/2010
TO MUM
Thank you for your care and protection since I was small I will cherish you forever.
MAY GOD BLESS YOU.
From Rebecca

This one makes Walt think of his own dear old mother, whom he really must go and see, she's down in Hampshire, an hour or so's drive, if he can remember where he left the car, let alone the keys – he pats down his pockets; what the devil has he done with his car keys? – and now he's frowning and fretting and I have to take him back to the house.

I spend the next two hours with Millicent trying to calm him down, leaving Rebecca to finish writing letters to her family, imploring her siblings to work and study hard, and thanking her parents for all that they've done.

Late that night, once everyone's in bed asleep, I sneak into Marguerite's study to use the printer. I make two copies of each of Rebecca's letters and run them over to James's room in the morning so that she can pass on her messages in hard copy.

8

THE RUSE

Marguerite is going away for a few days. She announces it over dinner. 'Cousin George from England has decided to come for a visit.'

'Who?' says Walt.

'Cousin George. The one you don't like.' She tells him matter-of-factly, then whispers across the table at me and Alice, 'Walt thinks George is a queer. Tell you what – I think he might be too. But I do love queers! They're *such* fun.'

'Oh, George,' says Walt vaguely. I don't think he remembers Maybe-Gay George at all.

'Oooooh, I know!' squeals Marguerite, a mouthful of roast chicken falling onto her plate. 'We'll spend a few days in Watamu. It's *just lovely* there – he'll love that.'

Watamu is a small, white-sand beach town about a hundred kilometres north of the main coastal city of Mombasa. It's where Kenyans go for a coastal holiday – to avoid the European tourists who flood Mombasa and 'don't know any better'.

'What a splendid idea,' Marguerite says. 'Oh, I *am* clever.'

I'm not sure how spontaneous this decision really is, though. I can't put my finger on it, but there's something about the way she's brought it all up that feels . . . contrived.

'You girls will be alright with Walt, won't you? Millicent can stay while I'm gone so all three of you are always around. Pass the gravy would you, darling?'

Two days later, she's gone, and I'm on night shift.

It's half-past one when the bed alarm wakes me. I check the monitor to see Walt is up pacing. I go through to his room to try to settle him – he's furious.

'I don't have five fucking pounds to rub together!' he says. Everyone's trying to screw him out of his dough. 'And I won't bloody hesitate to *physically exterminate* the culprits if that's what it takes!'

'Okay, Walt, it's okay. I think there's just been a mix-up, that's all.'

'What do you mean, a "mix-up"?' He holds his wallet out to me. 'Not a single fucking pound in there!'

'Well, the good thing is you don't need to worry about having pounds – we're in Kenya, remember?' I say, in the cheeriest tone I can muster at this time of night. 'We use shillings here. And look, you've got plenty of those – hundreds!' I show him the notes. 'You're loaded! You could take me out to dinner every night of the week with all this.'

Walt stares at me like *I'm* mad. 'Keen-ya?' he says. '*Keeny-ya?*'

'Yes, Walt. In your house in Nairobi.'

'No, we're not.'

'Yes, we are.'

'No, we're not.'

'Yeah, Walt, look – we are!'

'Why must you talk such nonsense. We are in *England*, you silly girl!'

And so begins a one and a half hour tour of his own house. I show him the labels on the Kenyan products in his bathroom, the cans of Tusker beer in the pantry, the Masai beaded doilies under the tray on his dresser. No dice.

We go through to the living room. I turn all the lights on and walk him around the place, trying to help him find his bearings. 'See, Walt – look around. This is Kenya. Don't you recognise it? We're in your house in Nairobi.'

Walt circles the room, takes it all in, shakes his head in disbelief. 'Well, well, well.' He chuckles bitterly. 'This has been very cleverly done indeed, I'll grant you that much.'

I've no idea what he means. 'What has?'

'I suppose it cost an awful lot to ship all this stuff out here.' He waves his finger at his furniture, the pictures on the wall.

Holy shit. He thinks I've recreated his Kenyan house somewhere in England.

I try to point out the more structural features of the house – things that can't be packed into a shipping container.

'No, Walt, look! Look at the fireplace, the skylight, the archway –'

'I'm no fool, I know just where I am!'

How do I prove this? Do we have to go outside? I open the curtains; the garden is lit blue by the beams of a full moon. 'Okay, Walt – here, come and have a look.' We've both got our faces pressed against the glass, foggy patches pulsing with our breath. 'There, see? That's your garden. See the bird feeder? And the trees where the monkeys play in the morning? And that's James's wheelbarrow. This is *not* England.'

He sees. He screws his eyes up and shakes his head, then looks and sees his Kenyan garden again. He's starting to come around.

I spy a newspaper on the couch. 'And here, see? This is today's newspaper. The *Daily Nation*. Look at all these pictures of fat politicians! Where else could you be?'

Walt flips through the pages, slowly becoming less sure of himself. 'Well,' he says, 'when the sun comes up, I'll be sure to take a long walk through "Nairobi".'

'Absolutely, Walt. I promise we can do that in the morning. For now, how about we go back to bed, though? It's three o'clock in the morning!'

He follows me reluctantly down the hallway, just as Millicent emerges from a night-time toilet trip. I shoot her a look to let her know everything's under control.

'Nighty-night,' she says, making a quick dash for her room to minimise the distraction.

'And who the bloody hell is that old woman?' Walt asks me, as I tuck him into bed and arrange his pillows just so. 'I keep seeing her everywhere.'

'She's an old friend of the family,' I say, astounded he's able to remember that, but not his own home. 'We can sort it out tomorrow.'

The next day, it's as though the night before didn't even happen. We spend the morning at home, reading the Kenyan papers, watching the Kenyan birds. Until he becomes restless, saying he feels like he's in prison, and I decide an excursion would be good for his head.

Peter drives us down to the Club for lunch.

It's just Walt and me, sitting at a table in the main dining room, surrounded by silverware and roast trolleys.

He takes my hand across the table, holds it in his, gazes at me intently. 'My darling,' he says, 'I'm so terribly sorry, I've made such a dreadful mess of all this. My wife is bound to find out. We'll have to deal with her gently, the poor old duck. I don't want to cause her any more upset than I have to.'

Oh shit. He thinks I'm his mistress.

At first, I try to hose it down. 'Oh – no, Walt – I think there's been a mix-up. I'm Kirsten, remember? I'm a friend of your daughter, Fiona.'

'Yes, yes,' he says, not really hearing me, 'we'll have to come clean to the whole family eventually. But I must talk to Marguerite first, I really do owe it to her.'

A waiter brings over Walt's Ribena in a wine glass.

'But once that's all sorted, my love,' Walt tells me, 'I've been wanting to ask for so long: will you marry me?'

I can see people at other tables watching us and judging me: a young gold-digger taking advantage of a sick old man. They're tutting and frowning and shaking their heads; they don't know that it's better for me just to roll with this, for Walt's sake. That I'm doing him a kindness. That it'll only be a brief engagement – he'll have forgotten me by the time we get back to the car.

He stares at me, lovesick.

I accept. 'Yes, Walt my dear, of course I will. I thought you'd never ask!'

'Oh wonderful, just wonderful.' He kisses my hand, clasps it between his. 'Splendid. I suppose the next step is to get you a ring!'

Towards the end of our celebratory meal, Walt excuses himself to 'use the little boys' room' around the corner. After some time, a waiter approaches me.

'Excuse me, madam,' he whispers, 'Bwana Smyth, I think he is lost. Could you come this way, please?'

I follow him through to the courtyard. Bwana Smyth is sitting at a table with a Swedish couple who look very confused.

'I'm sorry, sir,' the man says, 'have we met before?'

'Oh, deary-me,' Walt replies, laughing politely but ignoring the question. 'And are you both enjoying your stay?' I can see the panic in his eyes.

'Walt, there you are!' I swoop in to retrieve him. 'Hello, hi, how do you do?' I shake hands with the Swedes, wink. 'I'm Kirsten. Lovely to meet you both.' Then I turn to Walt. 'We can't go anywhere without you running into old friends, can we? Quite the socialite, *mzee* Smyth!'

He laughs, wags a finger and teases, 'Ohhh, not much gets past you!' When he grabs my hand, I can feel the relief flowing through his grip. I feel a sudden pang of sympathy and a surge of protectiveness. *It's okay,* I want to say, *I'll look after you, you're safe. You poor old bastard.*

The Swedes seem to have twigged to what's happening here. They smile kindly at us. 'Nice to see you,' they say, as I help Walt to his feet.

'Come on now,' I say to him, 'we'd best get back to our lunch – it'll be getting cold!'

But instead, I lead him out to the car park, where Peter is leaning against the Peugeot reading a newspaper. He sees us coming and races around to open Walt's door and help him into the car. 'There you go, *bwana* – how was your lunch?'

'Very good, very good, thank you very much,' says Walt, rubbing his furrowed brow.

'Home?' asks Peter, sensing lunch has ended a little prematurely.

'Yes, back to the house, thanks, Peter,' I say, where I put Walt down to bed for a long afternoon nap.

A text message from Sarah saves me from spending another Saturday night in my room. Do I want to go to the US Marine Corps' 235th Birthday Ball with her and Jack? I absolutely do. I haven't been able to catch up with them since our afternoon at the bar, despite plenty of invites to parties and soirees. This time, the event is not too far from Walt's house.

But I don't have a dress. Or shoes. Nothing that will fly at a black-tie affair. I have to borrow one of Sarah's gowns – a satin number that only just fits – and shuffle along to hide my hiking boots, while trying not to trip on the hem. It's not a good look, but

I'm not about to let a fashion handicap stop me checking out how the world's mightiest fighting force celebrates its anniversary in a foreign land.

Marguerite – back from her beach getaway – kindly lends me a string of pearls for the finishing touch. She thinks it's 'positively splendid!' I've been invited. So do I. Where else am I going to see a novelty cake cut with a ceremonial sword?

With the setting sun casting a golden sheen across the green of Nairobi's Windsor Golf Hotel & Country Club, I find myself clinking champagne glasses with the diplomatic clique of East Africa. We mill about on the slate pavers, nibbling at samosas and cucumber sandwiches, smiling at grey-haired men and their epaulets, eavesdropping on ambassadorial gossip.

Sarah and Jack introduce me to one of their Kenyan friends, a rapper and minor celebrity named Sauti. None of the VIPs recognise him; more than once he's tapped on the shoulder and asked to send for more refreshments from the kitchen. 'It's alright,' he says with a grin, when we gasp in embarrassment. 'The waiters know me, and that's what counts. We'll get first dibs on the hors d'oeuvres.' On cue, a server brings us a fresh tray of salmon blinis and asks him for a selfie.

This ball, Sarah tells me, is *the* event on the expat calendar. It's all anyone's been talking about for months. It all seems a bit buttoned-up to me, but I get it. Just about everywhere in Nairobi – except for the High Commission and private residences – is out of bounds to foreign office staff, an overly cautious approach to security that restricts their social lives to these sorts of cordoned-off occasions.

As dusk falls, we're ushered along a candlelit path to a glittering marquee set up on the fairway. There's some confusion when, at the third security check, Sarah sets off one of the metal detectors. The guard waves a madly beeping black wand over her chest until finally she remembers the mobile phone she has stuffed down her bra.

She pulls it out of her cleavage, holding it aloft in surrender. 'Relax everyone – I'm not a terrorist!' she says, and everyone laughs, but it's a bit close to the bone.

A few months earlier, jihadist militants killed seventy-four people watching the World Cup soccer final at a rugby clubhouse in the Ugandan capital, Kampala. Suicide bombers walked in and blew the entire crowd up, retribution for Uganda's military presence in Somalia, where Al-Shabaab is based and the African Union is running a UN-backed peace-keeping mission. Headless bodies were left sitting on white plastic chairs, while footballers carried on playing on a blood-splattered screen, oblivious to the carnage. Those sorts of horrors are now threatening Kenya, too. Nairobi, after all, was one of Osama bin Laden's early targets: more than two hundred people died when he sent a truck carrying a ton of explosives to the US Embassy in 1998. It's only a matter of time before the mujahideen strike here again.

My friends and I are sitting at a grab-bag table: a few Brits and Australians, a Swedish woman and her Dutch husband, a Rwandan and his German wife. The waiters bring rounds of drinks and hot towels, eucalyptus-scented to freshen our greasy fingers.

The lights dim. A man in ostentatious military regalia stands up. We hush.

We hush for nearly an hour, being told how the US marines are the finest warriors Planet Earth has ever seen. Flat screens are hoisted throughout the tent to ensure every table has a clear view of the birthday message sent from Commandant General James F. Amos to marines around the globe. It's a twelve-minute loop of American flags waving in slow motion, cross-fading through a montage of gun-slung heroism from Korea to Afghanistan, set to a stirring drumbeat and Hollywood strings.

The British woman beside me has had a gutful. 'Fuck me, it's like the trailer for a summer blockbuster,' she whispers.

'Subliminal retainment,' suggests her friend, summoning another round of gin and tonics for the table.

The emcee introduces our guest of honour, the US Ambassador to Kenya, Michael Ranneberger. He has quite the résumé: it seems he singlehandedly pulled Kenya from the brink of political chaos in the wake of the country's disputed 2007 election result. This outbreak of civil unrest saw around a thousand people killed and hundreds of thousands internally displaced as rival ethnic factions turned on each other, and police tried to quell the violence with bullets. We're told that while some people criticised Mr Ranneberger for 'overstepping the diplomatic mark' as he steadfastly drove the formation of a coalition government, ordinary Kenyans were grateful to have American guidance at that critical moment in their history. (The ordinary Kenyans serving us dinner tonight miss the opportunity to thank their saviours. I catch several leaning against the marquee supports, yawning as their legs tire beneath them.)

Throughout the tent, bemused eyes swivel around the room to find each other. A few throats are pointedly cleared, but they're drowned out by a frothing patriot in the corner, who whoops and claps at every comma. I don't fully understand the dynamics in the room, but it's clear Uncle Sam's version of events has pissed a lot of people off. 'What's going on?' I whisper at Jack.

'Pretty much everyone here was involved in sorting out the 2007 crisis,' he explains. 'But the Americans always take credit for it. It's kinda their thing.'

The band starts playing 'The Star-Spangled Banner'. Half the room stands, hands-on-hearts singing, while the remainder drain their glasses and grit their teeth, wondering aloud why their country even bothers being here, or anywhere, for that matter, when the Yanks can do it all so well themselves.

In reality, America isn't here just to help Kenya's fledgling democracy. That's a good cover story, but their main business is to surveil and assassinate Islamists, either with special forces soldiers sent into Somalia from this side of the border, or with air strikes and drones. When they're not doing that, they're trying to shut down the piracy and drug-smuggling operations that fund the jihadist groups. 'You wouldn't believe how much of Europe's coke and smack gets there via Africa,' the German tells me. 'And it's not just coming through terrorists – half the Kenyan parliament is involved.' Operation Enduring Freedom has been running here in the Horn of Africa since it was launched in 2002, just a few days after the US Senate authorised President George W. Bush's war on Saddam Hussein. It turns out Kenya is as much a part of the War on Terror theatre as Afghanistan or Iraq, it just doesn't make the news back home.

Eventually, alcohol kicks in to dilute the stifling atmosphere. A nearby table of American women takes over the dance floor, and the DJ plays the obligatory 'Africa' by Toto. Soon old white men are dancing with young black women, and old white women are dancing with young black men. I have a brief spin with an off-duty waiter who tells me he deals cars from the bar he works at and makes excellent cocktails – if I'd like to we could go try some? We could . . . but I'm on duty with Walt in the morning, and I don't fancy kicking my shift off with a hangover.

As I make my exit, a group of marines in blue dress are executing a choreographed rendition of Soulja Boy Tell'em's 'Crank Dat (Soulja Boy)', bouncing around the parquetry in perfect unison.

It's hard to leave.

One morning, I decide to use the many hours of sitting quietly while Walt reads the newspapers to read up on Kenya's history.

White guys weren't the first outsiders to pitch up in this part of the world. In fact, they were just about the last. Omani Arab traders had been visiting East Africa since Jesus was a kid, establishing outposts all along the coast and on the nearby islands of Pemba and Zanzibar, shipping out exotic treasures through a trading network that grew to reach as far as Indonesia. The Arabs didn't bother exploring the perilous interior themselves, instead recruiting locals to haul caravans laden with ivory, rhino horn, gold and slaves out from the uncharted land that unfurled to the west.

Over the centuries that followed, these coastal settlements were further populated by Persians and Gujaratis and South-East Asians, and gradually established their own distinctive Swahili culture, with Islam as the predominant religion.

The Portuguese were the first Europeans to arrive on Kenya's shores, showing up around 1500. They'd spent the better part of a century getting acquainted with the western side of the continent and, having finally rounded the southern tip, were now securing a route to India, setting up naval bases along the way and firing motivational cannons at anyone slow to acquiesce. The next few hundred years saw them squabbling with the Omanis over control of the coastal centres and the spice and slave trade routes that ran across the Indian Ocean. The port city of Mombasa changed hands several times before the English showed up, eventually taking formal control of it at the end of the 1800s. They'd emerged from the 'Scramble for Africa' with the East Africa Protectorate, a vast swathe of land with what they saw as untapped potential, ranging from arid desert to fertile highlands to Lake Victoria. Thought at the time to be the source of the Nile, the lake is a body of water so large it produces its own weather systems. But none of that potential would be tapped without a railway connecting the interior to the coast.

In 1896, construction began on the Uganda Railway, which soon became better known as the 'Lunatic Express': a single, metre-gauge track running a thousand kilometres from Mombasa to Kisumu via Nairobi – a city that did not yet actually exist – costing five and a half million pounds and four human lives for every mile laid. It was a hellish endeavour. The route was fraught with unforgiving terrain and wild animals, and while the Brits might have claimed the moral high ground for their part in ending slavery, they had no qualms shipping out tens of thousands of indentured labourers from India to lay a million sleepers across the savanna.

'Coolies,' Walt calls them when I ask whether he knows much about the track, though it was completed in 1901, a few decades before his time. 'They were used to the heat and knew how to build railways. Well, we couldn't have done it with the natives.' Walt sees the look on my face and throws his hands up defensively. 'They were barely bloody tame at that stage!'

I shudder, take a deep breath, and try to Zen away the sheer awfulness of his characterisation of human beings. *The world was a different place*, becomes my silent mantra. *You can't tell someone who has dementia to get with the times.*

'And all this stuff about man-eating lions?' I say. 'I thought that was just a silly Val Kilmer movie. Are you saying *The Ghost and the Darkness* was actually true?'

'Oh yes,' Marguerite chimes in from the study, where she's been writing emails to various cousins and friends. It's how she spends most of her downtime — emailing or Skyping or texting friends in the UK; she puts on a merry face about being back in Kenya, but I get the sense her heart is in England. She walks out to join us and pours herself a cup of tea. 'Nasty buggers, those Tsavo *simbas*. Still are. They're different to other lions — the males don't have manes! Something in the blood. High testosterone, they say. Oh!' She turns suddenly to Walt, giggling. 'Maybe the one that nearly got you was their great-great-grandchild?'

Suddenly, the lights in the living room go dark and the radio falls silent. Moments later, there's a symphony of beeps as the diesel generator kicks in and the fridge and microwave are powered back on.

Walt's up and out of his chair to investigate. I follow him and Marguerite into the garage, where she, James and David explain several times over that the generator is running because the power has been cut, but it should be back on soon and there's nothing to fret about. Eventually, Walt's satisfied that all's as it should be, and we return to the patio.

In the meantime, Magda has arrived. I'm thankful for the timing of the generator distraction – it's much easier explaining the generator to Walt than it is another car pulling in the driveway.

'Ohh, hello, Walt!' she says, greeting him with a warm hug.

'Ohhhh, well, well, well, it's *you*,' he says, smiling happily – she's one of the few people he seems to remember.

'I see the power has gone out here too again,' she says. 'At our place too. Yes. Every day this week!'

'Oh no, how ghastly,' says Walt, having already forgotten our recent trip to the garage.

'We were just telling Kirsten about the railway, the Lunatic Express,' says Marguerite.

'Oh yes, that awful train line! The poor people who had to build it. Really. They were treated very harshly,' says Magda, then turns to me. 'I have some wonderful books you can borrow, if you like. Have you read *Facing Mount Kenya*, by Jomo Kenyatta? Do you know who he is?' I do – but she doesn't wait for me to respond. 'He was the first President of Kenya.'

'Ho-ho, "free-dumb, and independent"!' Walt sniggers. I've come to recognise this as the ugly catchcry he favours whenever he hears the word 'independence'.

Magda ignores him. 'He was a very interesting man, Jomo Kenyatta. Yes. He studied economics in Russia and England.'

'*Did* he!?' says Marguerite.

'Yes.' Magda blinks at her, apparently puzzled that someone living in Kenya wouldn't know this. Then she turns her attention back to me. 'He was Kikuyu. The book is all about the Kikuyu people and their customs. Do you know of the Kikuyu? Peter is a Kikuyu, I think. They are one of the biggest tribes in Kenya. I will lend it to you – you will find it very interesting, I'm sure.'

'Yes thanks, I'd love to borrow that,' I say. 'And I've just read there was a massacre, while the train line was being built.'

'Well, of a sort,' Walt says. 'A skirmish.' He raises his eyebrows as though to play down a scandal. 'Some of the overseers had been "fraternising with the natives".'

'Fraternising' and 'skirmish' are quite the euphemisms, it turns out. The real story is that in a place called Kedong, five hundred men were speared to death by Masai warriors as revenge for the rape of two young local girls.

None of these horrors much slowed the track's progress down – nor did the malaria and fatal accidents that put more than two thousand skeletons into the ground by its side. The British were desperate to get the edge over their colonial neighbours: Germany was having a crack in Tanganyika (now Tanzania) in the south, the French were in the Sudan, the Italians were sitting on the Horn of Africa, ordering the Somalis and Eritreans around and lusting after Ethiopia. If Britain didn't secure an inland route, someone else would claim that advantage. So on and on the Kenyan track inched, each day more bolts, more wood, more tonnes of steel laid out, with over a thousand bridges built to carry a locomotive strong enough to knock elephants out of the way, climbing and winding up from sea level to the mountains and diving sharply back down into the Great Rift Valley – a feat of engineering designed to ensure the whole East African exercise would pay off for the British one day.

But paying *for* it was an issue in the meantime. The price tag was so great, in fact, that the Foreign Office begrudgingly decided they'd have to encourage Britons to come over as settlers to work the land. That hadn't been the original plan, but without a base of commercial farmers paying to send their product out to market and have other goods freighted in, there'd be no way to make the line profitable. The *mzungus* came pouring in, forcing Africans off their land and turning it into tea and coffee plantations, or growing sisal and other commercial crops. Meanwhile, a fair number of Indians exercised their right to stay and work in the protectorate once the railway was completed, inviting family to come and join them. Descendants of that early diaspora make up much of the thriving Indian community in Kenya today.

That crazy railway, more than anything else, is what set the course for the country's modern era. Or as the Commissioner and Consul General for the British East Africa Protectorate, Sir Charles Norton Edgecumbe Eliot, put it: 'It is not uncommon for a country to create a railway, but it is uncommon for a railway to create a country.'

The railway didn't 'create' the country though; European powers did, scratching out its borders on a map during the late nineteenth century's Scramble for Africa. Those arbitrary lines encompass a region home to over forty different ethnic groups, each with its own language, beliefs and customs. They placed Kenya in the embrace of Somalia, Ethiopia, Sudan, Uganda and Tanzania, splitting centuries-old ethnic alliances apart in some instances and grouping eternally warring tribes together in others, all under the banner of modern 'nationhood'. I'm reminded that when those of us in the West lament 'troubles' in Africa, it's worth bearing this history in mind.

Marguerite and Magda decide to head down to the Club – there's a special ladies' lunch on, with a matinee screening of the opera *Carmen* in the garden room. Walt says he'd prefer to stay here for a peaceful afternoon at home – he doesn't want to be 'wailed at' by a 'woman in too much make-up'. We sit reading together, chatting, quietly enjoying the day go by.

One of the more extraordinary stories I read about the country's pre-colonial history is that of a live giraffe making it all the way from Kenya to medieval China via Bengal – it was a gift for Zhu Di, the Yongle Emperor. The giraffe arrived in the early fifteenth century, after explorer Zheng He led a 30,000-man voyage that would dwarf any of Christopher Columbus's later undertakings – the Chinese fleet included over sixty enormous junks, each of which was large enough to hold all three of Columbus's ships on its decks.

'Hey, Walt,' I say, as he folds over the newspaper he's just finished reading for the third time that day and shifts in his chair, looking for something to do. 'You wanna hear a poem the Chinese wrote about a giraffe back in the 1400s?'

'Why not?' he replies, so I begin.

In the corner of the western seas, in the stagnant waters of a great morass
Truly was produced a qilin, *whose shape was as high as fifteen feet*

'A what?' Walt asks.

'A *qilin*. They'd never seen a giraffe before and thought it was a type of unicorn.'

'Bloody fools.' Walt chuckles. (He shouldn't be so smug – when the Romans first saw a giraffe they thought it was part-camel part-leopard, and literally called it a 'camelopard'.)

I continue.

With the body of a deer and the tail of an ox, and a fleshy, boneless horn,
With luminous spots like a red cloud or purple mist

'Sorry – *purple*, did you say?' Walt cuts in. 'A purple giraffe?'

'Yeah look, I can't explain that,' I say. 'Maybe the poet was colour-blind.'

'Artistic licence, perhaps?' Walt offers.

Its hoofs do not tread on living beings and in its wanderings it carefully selects its ground
  It walks in stately fashion and in its every motion it observes a rhythm,
  Its harmonious voice sounds like a bell or a musical tube.

'Well now, that truly is hogwash,' Walt says. 'Giraffes make no noise whatsoever!'

'Ha! You're right,' I say. Giraffes are notoriously mute.

'Who did you say wrote this?'

'A Chinese guy, hundreds of years ago.'

'Well, if anyone could make a giraffe scream it'd be an Oriental,' Walt says. 'They were probably trying to eat it!'

'And isn't that a better reason to kill something than just to keep it as a trophy?' I say, unable to resist the urge to challenge him.

'Depends on how nice the trophy is,' he replies, with a smirk. I can tell he's winding me up, now. I know he disapproves of hunting for the hell of it – the lion on the wall was a case of self-defence.

'Gentle is this animal, that has in antiquity been seen but once,
The manifestation of its divine spirit rises up to heaven's abode.'

'Clearly,' Walt says, 'they've never seen two male giraffes going at it. "Gentle", I can assure you, is not the word.' Then he picks up the newspaper he'd only just set down and starts reading it over again from the front page, as I watch clips of giraffes violently thumping each other with their necks on YouTube.

A year after the Chinese emperor received his first Kenyan giraffe, another was sent from Malindi, along with a zebra and an oryx. A subsequent Chinese expedition delivered their new African friends a boatload of silks and porcelain, and returned with an 'arkful of African animals', including leopards, lions, ostriches, rhinos – and more giraffes. We can only assume this motley crew of expats saw their lives out in the Imperial Gardens; not long after Yongle's death, China returned to a policy of isolationism, shutting itself off from the world and putting its budding relationship with Africa on ice for the next six hundred years.

By 2010, though, the freeze has thawed. The newspaper Walt's reading for the third time this morning has stories all the way through it of the Chinese investment boom sweeping Africa, especially Kenya. Photo after photo shows Kenyan politicians shaking hands with Chinese businessmen, announcing new developments, partnerships, roads and train tracks – including an ambitious plan to replace the now-decrepit Lunatic Express with a new standard gauge railway.

(Seven years later, this new line would be complete. The official opening ceremony would take place on Madaraka Day – marking the day Kenya first gained self-rule – with a Kenyan orchestra playing patriotic Chinese songs under a bronze statue of Zheng He – the admiral who'd first visited all those centuries before, and gone home with a purple giraffe.)

All that talk of trains has stuck. Later that afternoon, I find Walt sitting on the end of his bed, reading a newspaper and glancing at his watch.

'Oh, hello there,' he says when he sees me. 'Are you seated in this carriage too?' He shuffles over on the bed, so that I can sit beside him. 'Don't you have a bag to stow?' Walt points to show me his is stacked on top of the wardrobe.

This is a new development: he's having a full-blown hallucination. I decide to roll with it and see where things go.

'Oh – no, thank you,' I reply, settling in. 'I'm travelling light.'

I play along for a bit, but Walt soon grows impatient at the lack of motion. He huffs and sighs, pacing the room. 'When on earth are we going to get going? We've been sitting here for bloody hours!'

I figure it isn't wise to continue the charade, so I draw the curtains to point out his beautiful Kenyan garden and bring him back to reality. Walt sees not flowers but a station platform, bustling with people and luggage and announcements. 'Hurry up, would you!' he yells at James as he passes by with a wheelbarrow full of topsoil, only accepting we are finally on our way when I stand behind the door and make the sound of a departure whistle.

We ride the train mostly in silence for about fifteen minutes. Then Walt starts patting down his pockets and looking around the room. 'I'm terribly sorry – I must be going completely mad,' he says. 'I've forgotten *completely* where it is we're going. And I can't find my ticket!'

I tell him we're on our way to Dover and that I am a nurse, returning to visit my family after a stint in London. I prompt him to tell me again about his mother – isn't he on his way to visit her? When Alice walks past, I call her in to play the role of the steward; she asks if we are enjoying our journey, and takes orders for a tray of tea and scones.

It's only when Walt needs the loo that I'm able to break the spell. I use the toilet flush as a punctuation mark, then come barrelling into the ensuite with the dogs, saying it's time we go for a walk down at the Club.

Later, sitting by the fire after dinner, I stand up to go through to the kitchen to make myself a cup of tea. As I reach for the door handle Walt shrieks at me from his armchair, his voice blazing with panic. 'Stop! Christ, no! Dammit, girl – what do you think you're doing? Are you *mad*? You'll bloody well kill us all!'

I freeze, not sure what I've done wrong. 'What do you mean?'

'You open that cabin door and we'll all of us fall to our deaths! You there . . .' He points at Alice. This time she's a flight attendant. 'Come and sort out this silly woman at once.'

So she does – scolds me with a wagging finger as I sit back down and fasten my 'seatbelt', apologising for the disruption.

We fly for another ten minutes before landing safely in the living room, then give Walt a suitcase to wheel down the hallway to bed.

The night before Fiona is due back, Alice and I are sitting with Walt in the living room. She's cross-legged on the floor by the fire, reading him *Angela's Ashes*, I'm catching up on emails on my laptop. We've had a good day; he's been happy. We took a walk around the garden this afternoon, visited the owls at the back fence with James, and practised putting golf balls into plastic cups on the lawn with Magda when she came around for afternoon tea.

Walt loves it when Alice reads him this book. The miserable prose seems to soothe him. After a few more pages on damp houses and hungry children, he shuts his eyes and lets his head rock back into the top of the armchair. He soon starts gently snoring – he's asleep.

The first time I hear the tapping on the skylight, I dismiss it as a branch blowing against the glass. Alice doesn't notice it, it must be my imagination. But it happens again. It's insistent and steady, like someone knocking.

Rap-rap-rap . . . Rap-rap-rap.

I stop typing, look up. Alice hears it too this time. The tapping stops. There can't be anyone up there on the roof. We must be going mad. I turn back to my laptop.

Rap-rap-rap . . .

Could it be a monkey? I know they're cheeky shits, but could they be smart enough to mess with us like this? . . . It's stopped again. It *is* a bit windy outside . . . It has to be a branch. Why have I never noticed how creepy this house is at night?

Rap-rap-rap . . . rap-rap-rap . . . rap-rap-rap . . .

Ok, we're done with this. We wake Walt and take him through to bed, locking the hallway gate behind us.

But we're scared. And when the storm hits, things only get worse.

Flashes of lightning illuminate the yard and cast violent shadows across the walls. Something metal rattles and clangs as it's blown across the patio.

I get up to look out the window, and in the next blue flood of light I see a figure in the garden, walking towards the house.

Alice grabs a torch.

We've no idea what we should do. Is this when you hit the panic button? Is there any point in calling the police? Fuck, where are Walt's guns when we need them?

An almighty crack of thunder shatters the air and rattles my bowels.

We go through to the spare room to wake Millicent – we need a local, someone who understands the place, who'll know what to do. She opens her eyes the moment we creep into the sunroom, sits bolt upright and reaches for her glasses. 'Yes, girls, what's wrong?'

I've never been so grateful to have her around. 'There's a man out there,' I whisper. 'I saw him in the garden.'

She pulls her long hair up into a topknot bun, clasps it, and takes charge. 'Okay. Are all the lights off?'

'Yes.'

'Check the security gate is locked.'

Alice pulls the padlock, shakes the iron bars. 'Yeah, it's locked tight.'

Millicent pulls her phone out and calls KK Security, telling them to send the patrol car around at once. For now, my life is in the hands of a woman in a Victorian nightgown.

We sit there, all three of us, huddled on Millicent's bed, the storm raging outside. I check the monitor: Walt's sound asleep, breathing steadily.

Alice and I see the man at the same moment. He's coming towards us, down the path from the back of the garage. A tall, terrifying man in a trench coat and boots, holding a rifle under one arm.

Millicent grabs the torch. Fearlessly, she approaches the window just as he does – just as he raises the gun and points it at her face.

'Don't shoot!' I scream, as I close my eyes and hold my arms up in feeble terror.

But there's no gunshot, just Millicent's calm voice. 'Oh hello, Frank, it's just you,' she says, then with a polite giggle, 'ah, deary me, what a fright.'

I open my eyes to see Frank, the night *askari*, staring in at us earnestly. He's wearing a raincoat and holding an umbrella – not a gun – now open above his head.

'Madam, is everything okay?' he asks, cupping his face against the glass.

'The girls thought they saw someone in the garden. Have you seen anything?'

'Were you around the other side of the house just now, Frank?' I ask, realising my mistake.

'Yes, madam – I was doing my patrol,' he says. 'Then KK radioed to say they had a report of a disturbance. They are on their way now.'

'Yes, I called them,' Millicent says. 'Ask them to do a sweep of the property, will you?'

'Yes, madam. I will.'

'Thank you, Frank,' she says. 'Now you best get out of the rain – don't go catching a cold.'

Alice goes through to the kitchen to make Frank a cup of hot tea, and I feel a mix of relief and embarrassment. 'Shit, sorry about that, Millicent. We were really freaking out.'

'Oh, not to worry. Just a little excitement for the evening!' She chuckles, heading back to her bed.

I watch from the window as the KK guys take their dogs around the garden. And I realise, with some shame, that I'm a total wuss.

But it's not just phantom intruders keeping me up at night – it's also anxiety over how Fiona's return will go down. We've just settled into a nice rhythm here. I know what I'm doing with Walt now, and how to deal with Marguerite, and I'm starting to balance an outside life with my duties in the house. For Fiona, though, I suspect nothing we're doing will be quite up to scratch.

9

FIONA RETURNS

Fiona pulls up in a taxi just as we're sitting down to breakfast, and within minutes of her arrival she's making a show of resetting the standards.

She takes the seat closest to Walt at the head of the table, directly across from Marguerite, and sets about readjusting the world around him, correcting our mistakes. His pills aren't in quite the right spot on the table. His chair hasn't been pushed far enough in. There's too much sugar in his coffee ('Is it decaf? Are you sure it's decaf?') and it's not hot enough, so she asks Esther to make a fresh brew.

Marguerite mongrels through her muesli with a brave face and breezy patter, trying to pretend this isn't all an implicit rebuke of her spousal care.

Millicent – who is rostered on duty with Walt this morning – tries to help but is clearly expected to stand aside. Alice either doesn't notice or doesn't care about Fiona's pointed micromanaging. I do – but I try not to take it personally. I feel like we've been doing a pretty damn good job with Walt and it's not being appreciated.

On the upside, Fiona is keen to spend some alone time with Walt, which means we all get a free pass to do as we please for most of the day. Alice and I borrow the Peugeot and head over to Sarah and Jack's for a barbecue — as far away from the tension as we can get.

The security guards at the entrance to Sarah and Jack's apartment complex eye us suspiciously when we pull up at the gates. They're in paramilitary uniforms with guns slung over their shoulders. One circles the undercarriage of our car with a mirror as the other walks slowly over to my window.

'*Jambo*,' I say cheerfully. '*Habari ako?*'

He ignores my attempt at pleasantries. 'Who are you here to see?' he says, leaning closer and pulling his mirrored sunglasses down his nose to squint at me over the top of them.

'Um, Sarah and Jack at number 23?' I say, wondering if we're at the right address. I was expecting security but this seems . . . unnecessarily hostile.

He glances at a clipboard.

'We can call them if you like?' Alice offers from the passenger seat, holding out her mobile phone.

He frowns at her.

The guy with the mirror finishes his lap of the car. They fist bump as he passes on his way back to the guard hut.

'*Sawa sawa*,' says Guard Number One.

'*Sawa sawa*,' replies Guard Number Two, never breaking eye contact with us.

We stare back for a moment. 'Do you need to see our ID?' I ask.

'No,' he says, before breaking into a massive grin. In an instant, the surly facade evaporates. He holds his hand up for a high five; I obediently deliver one. Laughing, he clasps my hand warmly and mutters something in Swahili. The gates open up, and he stands aside to wave us through. '*Karibu! Karibu!* Say hello to Miss Sarah and Jack for me, please!'

I follow the paved road to Sarah and Jack's building.

Alice laughs. 'That fucker was fucking with us!'

'I don't blame him,' I say. 'White girls are so easy to scare.'

Sarah and Jack's 'apartment' is enormous. Bigger than most houses back home. Four huge bedrooms – each with its own ensuite and walk-in robe – over two sprawling levels of vaulted ceilings and polished wood and parquetry, with external iron bars caging in the huge bay windows, blighting the view of lush communal gardens.

'Well, la-di-da!' I say. 'All this just for a couple of scrubbers from Mackay?' This is much more the kind of splendour I'd expected from the Smyths' place; it seems new diplomats are outliving the old guard. A dozen or so people are sitting around, drinks in hand, talking, laughing. Normal people. Young people. White and black and brown people. Very un-Clubby people.

'Yep!' says Sarah. 'I know it seems like overkill. But it's much easier for the office to just keep a roster of properties that are suitable for whoever might be posted here next – usually it's a family. Besides, it's a third of what you'd pay for a two-bedroom apartment in Sydney.'

'What kind of family would need all this, though?' says Alice.

'Well, it's got to be suitable for "entertaining". Part of the job is hosting dinner parties and soirees for visiting dignitaries, all that bullshit,' says Jack. But today it's just their friends: a mix of expats, Australian development workers, and a few locals.

We make our way out to the verandah where I see Sauti – the rapper I'd met at the Marine Ball – and introduce him to Alice.

'So, what are you guys doing here in Kenya?' an Irish girl bringing a tray of meat out asks us. 'Are you with the High Commission too?'

'Ahhh, no . . .' says Alice. 'We're, ah . . .'

'These are the girls looking after that old man with dementia!' Sauti tells her.

'Oh man, that's you guys!?' she shouts. 'With the crazy old guy? And the scheming wife or whatever?' She calls over some friends: another Kenyan guy in a preppy get-up, and a bunch of Aussies. They've all heard about our ... situation.

They press us against the barbecue and pepper us with questions: 'Who is this guy?' 'Are you nurses?' 'How did you get the job anyway?' 'Do you have to wipe his arse?' 'So, wait – he thinks you're his granddaughters? Or his mistresses?' 'Oh my god – we've been dying to get into that Club!'

Eventually we manage to turn the conversation around to everyone else. Most of them are AYADs – Australian Youth Ambassadors for Development – here to help control diseases in chickens, or to provide contraceptives and sexual health counselling to women, or to set up microfinance loans for rural villagers. One guy, Alex, is a freelance journalist from Melbourne. He's currently working for an organisation in a refugee camp in the north of the country, helping the residents publish a community newspaper. When he hears I work in television, we swap details – there's a video project he's trying to get off the ground there, I might be able to help.

The preppy guy, Eric, is Kenyan-Australian. Having recently graduated with an economics and science degree, he's returned to Kenya to put his knowledge into practice, working on a local energy project. 'Oh man, I know exactly the kind of guy you're working for,' he says, rolling his eyes. 'One of those old-school colonial types from my parents' day.' He understands what we're dealing with better than any of the white Australians do. 'I find it very hard to feel sorry for those people!' he tells us.

'Yup,' I say. 'I get it.' Then I'm hit with that weird feeling of generational guilt – like I need to apologise for my ancestors, while at the same time feeling a bit defensive about it. I wasn't there – I know colonialism was fucked up. And so do they now. How much personal responsibility should people bear for what they're born into? Still, it feels like a confession of sorts when I tell him, 'My parents are from Zimbabwe – well, it was Rhodesia then. They left a long time ago.'

'When Mugabe came in?' he asks.

'Yeah, pretty much.'

'Man, he's a bad dude too, though.'

'Yep.'

Someone changes the subject: this isn't the time or place for an armchair analysis of Africa's political history.

One of the group, Meg, is stationed in a small town called Kitale, a few hundred kilometres north-west of Nairobi, close to the Ugandan border. She jokes that her middle-of-nowhere town is very exciting now that it has two tourist attractions: in addition to the Kitale Museum, there's the recently opened Kitale Nature Conservancy – a 'sanctuary for deformed animals', which apparently features a cow with two heads.

I'm as intrigued by this place as they've all been by our job with Walt. I just *have* to see it – I have to know who's behind it and why they've felt the need to collect the country's four-legged freaks and put them on public display. I make a mental note to add the KNC to my itinerary, for whenever I finally get a chance to do some travelling.

At some point in the afternoon, Alice gets a text message from Fiona:

Stay as long as u like. Dont need u back until tomorrow.

It's the green light to let loose.

Someone suggests we go to a bar where they've got a live DJ playing tonight. It's not too far to walk, and safe enough around these parts before it gets dark. We set off out the gates, past the prankster security guards, past the used car lots that line the main road, past the Masai tribesmen grazing their cattle on the verge, and into a shady beer garden filled with sweet shisha smoke and a dance hall rhythm. *Bend-over-bend-over-bend-over*, the music intones. *Now wibble, wobble, wibble, wobble, wibble!*

One of the AYAD girls sees how shocked Alice and I are by the moves being pulled on the dance floor. They are borderline pornographic: women bend over to touch the floor, pressing their butts into the crotches of men who grind and thrust against them, in time with the heavily syncopated beat.

'Yeah, this is pretty much the most massive song in Kenya right now,' the AYAD girl shouts over the volume. 'We call it the "fuck-miming" song. You may as well join in – it's actually pretty fun once you get into it.'

The last thing I remember is being sandwiched in the middle of a conga line of fuck-mimers, getting dry-humped and bumped along the bar.

I wake up in a four-poster bed shrouded by mosquito netting. *Shit, the bed alarm. Where is it? Did I sleep through? Is Walt up yet?* I feel for it under my pillow – nothing. My mouth tastes like I've been sucking on old socks and my head feels like a tin full of rocks. I can only see straight out of one eye. *Wait, which room am I in?*

Oh, right, I'm at Sarah and Jack's place. I stagger into the ensuite, lean down to drink some water straight from the tap, and feel a sharp pull on the back of my legs. Why are my hamstrings so tight? The reggae beat comes back: *Bend-over-bend-over-bend-over.* I bent over way too hard last night – that much is clear.

'Alice! Alice?' I plod through the house, squinting like a pirate, and find her in the next room in a similar state.

'I'm dying,' she moans.

'I'm dead,' I say.

'You're out of practice,' says Jack, appearing at the door. 'Come on, get up! We've got breakfast for you. And coffees.'

'Oi, mole, come in here – I've got Bridget on Skype!' Sarah calls from the living room. I stagger in and see my sister's face on the laptop screen.

'Biddy!' I squeal. She's sitting at home on the farm, on the verandah. I suddenly feel very homesick.

'I hear you had a big night?' she says.

'Sarah and Jack's fault,' I say. 'They busted out the Bundy Rum.'

Bridget has just got back from a year overseas. She was working as a carer in the UK and is now living at home in Mackay, trying to find a job, without much luck.

'Oh my God!' Through the brain fog I have a brilliant idea. 'Why don't you come here? Take over from me when I finish? If Walt's still alive, that is. I'm gonna have to come home in January and they've asked me to help find someone to take over.'

'Piggy, don't make your sister come and scrub an old man's balls!' says Sarah.

'We don't scrub his balls. But in any case, Bridget actually *has* experience scrubbing balls,' I say. The care work she was doing in England was much more hands-on than this: feeding and bathing quadriplegics, that sort of thing. 'She'd be perfect.'

'I dunno, it sounds hectic,' Bridget says.

'It's not that bad!' I say. 'And looking after Walt will be a piece of piss after the work you've done.'

'I guess so . . .'

'Righto,' I say. 'I'll ask the Smyths if they're up for it.'

I've just pulled an Alice on my own flesh and blood.

It takes us until lunchtime to recover from our hangovers, and by the time we get back to the house Fiona has fired Millicent.

'Dad can't stand her. She's simply too old to be a good fit for the circumstances,' she says.

FIONA RETURNS

It's true that Millicent didn't have the best rapport with Walt – he thinks he's thirty years younger than her, and whenever she was on duty he spent most of the time complaining about the 'old woman' following him around. But it still seems harsh.

Marguerite flies out for England the next day, so she's going down to the Masai Market to 'buy some lovely African trinkets for Cousin George, and the chubby chap who comes around to trim the hedges'. She takes Alice with her, 'to help carry my baskets and shoo all the pushy buggers away', but I'm on the afternoon shift, so I'm stuck.

Fiona is again worried that Marguerite will try to whisk Walt back to England. She breaks into Marguerite's safe and retrieves Walt's passport and hides it in my suitcase 'for the time being'. She's going to use that to smuggle it out of the house later; a friend across town has agreed to look after it.

Alrighty then.

Then she realises Marguerite will apply for a replacement passport once she finds his is missing.

That's why we've got Walt sitting with us at the kitchen table with a notepad and pen in front of him, wondering what's going on. Fiona wants him to write a note saying that he does not consent to having any travel documents issued in his name. Trying to explain this to Walt is impossible: he's flat out writing his own name. He'll have to copy it from a template – and Fiona reckons her writing is too hard for him to read. 'You've got lovely neat writing,' she says. 'Here, you do it.' So it's my hand he goes over the top of.

A few shaky takes later, and Walt's made it official. And he's right behind it now, too. 'I don't want to go anywhere, thank you very much!' he tells us. 'So don't try to bloody well make me! I'm quite happy where I am, here in Hampshire.'

'Yes . . . you mean *Keen-ya*, though, Dad,' Fiona reminds him, slipping his oath into a folder and tearing off the practice pages from the notepad. Then she orders me to destroy the evidence.

There's a moment, while I'm huddled over the burn pit at the bottom of the garden, striking matches and blowing oxygen into the flames that are swallowing the ball of scrunched-up pieces of foolscap, that I turn to look for the hidden camera, for the whacky host to emerge from the hedges.

But no one appears. It's just me and the dogs watching the paper unfurl to reveal a pile of pills hidden in the middle. I singe my fingertips dragging the tablets out to see if they're Temazepam. They're not. They're just multivitamins. Why Fiona feels the need to incinerate them, I'm not sure.

Marguerite leaves for the airport the next day after breakfast, and as soon as she's out the driveway Fiona's calling me and Alice into action on the patio. Walt's distracted, helping Esther scatter seeds and fruit skins around for the birds.

'We need to sort out your pay,' Fiona says. 'Marguerite's been telling the Trust not to pay you.'

Say *what* now?

'Why?' says Alice, astonished.

'Okay. Who or what is "the Trust"?' I ask. I've been trying to avoid learning too much about 'the Trust', but it looks like I might have to enter the fray if I want to see my wages. I've been here more than two months and we still haven't sorted them out.

'Dad's family trust,' says Fiona. 'I had him set it up a few years ago to protect him. Marguerite gets her very generous allowance paid out of that. And any expenses related to his healthcare need to be authorised by them.'

Do Alice and I really need to know this information?

'"Them" being . . .?' I ask.

'The Trust is administered by three lawyers. One of them is in Marguerite's back pocket, but I think I can trust the other two.

She's been talking about getting rid of you all and having a local in to do the job, you know?'

Nope. We did not know that.

'But Marguerite is constantly telling us what a great help we are to her and Walt,' I say, starting to feel like a bit of a fool.

Fiona can see we need some convincing. She pulls her laptop out and Skypes her husband, Jonathan, in the UK. She has him recount to us a conversation he overheard between the two women. Jonathan seems a little weary and harassed; I get the sense he enjoys being brought into this about as much as we do.

He rubs his temples, holding his head in his hands. 'So, I heard Marguerite saying that Walt doesn't like having the carers around because they're, quote, "too noisy", especially at meals.'

Alice and I look at each other. Too noisy? Our table manners have been impeccable. Marguerite's the one who's constantly hooting and hollering as she tells stories, and taking phone calls at the table, and ducking in and out of the room to check the tennis score.

'Tell them the other part, Jonathan,' Fiona says.

He continues as though he's submitting evidence to a grand jury. 'Marguerite also stated she'd prefer to have a "local girl" that Walt knew to help look after him. Fiona asked whether this would be Esther, and was told that it wasn't, but this person remained unnamed.'

'Thank you, Jonathan,' says Fiona, ending the call. Then she turns back to us, as though her point has been made. 'Well, Dad won't stand for that. Having an African carer. I mean, if he was still "with it" it wouldn't be a problem, but he's not. It just won't make sense to him.'

I wonder whether Walt would stand for an African carer if he could remember the last fifty years — whether his attitude was tempered over that transformative time, and he came to accept the people of this land as his equals, or whether he stubbornly remained of the view that white people's dominance over blacks was just the natural order of things. In his better moments he certainly seems a more decent man than I suspect he was in the past. But the past is where he exists, most of the time. A place where black people were only ever inside his house to wait on him — not to remind him to take his tablets and help him in the shower.

'I have to make the lawyers understand that.' Fiona pulls out a digital audio recorder. 'It's voice-activated,' she says, pointing to the microphone. 'We have to get Dad on tape making it clear how he feels about things.'

After lunch, while Fiona puts Walt down for a nap, Alice and I join the Kenyan staff on their tea break under the jacaranda tree. Esther, Patrick, Peter, David and James all sit with Khamisi, sharing the *ugali* and *sukuma wiki* he has prepared. David had asked us to pick him up some '*maziwa lala*' with the groceries that morning, and we're curious to know what it is.

'Ahhh! Yes! My *maziwa lala!*' he says, jumping up and taking the strange triangular shaped carton, clutching it to his chest. 'Thank you, thank you, *asante sana!*'

'So, what actually is it?' Alice asks him.

'It is like milk, but it is sour,' David says, seemingly excited to tell us about this popular Kenyan drink.

James eagerly joins in. '*Maziwa*, it means "milk". And *lala* — it means "slept". So it is "slept milk".'

'Like, it's gone off?' I say.

'No no, it is not off. We just say, it has been left out to sleep overnight,' James says.

'Sounds like "off milk" to me!' Alice says. The staff laugh at our apparent disgust.

'You must try it,' says David. 'Come – I will prepare some for you. Come!' We follow him into the staff quarters, where he sets up a *jiko* (charcoal burner) in the corner of his room.

We sit on small crates and watch as David snips off the corner of the carton, and pours the milk into a saucepan, turning the flame down low. The rest of the staff hover at the door, watching our demonstration.

'It is my favourite,' he grins. 'I cannot drink normal milk. It makes me feel no good,' he gestures to his stomach. 'But *maziwa lala* – no problem! You don't have to have it warm – but I think it is better this way.'

As the liquid starts to gently bubble, David pulls out a bag of sugar.

'I like it very sweet,' he says. 'Maybe you will try first, before I put this in?'

He pulls a couple of tin mugs out from a box beside him, pours a small amount into one for Alice and I to share, then fills the other up and passes it out to Peter.

'*Asante*,' says Peter, blowing the steam across the top and taking a swig before passing it on to Esther.

Alice takes a sip from our mug, then passes it to me. It's tangy, like yoghurt.

David looks at us, expectantly. 'You like it?' he says.

'Yeah, it's not bad!' Alice says.

'Kinda like yoghurt,' I say.

'Yes! It is similar to yoghurt,' David says. 'Now, with *sukari*.'

He pours what must be an entire cup of sugar into the pot, then stirs it with a sanded strip of timber.

'There. That should be done,' he says, topping up our mug again.

I take a sip first this time. It is sickly sweet. Like syrup. I screw my face up trying to swallow.

David thinks this is hilarious. So do the rest of the staff. They cackle and slap their legs with mirth. 'Okay, so for you next time, no *sukari*,' he says. 'And you?'

Alice takes a hesitant sip. She has a similar reaction. 'No thanks,' she says. 'I prefer the first kind.'

The staff suddenly turn around – Fiona has come to find us. I worry for a moment that we'll be in trouble – that she'll disapprove of our fraternising. But she's smiling. She doesn't seem to think there's anything at all amiss.

'*Jambo*, Fiona,' David says, standing up to meet her at his door. 'I was just showing Alice and Kirsten the *maziwa lala*,' he says.

'Ohhhh yes! I remember that!' Fiona says. 'Do you take it with sugar?'

'Yes,' David laughs. 'Too much sugar for them.' He passes her the cup.

'Yes, a little bit of sugar is okay,' Fiona says, taking a sip and recoiling. 'But I think that's a bit too much, David! You'll give yourself diabetes!'

David laughs, taking the cup back from her, then passing it on to James to share with the others.

'Girls, come,' she says. 'We should restock Dad's pills while he's asleep. I want to do an audit and see if there's anything I need to order in.'

We wave goodbye and thank David, then follow her back to the house.

'Isn't that name just so sweet? "*Maziwa lala*",' Fiona says. '"Sleepy milk". I'd forgotten about that. I love it.'

I love it, too.

I wake up early and lie in bed scrolling on my phone while the call to prayer warms the dawn sky. There's an email from the production company I work for in Sydney. It's confirmed: *Hungry Beast* has been commissioned for a third season on the ABC – I have a real job to go back to. The producers have called a meeting with all of us to discuss new ideas for the show and talk about where we want to take it next year. I'll have to Skype in.

I head down to the Club to dial in from the computer room. I sit with my laptop in the phone booth they have in the corner, my headphones in, waiting for the Skype ringtone. The Club attendant is helping an older white couple in matching sweaters print their digital photos out from one of the PCs on the glossy hardwood table; through the windows I watch a Kenyan family playing croquet on the lawn. This is such a strange place.

I've got mixed emotions about the prospect of going home. On the one hand, I'm keen to get back to reality, I realise how much I've missed making sense of numbers and words, rather than sighs and glances. But on the other hand, I'm just settling into life in Kenya – and feel like there's so much more to discover here.

The Skype alert bleeps, and I see a room full of my friends and colleagues. Their Australian accents echo, pulling me right out of Africa, back to a land free of security fences and attack dogs but full of rules and anxieties.

'So,' my boss says to me, 'we're all a little confused about what exactly it is you're doing there. You're a bodyguard to a sugar daddy or something?'

'Yeah.' I laugh. 'Look, something like that.'

In a couple of months' time, I'll be back to explain it all in person.

After dinner that night, we set about capturing a senile man's testimony. 'Dad,' Fiona says, balancing the recorder on the arm of Walt's chair while he sits gazing into the fire; he startles and looks back at her. 'Dad, you know how you've been quite unwell lately?'

Walt frowns, thinks for a bit. I wonder whether he does 'know' that — and what 'lately' means to him. It seems a bit unfair to be demanding this kind of self-assessment from someone so clearly incapable of it.

'Oh well,' he says, 'I suppose I've been a little off-colour, but nothing to worry about!' He laughs it off, but his face tightens up a bit. We're making him worry about whether he should, in fact, be worrying.

'No, Dad, I mean with your dicky heart and all the rest of it — you might not remember it all. But you've been very unwell, and we're wanting to have someone here in the house to help look after you. That's what the girls have been doing.'

'What girls?'

'These lovely girls, Dad. Alice and Kirsten. The *Or-stray-lyans.*'

Only now does he notice us sitting on the couch across from him. He stares at us blankly.

'Hi, Walt,' we say, waving.

'How do you do?' He nods politely, throws us a terse smile, then looks back at Fiona.

'Anyway, Dad, Marguerite has decided they shouldn't be here. She thinks she should get you a local nurse to help instead. Would you like that?' Fiona says the word 'local' with that special sort of intonation that people use to turn it into a pejorative. I actually don't believe she's racist at all — but she's more than happy to pretend to be if it helps bend Walt to her will.

'Would I like *what?*' he asks.

'Having an African in to help you?'

'Help me what? We have enough staff.'

Fiona angles the recorder towards him.

'Help you in and out of bed, to dress in the morning, shower at night — that sort of thing.'

The penny finally drops.

'Not on this side of hell!' Walt roars.

'That's okay. I didn't think so, Dad.'

'Whose foolish bloody idea is that? I won't have it, I'm telling you! There's no need. I'm perfectly alright.'

'I know, Dad. Don't worry. It won't happen.'

Fiona buttons off the device. Mission accomplished.

The audio file is emailed to a complex network of lawyers, mediators and trustees. I can't keep track of who's who and where their loyalties lie. Some are based in the UK, others in Kenya. Some seem sympathetic to Marguerite, others are clearly trying to remain neutral in the developing drama.

I know this because Fiona — for reasons that will never become clear — starts forwarding me and Alice all of their correspondence and cc'ing us into her emails. Several times a day my inbox pings with a new missive about how Walt must never be returned to England, or about how Marguerite has proven herself utterly neglectful, or about how she really is the only one with her father's best interests at heart. And the trustees repeatedly write back with the same weary warning that they 'do not do contentious family law', and that if things start 'getting litigious' they'll have to hand the matter over to another firm. I can only assume she's keeping us in the loop because she thinks we're her allies, or so that she has witnesses to her efforts to help her father. I'd rather not know any of it, but she is relentless. She hassles for copies of title deeds and wills, tells them Walt is 'constantly expressing a wish to leave Marguerite', urges them to visit the house in Nairobi and see for themselves. They say they're not in possession of the documents she's chasing, and in any case wouldn't be authorised to hand them over, and stress that this is something the family members need to sort out among themselves.

Meanwhile, we've still got Walt to look after. And without Millicent here, Alice and I are on duty every day, occasionally having to pull a double shift, making it even harder for us to get any kind of down time.

~

Walt's hair isn't going to cut itself, and it's my job to take him to the salon down the road. He *hates* having his hair cut, but the Kenyan ladies there are used to him, and know how to butter him up. I manage to get him to their door before he realises what we're doing. He hesitates, but the hairdressers spot us and immediately start making a fuss.

'Bwana Smyth! Bwana Smyth! *Jambo*, we have missed you!' they say.

Rose, the manager, wags her finger in his face, scolding him. 'And look how long your hair is!' She's a statuesque woman, wears a bright purple and yellow head wrap in zigzag folds around her soft Afro crown. 'We have to sort that out!'

'Oh hello, hello,' says Walt, affable but wary as we guide him to a seat in front of a mirror. 'What are you girls going to do to me today?'

'We are going to make you *handsome!*' Rose says, leaning over him as she drapes a cape around his neck. 'More handsome than you already are!'

Rose laughs. Walt laughs. I can see he's already submitting. God, these women are good.

Rose wets his hair down with a spray of water, while another woman brings him a cup of tea and some biscuits as a distraction. For a moment, I worry about the biscuits. Is that too much sugar? Would Fiona approve?

He sits patiently with his eyes closed, while Rose trims the grey strands combed across his scalp. She's done in less than five minutes.

'Now, what about these ears, *mzee*?' she says. 'Can you sit still for me to tidy these up?'

'If you must,' Walt scowls, shutting his eyes again, as she trims the wiry spikes sprouting from the side of his head.

'There. We are done!' Rose brushes Walt down, then whips the cape away. The other women gather around to coo at his new appearance.

'Ohhhh, very *maridadi!*' I say, remembering the Swahili word for 'stylish'.

Walt blushes, giggles, squirms out of his chair and past the fussing beauticians. 'Alright, alright – that's quite enough – you can set me free now! *Kwaheri*, goodbye!'

I leave a wad of cash – with a good tip – on the counter and chase him out the door, finding myself doubting Fiona's certainty that he'd never stand for an African carer.

10
BLOOD & BEERS

Sitting in the living room one evening, the dogs warming their bellies at the fire, Walt reading the newspaper for the third time, I get a Skype call from one of my aunts in Australia. She's discovered we've got long-lost relatives in Nairobi: one of Dad's cousins on his father's side, Claire. It occurs to me that I've never even thought of my dad having cousins. I know of no one beyond my parents' siblings – our family tree was ruthlessly pruned by distance when they left Africa for Australia. Claire is younger than my father; she left Zimbabwe a few years later than he did. It looks like she married a white Kenyan guy and has taken his name; apparently they run a bar in town.

When my aunt tells me the name of it, I'm astonished. It's the bar just down the road from Sarah and Jack's place. Could I have been drinking with family all along?

I manage to wangle an afternoon off a couple of days later to investigate. I find a good spot in the beer garden, down a schooner of Tusker, then ask to speak to the manager. A woman comes out, a stunner, well over six-feet tall. No one in my family is tall, and I'm only five-foot-two. Could we really be related?

'Hi there!' she says, smiling. 'How can I help you? Is there an issue with the service?' I see her glancing at my table, trying to work out what the problem might be.

'No, no, no – no, the service is fine, thank you.' I jump up from my stool to face her. It's a strange conversation to initiate. I'm not quite sure where to start. 'It's just – um – you're Claire, right?'

'Yes . . .' she says cautiously.

'So, I know this is a bit weird, but I think we might be related?'

'Oh?' she says. She seems intrigued, but still wary. I don't blame her – if some half-cut harpy came up to me out of the blue claiming blood ties, I'd be on high alert too.

'My name's Kirsten. I'm from Australia. You're a Drysdale, right?'

'Yes – well, I was. Married now!' She gestures towards the table for us to sit back down.

'Right, so . . . I'm a Drysdale, too. I think you and my dad, Bruce, are cousins?'

'Oh, go on. Really?'

'Yes!' I say. 'On my grandpa's side. He and your dad are brothers?'

'Uncle Ronny!' she says, shocked, 'Is he still alive?'

'Yes!' I say. 'He lives with us in Australia.'

'God, he must be getting on.'

'Yeah, he's nearly ninety. He's in pretty good shape, though, considering.'

We just stare at each other for a bit – searching, I suppose, for familial features, and marvelling at our crossing of paths. I sense she's relaxed now, feeling less like she's about to be hit up for a loan or a cut of a will. She seems like a lot of fun.

'So, what does this make us?' she asks.

'Second cousins? Or is it first cousins once-removed?'

'How bloody exciting – a long-lost rellie from Australia! How did you find me?'

'One of my aunts is doing the family tree and heard I was here. She tracked you guys down.'

'All the way here!?'

'Yep. Power of the internet, I guess.'

'Yah, it's frightening, hey?' Her Zimbabwean accent echoes my parents', and makes me think of home.

'The weirdest thing is I've been coming here not even knowing about you – my friends live just down the road, so this is their local.'

'You're joking,' she says. I shake my head, and we share another moment of staring silence, trying to comprehend the coincidence.

'Sorry,' I say, 'I didn't mean to interrupt if you're busy. I just wanted to come and say hello.'

'Of course! Bugger work for the day. It can wait. We should have a drink.' Claire stops a passing waiter and asks him to bring us a couple of beers.

'So, what are you doing in Kenya? Are you here on holiday?'

'It's a long story,' I say, then tell her how it all came about. 'We're not really nursing so much as . . . supervising. They're a slightly odd family.'

We drink and talk until it gets dark, my new cousin and I, filling each other in on the branches of family tree that have been grafted onto different continents, while fleshing out the new growth and tracing our roots back as far as we can to Scotland, England, Ireland and France.

Claire tells me about a whole offshoot of the family who ended up in Canada and the US, and how she and her husband, Robert, toyed with the idea of emigrating but now have three daughters, all at primary school here, all proudly Kenyan, here to stay. She can't help but worry about them, though – she still wonders now and then whether they should go somewhere safer.

I tell her how hard it was for my parents to start again in Australia, how Dad was twenty-eight years old and had nothing more than the twenty-four dollars in his pocket when he landed in Brisbane. They've done well there, though: decades of hard toil and good fortune have rewarded them with a wonderful life in what they see as a generous country. (Being migrants who don't 'look' like migrants was also no doubt an advantage; it's fair to assume black Rhodesians moving to Queensland in the 1980s wouldn't have had quite the same experience.)

When I wonder aloud about how things would have gone for my parents had they stayed, I discover that their leaving Zimbabwe was a slightly more urgent affair than I've been led to believe.

'They couldn't stay,' Claire explains, seemingly surprised by my naivety. 'Your dad, his brothers, all of those guys who were in the army, they really had to get out in a hurry after the war. Mugabe wasn't going to be kind to them. Even the blacks who'd fought with the government were scared.'

'You're lucky your folks got to Australia,' Claire says. 'They were smart to go when they did – it's virtually impossible to get in there now. So many ended up in South Africa – I did for a time, my parents went there, and my sisters – but it's got its own problems, too. I moved here when I met Robert. It's better here. Kenya has so much potential, so much hope.'

We're interrupted when I get a text from Fiona. She needs me to come back to the house as soon as I can.

My family is put on hold while I return to another.

The moment I arrive at the house, I'm dragged to the desk in my bedroom and dialled into a Skype conference call with the trustees. I tell Fiona I really don't want to get involved in her PR war, but she's insisting on it. She wants them to hear from me and Alice – her 'independent sources' – about how everything relating to Walt's care should be done exactly the way she's demanding it be done. 'It will help convince them to approve the payments for you girls, too,' she says. Hmmm, I've never been bribed with my own earnings before.

'So, Kirsten, how does Walt seem to you?' the trustees ask, also seemingly under professional duress.

I tell them the truth as I see it: that his physical condition has improved significantly since I arrived, but that mentally he seems to be in steady decline. That some days are better than others, but that a 'good' day in this context has come to mean 'incident-free', not that he's happy, per se. That a 'good' night means he's only up once or twice, and a 'bad' night requires resettling every hour. That he's anxious about something at least 80 per cent of the time, in my view. I tell them that Fiona is going above and beyond to make his world comfortable. That she has thought of everything – from his diet to his physical environment to his heart and his feet and his teeth. That he could not possibly ask for a better case manager – that it's a shame he doesn't realise his daughter is making sure he's looked after so well. I tell them he is hot and cold when it comes to Marguerite – that at times he claims to want to divorce her (or worse), but at others wants to know where she is and clearly regards her with great affection. I say that in my opinion, it does seem, generally, that he's better when she's around. That he misses her – wittingly or not – when she's not here.

No doubt this irritates Fiona, who's standing listening at the door. Eventually I'm released, my statement recorded, and Alice takes over. I assume she tells the trustees much the same thing, though I know she's less sympathetic to Marguerite than I am.

Whether or not our testimonies make the trustees more inclined to release the funds for our wages remains to be seen. I find myself – not for the first time – marvelling at my own idiocy. How did I get here? What am I doing? Who takes a job on the other side of the world without clarifying the details of pay?

We're all – Alice, Fiona and I – sitting in the living room reading one night after dinner. I'm on duty, next to Walt on the settee. The fire crackles, the opera CD plays softly, the dogs lie lazy at his feet. He kicks off his slippers and rubs his toes across Jua's belly. She lets out an easy sigh.

Then Walt's breathing changes. He lowers his newspaper to his lap, tilts his head back and shuts his eyes, pinching his eyebrows together ever so slightly.

'Walt, are you alright?' I ask gently, not wanting to startle him.

He opens his eyes and looks at me. 'Oh yes, quite alright,' he says, giving me a reassuring tap on my knee before closing his eyes again. But I can tell he's not.

I notice a light knocking sensation on the back of the couch, as though the taut upholstery is being struck with a tiny drumstick. Walt reaches one hand up to his shoulder.

It's his heart, I realise. The pacemaker. Pounding through his back.

'Hey, Fiona,' I whisper. She looks up from her book. 'I think Walt's heart might be playing up.'

She jumps out of her chair, shoos the dogs out of the room and kneels in front of him. 'Dad – Dad, are you feeling alright?' She takes his wrist to feel for his pulse.

He smiles, laughs. 'Yes, yes, I'm perfectly fine. Just the old heart getting a bit wound up.'

The bugger is stoic, I'll grant him that.

'It might be his blood pressure,' says Fiona. 'It can drop after a meal, which will trigger the pacemaker to kick in.' She stands to pull him to his feet. 'Come on, Dad, up you get – let's have you walk around a bit, get that blood flowing.' She locks her elbows through his and heaves him up. '*Harambee!*'

She walks him in slow circles around the room, talking to me and Alice all the while. 'You must be very careful when this happens – make sure you're supporting him. Ideally there'd be two of you, one on each side. We don't want him fainting. But moving around will help with circulation and should get that pacemaker to calm down.'

After a few minutes, it's settled and he's sitting back in his armchair, fussing over a dog with its muzzle between his knees.

'We'll ask Dr Andrews about it at Dad's check-up tomorrow,' says Fiona. 'You two should both be there, actually.'

It's another morning off I won't have – but I don't mind going. I now appreciate, in a way I didn't before, that Walt could die while I'm on duty with him. It would be good to know whether the doctor has any tips on how to avoid that.

Peter drives us to the Aga Khan Hospital after breakfast. It's one of the best private hospitals in East Africa; of course, only a lucky few can afford to be treated there. We've been here a few times before – but more just for routine check-ups and prescription renewals than anything this serious.

A row of leather chairs is lined up in the hallway outside Dr Andrews' office. We wait about fifteen minutes to be seen, while amputees and cancer patients and pregnant women are wheeled past. Walt thinks we're in an airport departure lounge. 'Have they called our flight yet?'

'No, Dad, we're here to see the doctor about your heart.'

'Oh. We haven't missed our flight, though, have we?'

An ancient African man with a wizened face shuffles past, skin shrivelled like a walnut, eyes somehow still sharp behind milky cataracts. He's impeccably dressed – spit-shined shoes, a three-piece suit – and two younger women accompany him. His daughters, perhaps?

The African man stops in front of Walt. He smiles, bending down to shake Walt's hand. Walt smiles back, grips him warmly.

'*Jambo, bwana,*' says the African man.

'*Jambo, mzee,*' says Walt.

Alice and I look at Fiona, who shrugs, as mystified as we are. The two women smile at us kindly, give a nod of solidarity, then usher their charge along. I'm sure neither old man actually knows who the other one is – perhaps they were just reminded of a friend from a previous life. Or perhaps it was just a moment of acknowledgment – that no matter the colour of our skin, age betrays us all in the end.

A receptionist steps into the hallway. 'Walter Smyth?' she calls.

'Oh blast, I've lost my bloody passport!' Walt says, patting down his pockets as we all troop through.

'No, Dad, don't worry, we're here to see the doctor.'

Dr Andrews leans back behind his big mahogany desk, makes a show of taking us all in. He's been the family doctor here for decades. He knows all about the 'differences of opinion' between Fiona and Marguerite when it comes to Walt's care.

'Well!' says the doctor. 'Quite a crowd you've brought with you today, hey, Walt?'

With a perplexed smile, Walt turns to look at us all seated next to him. 'Yes, well. To be totally honest – I've no idea who they all are!'

Something about the raw truth of this makes us all laugh, Walt included.

'Alright then, let's get you up here and have a look at what's going on.'

The doctor has Walt take off his shirt and sit on the examination bed, where he anchors half a dozen multicoloured leads to his chest with little rings of sticky plastic. The wires lead into a monitor and produce a rainbow of squiggly lines across a screen.

Then Dr Andrews helps Walt onto a treadmill. Alice, Fiona and I help hold him steady as he walks, very slowly, across the moving belt. He grumbles a bit but is surprisingly compliant for someone who can't understand why a group of strangers are asking him to undress and walk to nowhere.

Dr Andrews studies the monitor, adjusts some dials, consults his paperwork. Says 'mmhmm, mmhmm' a lot.

'Okay,' he says finally, 'thank you, Walt. You can put your shirt back on.'

We help Walt off the treadmill and back over to the bed, as he wags a teasing finger at us. 'But all these young women seem to prefer me with no clothes on!' he says.

I don't know that he even recognises Fiona as his own daughter right now. She always seems to quietly relish it when he doesn't remember Marguerite, and I wonder if it bothers her when she's the stranger. She betrays so little emotion, it's hard to tell.

'Okay,' says the doctor, 'so I've made some adjustments to the pacemaker. We do want it to be somewhat responsive to changes in blood pressure, but perhaps not quite so responsive as it has been.'

Fiona seems pleased that her diagnosis was right. 'Should we also run some more bloods?' she presses.

'Well . . .' Dr Andrews doesn't seem to think this is necessary. 'He had some done not too long ago,' he says, flipping through Walt's file.

'I think it would be best to get a good overall view,' Fiona insists. 'Urine, too. If you wouldn't mind?'

'Sure,' says Dr Andrews, pulling out his referral pad and scribbling some lab requests. Like us, he seems to realise it's easier to say 'yes' to Fiona's demands. 'Here, take this in to the nurses next door. They should be able to see you right away.'

They do. They prod and they poke him, they have him piss in a jar, and even though the results come back a few days later reporting all is as well as can be, Fiona still manages to find something to worry about: his iron – while within the acceptable range – is slightly lower than it was in his last test. This is a wicked problem. He can't take iron supplements, because they might constipate him. He can't eat more red meat, because of the fat that comes with it, and because he'll want to put salt all over it, which will sometimes actually be sugar, and we don't want him doing that because if he becomes diabetic he'll have to have a needle every day and he won't understand why and if he refuses we'll run the risk of him going into a coma.

Fiona tells Khamisi that from now on, we are to have spinach with every meal but breakfast.

It's a rare grey, drizzly day. Alice is out on the patio with James and David, helping them repair a loose railing. Fiona and I are in the study, watching a documentary about the great migration with Walt. She brought the DVD over from the UK in the hope of entertaining him on days like this. He's gripped by it, even though he's seen it a dozen times before – even though he's seen the real thing many times before.

'Oh, they are marvellous creatures, aren't they?' he gushes about the baby elephants rolling around in the mud. Then with a fatalistic sigh, 'Well, nature is cruel,' when a young impala is taken by a cheetah.

The phone rings in the dining room and I go through to answer it. It's Marguerite, in a real state.

Apparently she's emailed Alice to ask what's going on, as Fiona hasn't been replying to any of her messages, and Alice has replied asking her whether it's true that she told the Trust not to pay us, because Fiona is threatening to fly us out to Zanzibar until it's sorted, if that's the case. (The Zanzibar strategy is news to me. And frankly, it's quite appealing. I'd better make sure I get my passport back in case she does follow through.)

Marguerite is defiant. 'Absolutely not!' she says. 'In fact, I've been asking them to make sure you're paid! And I've never told the lawyers I want you gone, never in my life! I tell you, I am totally fed up with the way Fiona treats me. Telling all these dreadful, dreadful untruths! If it wasn't for dear old Walt, and you and Alice, I'd just run away. Do you know what else she's done? You won't believe it – she's told the trustees that she thinks my doctor and I should be called in for police questioning! I'm starting to think I may as well just top myself. The sooner the better for everyone!'

She hangs up, sobbing. It's awful, but Fiona says it's all just for show – that I shouldn't be sucked in by her histrionics. I dunno . . . The suicide threat might have been exaggerated, but her distress sounded pretty authentic to me.

At breakfast two days later, the phone rings again. This time Marguerite delivers the news of her impending death in a much more upbeat tone. 'Oh, helloooo!' the voice sings. 'Now, I'm calling to let you know that I've just accidentally drunk a cup of "mothball tea".'

I am so fucking over this bullshit. Accidental death by a warm cup of camphor? This is it – I've reached the point where nothing anyone in this family says or does can shock me anymore.

'Right,' I say. 'I see. Just out of curiosity, how did the mothball end up in your tea?'

Alice and Fiona look up at me, confused.

'It was on the floor, you see!' says Marguerite.

'Mm-hmm. So, you picked a mothball up off the floor and put it into a cup of hot water?'

I shrug back at them.

'Yes,' she says, 'well, you know, it looked awfully like a tea bag.'

'Right. Yes. I can see how that could happen. And you didn't notice that the tea tasted funny when you started drinking it?'

'Well, do you know, it was the funniest thing – I was so jolly thirsty that I just gulped half of it down in two swigs and it was too late by the time I realised!'

'Alrighty then,' I say. 'Well, let us know if you take a turn for the worse.'

'Will do. I say, is Walt there?'

'He is . . .' I say, hesitating. Walt woke up in a dark mood and has spent the past hour telling us how he's going to 'shoot that bitch wife of mine in the head' the moment he gets the chance – much to Fiona's delight. I'm not sure that now is the best time for them to talk.

'Would you put him on for me, please?' Marguerite asks. 'It's been an age since we spoke.'

What can I do? She's his wife. I pretend not to see Fiona signalling for me not to, and I pass the phone to Walt, who for all his tough talk earlier is now sweet as pie.

'Hel-*loooooooo*, darling,' he says. 'Where are you?'

A tinny squawk garbles through the earpiece.

Walt pulls the curtain aside and peers out the window. 'Oh yes, all's well here. Lovely blue sky.'

More squawk.

I sit back down at the table to continue my breakfast, but moments later Walt is holding the receiver up to me, his arm outstretched, looking exasperated. 'Could you please explain to my dotty old wife that I'm in England?'

'But you're not, Walt. You're in Kenya.'

'What?'

'*Keen-ya*,' I say again, this time with his pronunciation.

I hear Marguerite's faraway voice coming down the line, sounding like a mosquito stuck in a thimble. 'Yoo-hooooo! Is anyone there? Yoo-hoo?' She starts whistling.

'Look out the window, Walt,' I say. 'See, there's the *askari*.' Patrick is standing at the gate, fiddling with his slingshot. 'We're in Africa.'

Walt puts the receiver back to his ear. 'Oh – apparently, I'm in *Keen-ya*,' he concedes.

He's nowhere and everywhere all at once.

Fiona decides she wants to buy Walt some new slippers. And he can't just have any old slippers – they must be podiatrist-approved slippers. Fiona thinks you can buy some at Nakumatt, so that afternoon we all pile into the Mazda: Walt in the front with Peter driving, and Alice, Fiona and me in the back seat, like we're on a family road trip. We make the short drive down to Village Market, the upmarket shopping complex near the UN headquarters. We pass dozens of sinewy marathon runners on their training route, and the furniture sellers with their polished wood four-poster bed frames and plush recliner armchairs, and the nurseries full of potted plants and bunches of fresh-cut flowers. I'm fascinated by these open-air roadside businesses.

'What do they do with everything at night?' I ask Peter.

'They have an *askari*,' he says, glancing up at me in the rear-view mirror, careful not to divert his attention from the road for too long.

'A lot of the stallholders in a particular area will pool their money to pay for a night watchman,' Fiona explains. 'But every now and then even they get held up.'

'Yes, it is very-very bad,' says Peter.

'What's bad?' asks Walt.

'The bandits,' says Peter. 'The bandits who rob the stalls.'

'Oh no, how dreadful!' says Walt, looking intently at Peter with a surprising amount of sympathy. He thinks Peter's saying he's been robbed. 'Did they steal much?'

Peter catches on quickly to the misunderstanding. 'Oh no, *bwana*,' he says. 'No, no, they didn't get anything. I am fine.'

'Oh, thank goodness for that,' says Walt, sincerely relieved.

'Nothing to worry about, Dad – look, here we are!' says Fiona, trying to distract him from worrisome thoughts as we pull up at the boom gates. Security guards have us pop the bonnet and boot, and they run the mirror around the car before waving us through. Peter drops us at the entrance then finds a shady spot to wait in the car park.

Village Market is where expats and wealthy locals come to enjoy sushi in the open-air food court, set against a waterfall feature and terraced gardens. It's a mecca of Western-style comforts and wealth, full of rich Kenyan kids eating frozen yoghurt, teenage couples going to see the latest Hollywood blockbuster, conspicuous US special forces soldiers playing mini-golf, and guests staying at the adjacent five-star hotel buying expensive souvenirs and having coffee and cheesecake at Artcaffe. Just outside the gates, Coca-Cola is sold in dusty *dukas* for thirty bob a bottle; inside, it's ten times the price.

Fiona says we're not supposed to bring Walt to places like this — that they're too busy, too unfamiliar — but today she says it's fine because the three of us are there to look after him. I can't help but notice that she's more than happy to bend her hard and fast rules when it suits her. And apparently she's forgetting that it is *technically* Alice's afternoon off.

Fiona and Alice walk ahead to scout for the footwear department, leaving me to wander around with Walt until we know where to take him. I'm happy to be assigned that role. I enjoy coming to Village Market just for the people-watching aspect — and Nakumatt, the country's largest department store chain, is a great place to watch Kenya's small but growing middle class browse the shelves of modern promises.

Walt is similarly fascinated by this wonderland of colourful stuff and noise. He grabs me conspiratorially, holding up a purple nylon wig. 'This place is an absolute asylum!' he whispers. 'Are we at the circus?'

A group of Kenyan teenage girls come around the corner, giggling hysterically. They're each wearing a different coloured wig and are draped in rainbow strands of metallic baubles.

'Look at these people!' Walt says, gobsmacked. 'They're completely mad. Stark. Raving. Mad!'

'Oi!' Alice hollers from the other end of the store. 'Down this way – we found them.'

'Come on, Walt, let's head down here,' I say, taking him by the arm and reaching for the purple wig to return it to the rack. He pulls it back, makes as though he's going to try it on, then breaks into a fit of mischievous giggles.

I'm touched by his expression of pure, childlike delight. It reminds me of how my grandmother loved visiting the pet store in Mackay, because she thought she was at the zoo. *We actually should bring him here more often*, I think. *He gets a real kick out of it.* But Fiona would never agree. To her mind, it seems, almost no moment of joy is worth unwrapping him from his cotton-wool cocoon.

The new slippers don't do anything to stop a run of tricky days with Walt. He's fixated on the idea that his mother has died, and that he needs to go to her funeral.

One particularly long and difficult day, while Fiona is taking Walt's passport (still hidden inside my suitcase) to 'somewhere safe on the other side of town', he is so determined to drive down to Dover to farewell his dear old mother that he becomes aggressive when Alice and I won't give him the car keys.

'I reckon we should just take him for a drive,' Alice suggests, as he storms after her through the sunroom. 'He'll forget where he's going as soon as we get halfway down the road. Let's just take him for lunch at the Club.'

'Okay, I'll let Khamisi know not to worry about lunch.'

I'm too late: he's already made a start on a curry. He's humming as he stirs the pot on the stove. And he is very upset when I tell him we won't be having lunch here after all. 'But I am making the Indian curry today!' he protests. 'I have prepared it with all of the spices.

Look – I have the cumin, and the ginger and mustard seeds.' He lines them up on the bench.

It does seem a little sacrilegious to miss out on one of Khamisi's meals. He was trained in a five-star hotel and is immensely proud of his mastery of European cuisine. Before the Smyths, he'd been working for a Swiss family, until they returned to Geneva. Fiona found his résumé and letter of recommendation among the dozens of flapping papers pinned to the noticeboard at the shops. Most expats and wealthy families find their Kenyan household staff by word of mouth, but occasionally get lucky picking from the hundreds of pleas for a livelihood thumbtacked to crumbling cork.

'I know – I'm so sorry, Khamisi.' The smell is making me salivate. I really would much rather stay and eat his curry than drive Walt to his mother's funeral. 'Maybe we can have it for dinner instead?'

Khamisi throws his hands in the air.

I feel terrible for having offended him – he takes his work very seriously. 'Why don't you have it for lunch?' I suggest. 'You could share it with the other staff!'

Khamisi laughs, pulls a face. 'No, no, no, you know – we Africans, we do not like these flavours.' Well, he can't be speaking for all Africans, I think. Esther's in the laundry folding washing, so I call her in. 'Hey, Esther – do you like curry?' She gets all bashful, covering her smile with her hands while she shakes her head. I realise it's probably rare that she's asked to offer an honest, personal opinion on anything in the Smyths' house. 'You can have this for lunch if you like – here, have a taste!'

She comes over to the pot, smells the spoon in Khamisi's hand, and screws up her face. 'No, no thank you. *Asante.*' She breaks into a fit of giggles.

'You see?' Khamisi says. 'It is too rich. I prefer to have my *sukuma wiki.*'

'Huh?' I say. 'How can you cook so well if you don't like the taste of what you're making!?'

'I had very good training in the hotel kitchen,' he says proudly. 'I know all of the herbs and spices. I make this for *you*,' he pleads.

'It's the *bwana*,' I try to explain. 'He is very *wasi-wasi* today — we have to get him out of the house for a bit.'

Khamisi softens and comes to a compromise. 'I will make the curry and I will keep it warm. You will try some when you come back.'

'Yes, okay, deal,' I say. If I have to eat lunch twice to keep the peace, I'll do it.

He resumes his humming and stirring, though in a decidedly morose tone.

I find Alice waiting by the car with Walt dressed in his crumpled suit. 'He insisted on wearing it,' she says. 'And I promised we'd stop to buy flowers on the way.'

Walt is pacing, frowning, rubbing his face, sighing. 'Oh no, oh no,' he keeps muttering. 'My poor, dear old mother.' He's grief-stricken, I realise. What an awful mental place to be stuck at.

'Should we drive ourselves, or get Peter to take us?' Alice asks.

'Peter,' I say. 'That might help remind Walt he's in Kenya.'

We wave Peter over from his chair under the tree near the staff quarters, and pile into the Mazda. And sure enough, by the time we're through the gates and turning onto the road towards the Club, Walt's asking who we're meeting there for lunch.

His mother is long dead again, may she continue to rest in peace.

Marguerite is due back in a couple of days. I find the thought of it exhausting. On the one hand, having her around can sometimes make Walt easier to handle in times when he's searching for a familiar face. On the other, Marguerite often requires her own handling – help resetting her Kindle or finding files on her computer, or explanations of the carers' roster and how it all fits in with her diary, even if we've been over it a dozen times before. Not to mention the ongoing family tensions that she doesn't know we already know about, meaning we have to feign ignorance when she complains to us that Fiona is making her life very difficult. The most draining part of this job, I realise, is the psychological juggling act of trying to keep these two women happy.

Around eleven that night, Alice and I finally collapse into bed. But we've barely closed our eyes when the door opens and the light turns on. It's Fiona. She's got another plan.

Step one is to make Marguerite realise just how bad an idea hiring a local nurse is – by hiring one. She calls a friend who's involved with an aged-care agency in town, asking if they've got any 'big, fat African men' on the books who could come and do a stint with Walt next week, once Marguerite's back.

'That should call her bluff once and for all,' Fiona says.

I wonder if the big, fat African man they send out will be in on it. I wonder how much more of being complicit in this terrible shit I can take.

Step two is to disappear me and Alice before Marguerite gets back, but that all goes out the window when a taxi pulls into the driveway on Tuesday morning.

It's Marguerite, a day early. Alice and I look at each other, confused.

'I thought she wasn't due in until tomorrow,' I say.

'She wasn't,' says Fiona, apparently unfazed, pouring herself another coffee.

'Surprise! I'm back!' Marguerite sticks her head sideways through the doorway. 'Did you miss me? I know I'm early – I just had a spur of the moment brilliant idea to leave before the snow got too much. Couldn't bear the thought of getting stuck at Heathrow with that ghastly blizzard on the way. So, here I am! Oooh, is that a fresh pot of coffee? I'll have one, please. How lovely.'

But later that day, on the baby monitor, I hear Marguerite telling Walt how great it was to arrive 'when they were least expecting me, so that I can see what they're up to'.

So, both women are right to suspect the other of plotting against them. And I'm about to become a domestic mercenary double agent.

The next morning before breakfast, I go into Walt and Marguerite's room to help Walt get ready for the day. I make sure his clothes are laid out in order on the bed, that his razor and comb are carefully placed in just the right spots on the ledge above the basin.

Marguerite faffs about in her nightgown, setting her own toiletries out on the dresser. I still feel a bit weird about looking after another woman's husband when she's right here beside us, but she seems to have accepted Fiona's insistence that a carer should always run him through the morning routine. To be fair, Marguerite would probably struggle to remember every last detail of the regimen. And maybe she finds it actually is easier having us in there to help.

'Now, tell me,' she says, 'is it *your* sister Brenda who's coming to stay in January? Or the other one. Alice. Does she have a sister? Oooooh, you *must* smell this *lov-er-ly* new hand cream I bought at a nice shop in Heathrow.' She holds out a pink tube of Crabtree & Evelyn moisturiser.

I take a sniff and am overwhelmed by the floral scent. I sneeze.

'Bless you,' comes Walt's voice from the bathroom. I look over and he's still emptying his bladder.

'Um, yes – that's my sister. Bridget, not Brenda,' I say. 'But she'll only come if you want her here – you can talk to her on Skype first if you like.'

'Oh, bit late for that – Fiona says it's all arranged,' says Marguerite, only just masking her annoyance. Then she immediately brightens up again. 'I say – will Brenda be any good at fixing the printer and all those computer things for me? Like you girls are? Oh that *does* smell nice, doesn't it?' She rubs the rose moisturiser into her hands, then smears them across her face.

'Bridget. Um, yes . . .' I say, noticing Walt start looking a bit lost as to what to do next. I go through to the ensuite to reposition him at the basin. I put the plug in and run the taps – just hot enough – for him to have a shave. 'She should be able to help with all that. And I think she'd be very good with Walt – she's got a lot of experience with this sort of thing.'

'Oh, splendid!' says Marguerite. Then to Walt, 'Do you hear that, darling? You've got *another* nice Or-stray-lyan girl coming to help look after you.'

'What's that?' Walt turns around, shirtless, pyjama pants tied around his waist.

'Kirsten's sister, Brenda.'

'Bridget.'

'She's coming to help when Kirsten goes home.'

'I don't need any help!' says Walt.

'Yes you do, darling. We all do. We're both getting on a bit.'

Then, while Marguerite is in the shower and Walt is shaving, Fiona beckons me out into the hallway, where Alice is waiting with a bag.

'I packed your joggers, togs, some gym clothes. And is this the book you're reading?' she says.

'Yeah . . .' I say, 'Where are we going?'

'Down to the Club. Quickly – let's go,' says Fiona, pushing us out the front door.

'Shouldn't I tell Mar–'

'No,' Fiona says, 'I want her to realise just how hard it is to look after Dad on her own – then she'll have to admit that she needs you around.'

She just did, I think, as we pile into the Peugeot and take off, without telling anyone – not even the Kenyan staff – where we're going or when we'll be back. 'Don't answer your phones if she calls,' Fiona says, as we pass a group of Kenyan women walking along the red dirt on the side of the road, balancing baskets of fruit piled high on their heads. 'She needs to learn this the hard way.'

We spend nine hours hiding out at the Club that day. Hardly a prison camp, granted, but that's a long time to twiddle your thumbs in the shade. I read a whole book. I email friends. I go to the gym. Fiona spends a lot of time in the computer room, Skyping Jonathan in England. By lunchtime, we've run out of wholesome things to do, so Alice and I spend the afternoon sunbathing and drinking gin by the pool.

Marguerite only messages us once, around three o'clock – 'Hi where everyI at?' – and doesn't persist when she gets no reply.

'She probably knows what's going on,' Alice says, rolling over to get some sun on her back.

'I still can't believe the big-fat-African-man thing,' I mutter, pulling my hat down over my face. 'Deliberately setting the poor bastard up, to be subjected to a demented old man's rudeness, just to prove a point to Marguerite.'

'I know,' Alice murmurs back. 'That's really quite disgusting, isn't it?'

Lots of this, let's be honest, is really quite disgusting.

Close to sundown, Fiona decides it's time to pack up and head home. Via Michael and Lorraine Kirby's house. Unannounced.

Alice and I barely know the Kirbys. They're acquaintances, more than actual friends of the family. I think we've met them twice, at the Club. Michael's the guy Marguerite calls when we need a *fundi* (a handyman – literally an 'expert') to come around and fix things at the house.

But Fiona pulls me and Alice out of the car and has us stand on their driveway like unwanted children, pink-skinned and red-eyed, sunburnt and half-cut, as she tells the bewildered couple that they might like to have us stay in their cottage a few nights a week.

It's pretty clear that Michael and Lorraine wouldn't like that at all. They wring their hands and shuffle their feet and bite their lips. Neither of them can bring themselves to make eye contact with us. It doesn't help that I start hiccuping.

They use the guest cottage quite regularly for their own visitors, for a start. And you know, it's not really set up for a long-term thing – just the one bed and a small bathroom! They'd have to light a fire in the afternoon to make sure the water was hot. And they wouldn't always be around to show us in.

'Oh, that's not a problem – the girls can look after themselves. Tell your *askari* to let them in,' says Fiona, either not detecting or not yielding to their reticence. 'Just name your price. I can have them bring their own linen, and make sure they're gone by nine in the morning?'

This. Is. Mortifying.

Eventually, she wears the Kirbys down. Or maybe they just take pity on us. 'Well, look, alright then – but only when we don't have visitors,' Michael says. 'Shall we say a thousand bob a night?' I suspect he is trying to price himself out, but Fiona readily accepts.

'And only if Marguerite knows about all this,' Lorraine adds. 'Please, Fiona, we really don't want to get involved with any of the drama between you two. You know, we got that letter you sent –'

Oh my god. The letter. The Letter. That letter. I feel sick with guilt.

'Yes, of course!' says Fiona, cutting her off. 'Wonderful, then. Can they come tomorrow?'

'No! Not tomorrow,' says Michael, letting his irritation show. Christ, it's excruciating for us all. He pulls himself back and says, apologetically, 'We'll need to clean it up for you first, it's not ready.'

By the time we get home from our AWOL adventure, Walt and Marguerite are having dinner. Marguerite acts like nothing's amiss; doesn't ask where we've been or admit it's been a difficult day without us.

But Walt is wearing a tie with his pyjamas, and all his tablets for the day are still in the dispenser.

The next morning, things escalate. Fiona bursts into my room before breakfast, this time with a fistful of cash and another order to evacuate. 'Pack your bags. I need you to go away for a few days,' she says, handing over a wad of US dollars to cover the time I've been working.

I don't know whether it's sheer spite, or a genuine effort to demonstrate just how vital Walt's carers are, but this time Fiona is forcing Marguerite into a weekend-long crash course on 'Life Alone with Walt'.

Which means Alice and I need to leave the house, and we have about five minutes to figure out where we're going to exist for the next seventy-two hours.

Alice has a friend growing oranges in Tanzania she's going to visit. Of course she does. Alice has random friends doing random shit in random places all over the world.

'You should come!' she says. 'We can take a bus to Arusha, and he can pick us up from there.'

'I can't!' I moan. 'My passport is still with the Rwandan Embassy. I can't leave the country.'

Now would be the perfect time for me to lean on my newly discovered cousins – but they're out of town on a camping trip.

I text Sarah and Jack, desperate.

oi. we've been kicked out of the house – long story. can I crash at ur place for a few nights?

we r flying to mombasa for the weekend. wanna come?

ummmmmmmm YES

Within the hour, Jack has booked me a seat on their plane, and I'm on my way to Wilson Airport with a sunhat and a beach bag.

What a turn of fortune.

We take off and fly low over Nairobi National Park, giraffes and herds of elephants scattering as they're touched by the plane's shadow. A smoggy haze hangs over the city behind us but it's clear blue sky ahead, and to the south the plains stretch for miles. Suddenly I hear the riff from 'Africa' by Toto – Sarah's playing it through her phone, holding it up to my ear. Jack pulls out a cold Tusker from his backpack and passes it to me. Only a beer could make this moment even more glorious.

The pilot pokes the plane up above the clouds and there, just out the window, is the snowy top of Mount Kilimanjaro. What's left of the snow, anyway – the famous white caps have shrunk dramatically over the past few decades.

The drone of the props, and the fresh air and sunshine and alcohol all combine to replace my sense of frustration with one of frothy elation. In that moment I don't ever want to leave. I commit to putting up with the Smyths as long as I can stand to, and to trying to find another job in Kenya.

It's about an hour's flight time to the coast. The air changes before the landscape below does, and I feel my hair frizz up in the humidity, the way it does during summer in Mackay. The ground starts to appear slightly swampy – damper and greyer than before. We fly over a smattering of white buildings with blue roofs, bendy green palms and shrubs, then over a cluster of buildings jammed onto a small island. This is Mombasa, Kenya's second-biggest city and the main contact point between East Africa and the world for centuries.

Everything is a bit slower here, like it always is where the tropical air is heavy. The garb of the people is different, too: more women in hijabs, more men in white *kofias*. Much of the city feels like anywhere in the urbanised world, but in the Old Town the buildings have a distinctly Islamic aesthetic: smooth domes and archways pierce the Swahili whitewashed coral stone and lime mortar walls, mysterious rooms are hidden behind brass-studded Gujarati doors thanks to the Indian influence. Faces peer down from ornate balconies at the twisting, meandering streets that stretch and narrow on a whim. At first glance it seems as though the Old Town sprung up in a disorganised mess, that it's just a chaotic cluster of structures. But if you look carefully, you realise that's a design feature – the angle of every facade, double-louvred window and courtyard has been set to corral coastal breezes through the buildings and flush out the heat.

The city itself is separated from the mainland by a channel and a creek. It was originally inhabited by the African Bantu people, though Persian and Arab traders have been coming here since at least as far back as the tenth century. Since then, Mombasa has been repeatedly squabbled over by the Portuguese, Omani Sultans and the British. Its Swahili name – Kisiwa Cha Mvita – means 'Island of War', reflecting the many changes in its ownership throughout its history. The shadow of these conflicts is most pronounced at the outer edge of the harbour, where children play soccer on the sand and the Indian Ocean kisses the feet of Fort Jesus. This imposing fortress was built by the Portuguese in the late sixteenth century and bears the hallmarks of each power to have since controlled it: Koranic scripture is carved into wooden doors and beams while creaky British and Portuguese cannons still point out to sea. The English used the fort as a soldiers' barracks and then a prison when they first colonised Kenya, before declaring it a national park in

1958 and turning it into a museum a few years later. (In 2011, shortly after our visit, Fort Jesus was declared a UNESCO World Heritage site.)

When we turn up that afternoon, the queue of visitors is mostly Kenyan couples with school-aged children, on family holidays from Nairobi. We see only a handful of other *mzungus*, to my surprise. Then Sarah reminds me that I'm only seeing Mombasa because I'm not here as a regular tourist; most visitors to Kenya don't realise there's much more to do than go game viewing on the Masai Mara.

The next day, I see the modern side of Mombasa. Our hotel – a modest but secure mid-market lodging boasting a 'Sports Bar' that we never manage to find – is set a couple of streets back from the beach, to the north of the city. We head down in the morning for a walk along the sand, past the luxury resorts right on the shore. The sunbeds are full of middle-aged European women lying like frankfurters in the sun, while their fit black toy boys deliver rounds of drinks and rub suncream on to their shoulders.

Sarah and I find ourselves giggling at a man walking towards us. He's wearing a jaunty captain's hat with a pair of aviators, an enormous white stomach hangs over his tiny white shorts and white espadrilles. He's roasted pink and holding the hand of a stunning black woman in a bright green sarong. Then we're approached by a pair of young 'beach boys' who ask us where we're staying. Sarah knows immediately to ignore them, but I unwittingly engage them in the prelude to a proposition. 'Ohhhhh – nooooo, no no no no, no thank you! *Asante*, no, no,' I say when I realise where this is going. They aren't even dissuaded when Jack catches up and puts his arms around our shoulders.

A pair of scrawny old fishermen come to our rescue – '*Hapana!*' they shout at the boys, and tell us to do so too, if we want them to go away. '*Hapana! Hapana! Hapana!*' we yell, the fishermen elaborating on our behalf in more complicated Swahili, even writing it out in the sand. '*Asante sana!*' we thank them, when the gigolos finally give up and slink away.

Then we see that the fishermen are doing something quite curious: throwing clumps of wet seaweed up at the dunes. One of them sees us staring and gestures to show that they're enticing the tiny ghost crabs that scurry down from their holes when each clump lands. The crabs are almost invisible against the white sand, only detectable when they're moving. We're astounded to realise there are hundreds of them on the beach, virtually scampering under our feet.

The fishermen let us tag along with them as they walk along the beach, showing us every critter they can find along the way. The tide is a long way out, stretching back hundreds of metres over the gentle slope of the continental shelf before it drops off into a cobalt abyss. We plod through ankle-deep water and stop at rock pools and coral clusters for each show and tell. Out comes a starfish. Then a blobby mop of neon green polyps. And a terrifically spiky purple-black sea urchin, along with a whole lot of miming about how standing on one will cause our feet to be poisoned and rot off. The warning comes too late for Sarah: she points to the black spines stuck in her heel. The men react with mock horror – then tell her what she must do. '*Maji, moto maji,*' they say, dipping their feet into imaginary buckets. One remembers the key English word: 'Vin-gah! Vin-gah and *moto maji*.' She's to soak them in vinegar and hot water then pull them out carefully with tweezers. For now, she keeps limping along.

We're summoned with great urgency when the fishermen find a cowfish. It immediately becomes my favourite-ever sea creature. It's only a few inches long, bright yellow with white spots, aquamarine eyes and puffy sucker pout lips, yet somehow, incredibly, it does indeed look like a cow. The taller man rests it on his palm and holds it out to show us its little 'horns', sticking up from the top of its head. The shorter man moos at us and stamps his foot, like a musty bull. Eventually the cowfish flops into the water and swims indignantly back to its little cave.

A full two hours have passed by the time we find ourselves at the other end of the beach, where the men have left their fishing boat. Although they don't seem to expect a fee, it feels like we should offer them something for being so generous with their time and knowledge. We scrape together all the cash we have on us: a few thousand shillings, about forty dollars, roughly a fortnight's wage. They seem pleased.

We head back towards our hotel across the soft sand, in the shade of the palms that lean over the high-tide mark, passing parked banana-boat rides and fresh coconut stands and men leaning against a rock retaining wall in front of a posh hotel, half-heartedly spruiking curios and trinkets. Their wares are laid out on the beach in neat rows of propped-up paintings and rails of colourful scarves. A procession of carved wooden animals make their way along the shore in single file, all mid-step marching on a motionless journey; lions and baboons and giraffes stand from knee to shoulder height, oiled haunches shining in the sun. A sign points to a shop beyond the dunes – 'THIS AND THAT SHOP' – but when we pass by, to my disappointment the roller door is down, all the this-and-thats locked out of view.

The girl at the hotel reception manages to find us some vinegar in the kitchen, and we spend the rest of the afternoon painstakingly removing the tiny splinters of sea urchin from Sarah's aching foot.

That night, over a seafood dinner in a restaurant on an old *dhow*, Sarah and Jack stage an intervention.

'Piggy, you need to leave those nutters,' Sarah says. 'It's such a waste of time. You should be focusing on your real career. You've got a job in television, for fuck's sake. Why are you wiping an old man's arse in Kenya?'

'I don't wipe his arse.'

'It doesn't matter! You may as well be. Why don't you try to do some reporting or something? At least make the most of the fact that you're here.'

'Alright, shut up, I get it. I'll find something real to do.'

I find something real to do later that night, at 'The Hottest Place in Africa': the Tembo Entertainment Plaza, the greatest pizza parlour/Bavarian beer garden/pole-dancing arcade you'll ever visit. Tonight, it's hosting the Miss Tembo 2010 Beauty Pageant – a bold euphemism for what turns out to be a good ol'-fashioned wet T-shirt competition, with a 15,000 shilling prize going to the girl who can pull her G-string the highest above the waistband of her jeans. But it's the poster for next week's event that catches my eye: the Mr Tembo Bodybuilding Competition, organised by the Kenyan Bodybuilding Federation. I'm intrigued by the existence of a subculture dedicated to bodily perfection in a part of the world better known, at least in the West, for physical struggle and deprivation. I take down the number and vow to follow up when I get back to Nairobi.

But then I drink too many Tuskers and forget.

I wake up with cotton teeth and a tender blue bruise on the top of my pelvis.

'You were doing the worm,' Jack tells me.

'You weren't very good,' Sarah adds – which is bullshit, I'm great at doing the worm.

We spend most of the day in and out of the hotel pool, trying to rehydrate with cold lemonade and electrolyte sachets from my traveller's first-aid kit. By the late afternoon we're well enough to go for another walk. This time we head north up the beach, past the striped-umbrella resorts and a man selling camel rides to a point where a small cliff hangs over the water.

A group of local boys is playing up there, goading each other into jumping from the ledge into a small rock pool. It's only a couple of metres across, and about the same deep. The water is clear as glass; you can see the grainy sand at the bottom. 'Hell-lo-how-are-yooooooo?' the boys over-enunciate in singsong voices, eager to show off their English when they see us picking our way over the rocks beneath them.

One of them has a snorkel. He lets us use it to see the tiny seahorse he's found shivering in a crevice on the inside wall of the hole. He's bursting with excitement when we emerge from the water together: 'Did you see it? Did you see!?'

'*Ndiyo*,' I say, giving his snorkel back. '*Ndiyo*, yes, we saw!'

Flying out of Mombasa the next morning, I look down at the impossible blues, greens and violets swirling at the edge of the ocean, the white crust of sand holding it back. Further out, where Chinese and Dutch companies have been dredging, the colours go a murky, grey-brown.

Mombasa is a paradise crawling with parasites. I suppose it's always been that way.

11
THE FINAL STRAW

The day I finally quit, I don't see it coming – though in hindsight, it was only going to be a matter of time. I'm fresh back from Mombasa, with sand in my hair and a spring in my step. The taste of the outside world – of real Kenya – lingers.

But not for long.

As the taxi turns down the street to drop me back at the house, Fiona is waiting at the corner in the Peugeot to intercept me and whisk me away to the Club.

'We're just going to kill some time until dinner,' she says, beaming, as I transfer my bags from one car to the other on the side of the road. The Kenyans who gather for lunch under the tree at the turnoff – mostly domestic staff from all the neighbourhood houses, here on their break – must think we're mad. 'I've told Alice to stay away a bit longer. I've been having such fun.'

The whole time Alice and I have been away, Fiona's been stirring Walt up – literally whispering into his ear about his meddling, gold-digging wife, then disappearing unannounced, phone off, for hours at a time, leaving Marguerite to deal with him unaided, with no one to even stand in for two minutes if she needed to go to the loo.

'Then I got the big, fat African man in.'

Oh god, she actually did it.

The man didn't last a day. 'Dad thought he was a politician,' Fiona crows, 'coming to repossess the farm. It couldn't have gone any better, really! Marguerite's in an absolute tizz.'

So, we spend another whole day sitting at the Club, my Mombasa glow rapidly fading, and this time when we get back to the house Marguerite is livid. Walt is following her around the place, carrying his best suit on a hanger and saying, 'When are we leaving? I can't be late – it's my dear old mother's funeral!'

Dead mum again. Apparently it's been going on for hours. It's Jua the golden retriever's fault. Absolutely convinced him he was in England.

'There's no funeral today, darling! I've told you a hundred times!' Marguerite shrieks. Then to me, while Walt anxiously checks his watch, 'He's been like this all day. And not a jolly soul around to help!' It's the first time she's openly expressed anger towards me – and I don't blame her. 'Where have you been? I thought you were due back this morning? I missed my computer lesson! Alan was supposed to be coming around at four to show me how to connect the doodad to the whatsit, because you know I am quite quick to pick up these things as long as I have someone to teach me. Well, I had to tell him not to worry, didn't I? It'd have been pointless with Walt hanging around in this state.'

'Is Alan coming around, is he?' Walt asks.

'No!' Marguerite screams. Then all of a sudden, out of nowhere, a smile reclaims her face. The woman can switch gears so swiftly and severely it leaves me reeling sometimes. 'Oh, I say, did you have a lovely time in Mombasa? You must tell me all about it. It is marvellous on the coast there, isn't it?'

I snatch a moment before dinner to catch up with the staff around the side of the garage. David and Esther are there with James, helping him fill the wheelbarrow with firewood.

'Hello! You are back! You disappeared!' David says, shaking my hand. 'We were wondering what happened to you! And where is Alice?'

'I know, I know,' I say, 'sorry we didn't get a chance to say goodbye. Alice is visiting a friend in Tanzania. I was in Mombasa with my friends.'

What must they think of this – of our ability to just up and go on spontaneous trips to far-flung parts of the country on a whim?

'But you are back now?' James says.

'Yes, yes, I'm back. And Alice will be too, in a few days.'

'Oh good, good.'

'Yoo-hoo!' we hear Marguerite calling from inside the house. 'Supper's ready!'

And I leave my friends outside, while I go in to eat at the table with our employers.

Over dinner, I answer Marguerite's questions about where I went and who I saw and what we ate in Mombasa, while Fiona sips her soup in smug silence and Walt asks what time we're leaving for Nairobi in the morning, over and over and over again.

As soon as it's polite enough to do so, I excuse myself and hide in my room. I start waxing my legs, figuring the pain will be a good distraction from the unspoken tension. Maybe there's an element of self-flagellation in it, too. I'm growing ashamed at my spinelessness.

But the confrontation that's been inevitable for weeks gathers pace, until they're both at it in the hallway, right outside my door.

'Fiona, this is *my* house and I do find it awfully rude for you all to just disappear without even telling me what's going on!' Marguerite says.

Good on her, I think. It's the first time I've heard her really arc up.

'And by the way, I wasn't going to say anything, but I feel now I just have to. I know about that awful letter you sent around town. I think it's dreadful. Really, I do.'

Holy. Shit. This is about to get wild.

Except it doesn't. 'Well, Marguerite, I felt people needed to know the facts,' says Fiona, cool as ever.

'They are absolutely *not* the facts! They are outright lies, and thankfully all my friends know me better than that, and do you know they all binned it straight away and called to tell me they thought it disgusting of you to do such a thing?'

'Well, that's their prerogative. At least they know my point of view.' Fiona sounds barely rattled at all.

'And I've got a copy myself. Dolly brought it over. I'll be showing it to the lawyers.'

'You're entitled to do that.'

'I just don't understand you, Fiona!' Now Marguerite's voice starts to wobble. 'I brought you up, I cared for you when you were sick. I don't know why you'd treat me like this.'

Part of me wants to put earphones in and drown this out. The other part desperately wants to get to the bottom of what's going on between these two.

'I'm just trying to look after my father in his final years,' Fiona says.

'Yes, and for that I'm very grateful! I'm trying to look after him too! But this would all be so much easier if you would just tell me what is going on. This is my house and you're just walking all over me.' My door swings open. Marguerite's on the verge of tears. 'I suppose you've just heard it all,' she says to me. 'Well, I'm sorry but I must say I do think you've all treated me terribly badly.'

She's right. I'm mortified. 'I know. I'm sorry, Marguerite. Really, I don't want anything to do with this . . .'

'You know this is my house. You all just arrived here – no one asked me – and that's fine, you're a great help, but to be mucked around like this by everyone . . .'

I feel my face flush with shame. This poor woman. She really has been treated appallingly. And I've been a part of it.

Then Fiona rolls her eyes at me from the doorway, and something inside me snaps.

'You know what, guys?' I say, struggling to stand up as my half-torn wax strip binds me to the carpet. 'I'm done. I'm out. I can't take this anymore.'

I pack my bags and leave first thing the next morning for Sarah and Jack's place, wondering what the hell I'm meant to do with myself now. It's two months before my job in Sydney starts up again. My friends convince me there's no point in going home early – that I may as well make the most of being here. At some point in the midst of a Bundaberg Rum–induced haze, I book myself a last-minute spot on a two-week overland safari to see the mountain gorillas in Rwanda, leaving in a few days' time.

Best decision I ever made.

The next day, I have a chance to visit Claire again. Her girls have their school cross-country, and we head down to watch the race. Hundreds of children in house shirts of purple and green and orange run around, following the red flags that mark out the course. They're black kids, white kids, brown kids. They're African and European and Indian kids. They're kids who seemingly don't notice or care about skin colour – kids of every race, racing around a school oval, equals, competitors, friends, while their parents laugh and cheer and watch the next generation take for granted what in their day could barely be imagined.

'It's lovely, isn't it?' Claire says. 'Even when I was at school in Zim, what, twenty-five years ago, it was nothing like this. We had one or two black kids in our class, but that was it. For these kids there really is no segregation. Well, look, at least not for the middle class. There are no whites or Indians in the slums. But these kids will grow up and this will be the norm to them.'

I think back to a conversation I had with my mother once, about whether she — growing up in Rhodesia — knew there was something wrong with their society.

My mother is a good, kind, decent person. She was about to hop into the shower when I asked her, in our poky little bathroom on the farm in north Queensland, the one we always shared with green frogs and insect invaders. She stopped, stood stark naked on the bathmat, tilted her head to the side to think about it. Then she pulled the toilet seat down, sat on it, stared into the distance and the past. 'You know, it was just the way things were. We were born into it. We didn't *hate* Africans — well, maybe some people did. I didn't. I didn't know anyone who *hated* them. You must remember, it wasn't like South Africa. We never had apartheid in Rhodesia. It was just — they had a different place to us. That's just how it was. You know, black people didn't come to the front door of our house — I only realised that many, many years later, when I read a book by an African maid about what it was like working for a white family. I don't remember anyone ever telling me that was a rule. But when I thought back on it I realised that if anyone black ever came to the house for any reason, they knocked at the back door.' Mum held her hands up in the air, in disbelief. 'I mean, how bloody stupid! How awful! But you know — we were kids. It just seemed normal at the time. It wasn't until I was much older — in my twenties, I suppose partly because of the war — that I really started to analyse things. My mother, being English, was far more progressive than my father. They'd have debates about it. She was on the side of the independence movement, but Dad would say "They're just not ready to run a bloody country!" They used to cancel each other's votes out. But I never really got involved in any side of it. I mean, obviously now, in hindsight, I can see how wrong it was. But not everyone is naturally political, you know?'

'Did you have any African friends?' I asked.

'When we were little we did. We all played with the "piccanins" – the servants' children, most white kids did, especially if they lived on a farm. Your father learned to speak their language before he could speak English! But as we got older that sort of fell away. You know, you went to school and life just became more segregated.'

Mum thought for a moment. 'The only person I knew – white person, that is – who really truly didn't seem to see colour was my friend Irene. It was like she was immune to it. She even had a black boyfriend in high school. But that was very rare. And, of course, her parents could never have known about it.'

It's astonishing, I think, my attention returning to the cross-country, how much has changed in this part of the world in just a few decades.

Back at Sarah and Jack's place, I start to have second thoughts about quitting – I wonder whether there's a way I can make things work. At the very least, I need to make sure I'm not bringing my sister into an intolerable situation. I send Fiona an email, trying to make her see sense.

Hi Fiona,

I hope things have settled down at the house and you and Marguerite have been able to have a discussion about everything and come to something close to an agreement about Walt's care.

THE FINAL STRAW

Remember Bridget needs to know by Friday at the latest whether she is required here to help care for Walt next year. She needs to be assured about the working conditions here — i.e. she is here as a carer for Walt and will not be dragged into the family disputes and will not be required to lie to or deceive Marguerite or anyone else about her whereabouts and activities. All parties have to agree to her presence here and she can expect a set amount of work and can budget and arrange holidays around that, and if she has to be sent away at short notice she will be paid for that time as work. Obviously she is open to a reasonable degree of flexibility regarding time on/off. If she is to stay in the cottage at the Kirby's then it would be good if she could also know that now.

I hope that by the time I return from my trip away something close to these conditions can be achieved, because I am finding the current situation intolerable. I know you have your issues with Marguerite, but I feel extremely awkward being in her & Walt's house and treating her the way we have, regardless of her ineptitude as a sole carer for Walt. Whatever the family history may be it needs to be recognised that for outsiders, she is his wife of almost 40 years and has lived there with him for over 25 years and it is not our place to assert ourselves in their world beyond what is necessary for Walt's health.

Cheers
Kirsten

My safari leaves the next day. Fiona's got two weeks to get back to me.

I sit on a bright red overland truck and I stare out the window at Africa. I make friends with the twenty other foreigners on board — Americans, Brits, Swedes and Germans.

We go whitewater rafting on the Nile, camping at Lake George, and on a walking safari at Lake Elizabeth. We see hippos and crocodiles and lions, flamingos and elephants, topis and zebras and giraffes. It's all pretty standard Instagram fare: white people in sunglasses, gazing out the window at a land of contrasts.

In Rwanda, something magical happens. We climb a mountain and find a family of gorillas. An enormous, grunting silverback sits not five metres away from us, chewing on a fistful of grass as his dozen wives mind his dozen children. We sit and watch them for hours in silence, in awe. There are only a few hundred of these creatures left in the world. This is something only a handful of very lucky people will ever get to see.

A baby gorilla playing nearby suddenly decides to cross in front of where I'm standing. The Rwandan guide tells me to stay still – not to back away, to just let it pass. The misty air swirls with my breath. My knees tremble. The baby gorilla somersaults across the forest floor, tumbling and rolling over the leaf litter. Its mother follows close behind, and as she passes she grabs hold of my shin with her left hand to keep her balance. I freeze, heart pounding, equal parts terrified and elated. She lets go of my leg, carries on her way, apparently unfazed by our encounter.

There is something indescribable about the experience of coming face to face with a creature so closely resembling our own kind, and knowing that in all likelihood, it will soon no longer exist because of what we have done. I can't tell if I'm overcome by beauty or sadness. All I know is that every tedious, compromising experience with the Smyths feels worth it in this single, life-affirming moment.

I get back from the safari on Christmas Day.

My demands have been met. Fiona's virtually begging me to come back. She's responded to my email, assuring me that she and

Marguerite have thrashed it out and that things will be better. She's returned Walt's passport. She promises she won't do that again. She assures me that Bridget won't be put through any of the drama Alice and I have had to endure.

I get a text from Marguerite.

Hi! U back from trip? Hope had lovely time. Will u be here for lunch? Khamisi has done fab feast.

I guess we're all pretending none of that bad stuff ever happened.

I'm back at the house just in time – the table is groaning with roast turkey, roast ham, roast chicken and roast vegetables, gravy, Yorkshire puddings and eggnog. Magda's here, and the Kirbys, and Harry from down the road, and the couple from the granny flat out the back, and Millicent and her mother, and Marguerite and Alice, and Fiona. Even Fiona's husband, Jonathan, is here from England. Jonathan seems to be an easygoing, jolly kind of guy who doesn't take anything too seriously. I wonder how it is he ended up with someone as intense as Fiona – although even she seems to have relaxed into the occasion. The two of them are going on safari before they go back. Marguerite's treat! (What the fuck is that about? A reward for cruelty? A peace offering? Is it possible that while I was away Marguerite and Fiona sat down and thrashed it out – accepted that they both had Walt's best interests at heart, just different ideas about what he needed? I really, truly, will never understand this family.)

Everyone's getting along – we're all pulling crackers and wearing the paper hats that fall out of them, and Walt is thrilled to be hosting such a great party even if he doesn't recognise any of his guests. We sing Christmas carols and groan at the bad jokes from the crackers and drink far too much champagne, and by three o'clock we're full and retire to the living room, where half the greying crowd promptly falls asleep in their chairs, mouths hanging open, catching flies.

In a weird way, after two weeks of being on the road, and showering under the stars, and sleeping in tents to the sound of grunting hippos, I'm relieved to be back.

January passes with no major incidents. Fiona still checks in from her safari every day to see how her father is going, but, true to her word, makes no more requests of spying or deception. It's just me and Alice and Marguerite now, working together with the Kenyan staff to look after a man who's lost his mind. It's almost – *almost* – the 'cruisey' gig Alice promised me in the beginning, except that Walt's outbursts of anxiety over car keys and dead mothers and money are becoming a little more frequent.

By the end of the month, my time with the Smyths is up. It's time to go back to Australia, back to Sydney, back to the world of TV. But first, I have to pass the baton to my sister, and Fiona will be back from her trip to help with the handover. I suspect she'll find it difficult not to fall into old habits.

The day Bridget arrives, Peter and I drive out to the airport to pick her up. Peter spots her before I do, emerging from the chaos that is Jomo Kenyatta's arrivals hall. He grabs me, points her out. 'That girl, she is your sister!?' he says, looking astonished.

'Yeah, that's her – Biddy!' I wave at my little sister. I feel a brief wave of anxiety about pulling her into this, but also excitement at being able to share Kenya with her, the good and the bad.

'She is exactly like you!' Peter says, looking back and forth between us after we've hugged. 'You are twins?'

We do look quite alike, though Bridget is taller than me. And much sweeter. You can tell that much just by looking at her.

She's got one of those warm, open faces; she doesn't have the semi-scowl that seems to be my default resting expression. I wonder whether Walt will detect anything familiar in her when we switch places – whether on some subliminal level, he'll remember that he knows someone who looks a lot like her, and whether that will bring him any sense of comfort or trust.

'No, not twins,' I tell Peter. 'She's two years younger than me.'

'Hello, Miss Bridget!' he says, taking her backpack and suitcase. '*Karibu* to Kenya!'

As we're driving away from the airport down Mombasa Road, Bridget suddenly squeals and points out the window. 'Giraffes! Oh my god – are they real?' I'd forgotten how excited I was to see the same thing the day of my arrival.

'Yes, they are real!' says Peter proudly. 'That is Nairobi National Park.'

'And there are monkeys in the garden at the house,' I tell her.

'Argggh, this is going to be the best!' she says.

Yeah, it'll be the best, I think. *But probably the worst, too.* Along with the rest of my family, I've kept Bridget updated on the twists and turns of my time with the Smyths, but I haven't been totally honest with her about my doubts that the truce between Fiona and Marguerite will remain in place. I've pulled a bit of an Alice, really. I've said as much as I had to in order to get her here.

Walt is at the gates when we get back to the house, shouting at Patrick to let him out. Fiona and Alice come racing out from the house, trying to round him up. He marches alongside the car as we roll into the driveway, rapping on the window.

'What are you doing driving my car?' Walt says to Peter – then, peering over at me in the front seat, and Bridget in the back, 'And who the hell are you?'

Bridget shoots me the kind of look only a sister can understand.

'You'll be *fiiiiiine*,' I say, as Peter lifts her bags out of the boot.

I give Bridget a quick tour of the house, introduce her to the staff, explain the locked suitcase, the fake wine and fake salt, the handwashing-of-undies-because-Mum-said-so situation. We run into Walt again in the hallway, on his way to the bathroom. He does a double-take of the two of us, says nothing, just scowls and carries on. It doesn't appear that our likeness will be of any benefit to Bridget.

Then, only a few hours after she set foot on Kenyan soil, I abandon her. Fiona wants us – Alice, Marguerite, Jonathan and me – to go to the Club for dinner. 'It'll be a good, neutral space to discuss Walt's new care plan, before I go back to England tomorrow,' she says. 'You'll be alright with Dad, won't you, Bridget? Esther will be around to help.'

Bridget shoots me that look.

'You'll be *fiiiiiiine!*' I say again. I am such a bad sister.

I do try to suggest that one of us should stay back to help, but Fiona insists it's more important that Alice and I both be at the dinner. 'I need you straight-talking Aussies to act as translators and witnesses for me. To make sure Marguerite understands how things are going to be. Also there's less chance we'll have a row if you're both there as a buffer.'

'We'll only be a couple of hours,' I assure Bridget, who stares at me in disbelief upon hearing she's about to be left alone with Walt for the evening because things between Fiona and Marguerite are, in fact, still so touchy that they need intermediaries to facilitate discussion. 'Khamisi's cooked dinner for you. And Esther will be around to help if you have any trouble. We'll be back before Walt's ready for bed.'

Dinner goes far more smoothly than anyone anticipated it would. Marguerite readily agrees to the new terms of Walt's care – that he is to have three full-time carers employed to look after him, chosen by Fiona and agreed upon by Marguerite; that only the carers are to administer Walt's medication; and that no changes to his medicinal regimen are to happen without Fiona and the Trust first being consulted. In return, Fiona promises to communicate more clearly with Marguerite about the young women being sent to live in her house and look after her husband, instead of just installing them without warning. The Club's secretary is sitting at the next table and insists on shouting us a bottle of champagne. Jonathan insists on following that up with a good South African red and telling us about how a recent MRI scan had made his balls feel so warm he thought he'd pissed himself. I insist on following that up with a round of whisky and telling everyone how I accidentally shouted the word 'vulva' in the Club computer room while discussing a story about labiaplasty with my *Hungry Beast* colleagues on Skype. Oh, how we laugh.

We have dessert. We have cheese. We have brandy, port and cigarillos. The waiter tells us the kitchen is closed and they need to pack up the dining room. He gently points out that we are the last remaining guests, and that it's nearly midnight and that –

'Holy fuck, it's nearly midnight!' I yell.

Bridget has been trying to call all of us, but of course our phones are all switched to silent. She's sent me several text messages:

9:35 oi where are u? Thought ud be back by now

10:12 Oi. Walt doesn't know who I am. What do I do?

10:38 Oi!!! ANSWER ME! Walt has put a suit on and is asking me for the car keys!!!??

11:20 ok well now we r sitting in the living room but he thinks we're on a plane and won't let me open the door to the hallway because we'll all die but Im gonna have to soon cos I REALLY NEED TO PEE!!!!

11:32 what r these red buttons on the wall for cos he wants to push one

I round us up and bundle us out of the dining room. On our way past reception, Marguerite leans over the front desk and starts rummaging around the mail drawer. 'Just going to see whether my newspapers are in yet!' She folds the *Tele* into a peaked crest and wears it on her head, then struts around the foyer flapping her arms and clucking like a chicken. The rest of us – even Fiona – form a conga line and parade around the parquetry floor while the Club staff watch on, part amused, part appalled.

I feel my phone buzzing again. I answer it, trying to be inconspicuous.

'Heyyyyyy, Biddy!'

'WHERE ARE YOU?'

Hoo-boy, she is mad.

'We're coming – we're coming now, I promise.'

'THIS IS BULLSHIT!'

'I know, I know – I'm sorry. We lost track of time.'

'Excuse me, madam – no phones in the Club, please!'

That's it. We've crossed the line. Moses ushers us out the door.

In the car park, Fiona pulls me aside for a heartfelt embrace. She tears up, thanking me for 'the excellent job you've done looking after Dad, especially in such trying circumstances'. It's the first time she's expressed any kind of gratitude or appreciation for how difficult the task has been. I feel a sudden rush of warmth for her in return. Or maybe it's just the whisky repeating, hard to tell. *She's not a monster!* I think. *She's just a daughter terrified of losing her dad.* These poor, lovely people.

When we get back, Bridget is in the dining room with Walt, helping him zip up an overnight bag. She glares at me. 'You'll be *fiiiiine!*' she mocks.

Marguerite waltzes him down the corridor to their bedroom, where she puts him to bed as he giggles like a little boy.

Bridget sits on the bed across from me in our room, fuming.

'You will be *fiiiiiine,*' I tell her. 'Trust me! Look, I am!' I hiccup and swallow a bit of vomit. I have to close one eye to see straight.

Bridget is fine. But she doesn't stay a day longer than the three months she agreed to.

~

In the meantime, I go back to Sydney. I do the final season of *Hungry Beast*, and when it's all over I find myself . . . still lost.

Hungry Beast has given me a taste for stories about people and places that aren't often covered, about things that aren't what they seem. And I can't stop thinking about Kenya. My time there has shown me just how deeply misunderstood the place is — how all we see in the West are stories about famine and disaster, war and disease, horror and poverty and violence. Those things happen there, yes, but we have no context for it. We don't see the everyday life around it, the ordinary (and extraordinary) human endeavours. The art exhibitions, the fashion shows, the schoolkids on class excursions to museums, the FM radio hosts, the film festivals and Sunday afternoon picnics.

An idea starts to form. There are hundreds of stories I can write — I can try my luck freelancing for a while.

Plus, Australia is giving me the shits. Who'd have thought the culture shock would be worse coming home? I'm far safer here than I was in Kenya, but in a strange way I feel less free. Since returning to my country I've felt the oppression of order far more keenly than I did before. Australia likes to think of itself as a 'laid-back' place. It's anything but. It's a nation obsessed with rules and control.

Everything seems ugly. I get righteous at all kinds of things. Like people spending twenty-five dollars on hot breakfasts and complaining about the cost of living, while reading newspapers full of paeans to strong border control. Border control! Here, on this island at the bottom of the Earth, one of the richest countries in the world, where we panic because a few thousand people have shown up uninvited and completely miss the irony given how things went down in 1788. Although I'm equally irritated by the naive progressives who tell me that Australia is a 'racist country', and act as though desiring any form of a system to decide who gets a humanitarian spot makes you a bigot who hates people of colour. 'There is no queue!' these people insist. But there are heaps of queues. There's a refugee camp in northern Kenya – Dadaab, the world's largest – where people have been queuing for twenty years. I read about it every day in the papers there. Dadaab is so established that it functions like its own city, with its own economy and a population including adult residents who were born there and have their own children. By size, it would be Kenya's third-largest city (indeed, many Kenyans think the fences should be torn down and the place made official), but its residents are imprisoned in limbo, homeless and hopeless. And they just aren't close enough, or rich enough, to reach Australia by sea.

Then, at just the right moment, Alex – the journo I'd met at Sarah and Jack's – emails me to ask if I'd be interested in doing some short journalism workshops for FilmAid, in Dadaab. The idea is to get different kinds of media practitioners in to teach residents how to produce their own content. I could run a few classes on video production – they have some recording equipment and keen students; he's already helped them set up their own newspaper.

I really want to do this. But the workshops only run for a couple of weeks at a time and are unpaid, so I need something to sustain me financially.

You won't believe it. Or maybe you will.

I go back to the Smyths. Six months after I left, I go back to the asylum for more.

12

TOUCHDOWN TAKE 2

Over the six months I was away, the old man in Kenya's rotation of carers included my friend Alice, my sister Bridget, an aspiring actress from London, Walt's own granddaughter, and then, finally, one of my friends from uni: theatre graduate, trainee clown and professional circus performer, Ruby.

By the time I returned to Nairobi, only Ruby remained. Alice was over it – not long after I left she'd gone to Norway to train husky puppies how to pull sleds through the snow. (Of course she had.) Walt's granddaughter had gone back to England for uni, the actress had gone back for an audition, and Bridget had gone back to Mackay saying she would 'never trust any of my recommendations ever again'.

Ruby, however, was loving it. I knew she would. When Alice got in touch to say she was leaving and needed to find a replacement, Ruby was the first person I thought of: she'd visited Kenya before, she was in between jobs, and – being slightly mad herself – she was up for anything out of the ordinary.

When I touch down in Jomo Kenyatta International Airport for the second time, she and Peter are both there waiting for me, grinning and waving madly from the back of the arrivals floor.

'You are back! You are back!' Peter says, hugging me and smiling and insisting, like he did the first time, on carrying my bags for me as we battle through the crowd. I've missed him, I've missed all of this.

'Yeah, I'm back!' I say, the reality of it hitting me as I find myself immersed in the sounds and smells of Africa all over again. There's a moment of dizzying ecstasy – the feeling that everything is exactly as it's meant to be, that this is precisely where I should be right now – followed by a slap of sickening doubt as I remember the madness of the Smyths' house. *Fuck, is this really a good idea?*

I pull myself together. *Yes, of course it is. You're going to make the most of being here this time. They've surely sorted everything out now. They're just a means to an end.*

'We have missed you very-very much,' Peter says, grinning, with his head tilted to the side in that funny way of his. 'All of us! Even the *bwana*!' Well, I know that part's a lie, but it's sweet of him to say so.

'Piiiiiiig!' says Ruby. 'So good to see you!' It must have been a year since we were last face to face. 'I have so much to fill you in on – this place is fucking bananas!'

Ruby has been here a few months and is fully acquainted with all the bizarre details of this very particular world: the ins and outs of Walt's care, the power dynamics within the family and their lawyers, the quirks of daily life in Nairobi, the strange time capsule of the Club, and the loveliness of the Kenyan staff. Where Alice was uninterested in the Smyth family's internecine personal dramas, Ruby can see – and takes great delight in – the many small peculiarities of people and places, including our own. We're much more on the same page in that regard.

The whole way to the house, she's filling me in on the highlights of her time here so far. 'The Royal Wedding! Prince William and Kate – it was the best! Marguerite insisted we go to the Club to watch it.

They'd decked out the entire place with flowers. Like, *massive* bouquets of roses, fucking everywhere. *So. Many. Flowers.* And huge pictures of the Queen and all the rest of the royal family stuck up all over the place. And they set up this massive projector screen in the tearoom, blacked out all the windows and made it a formal event. Like – you had to buy tickets to go. Dinner and canapés and all that. So all these old biddies dressed up and went to watch, and all the waiters were wearing white gloves and everything, and Walt,' she doubles over laughing, 'poor old Walt thought we were at the cinema, watching a movie. 'Cos, you know, all the chairs were in rows for the live broadcast. And you know what that coverage is like – it just dragged on and on and on, it was *soooooooo* boring. Just empty shots of the front of the palace waiting for Kate to arrive. And then when she finally did, all that boring shit of them standing in the church. And Walt just kept sighing really dramatically and saying over and over, "What are we watching? It's bloody slow going!" And Marguerite kept hushing him even though she was talking louder than everyone! About how Pippa had upstaged the bride. And how Camilla looks like a camel with those "big old chompers of hers". And how Harry is "definitely that other chap's son – the good-looking one Diana had an affair with". And then some people in the front row turned around and hushed *her* and she was so mad. And then they all sang "God Save the Queen", and she got drunk on champagne and started walking around holding a picture of the Queen over her face, with holes poked through for the eyes. The waiters were pissing themselves. Walt thought it was hilarious too. Honestly, the whole thing was just the best.'

'Argggh, man, I can't believe I missed that!' I say.

'I *knowwwwww* . . . you would have loved it!' she moans.

'So, who's at the house now?' I ask.

'Fiona and Marguerite. Fiona's got some nurse friend of hers coming from England to be the third carer – Annette. But it will just be you and me for the next couple of days.'

'Righto. And how's it been with her and Marguerite?' Ruby is across all the goings-on of my first stint with the Smyths – I'd sent a small group of friends regular email updates as it all unfolded.

'Actually, pretty good! Oh, also, she's got this whole new thing about how to deal with Walt's dementia now. She read some book about it. Anyway, she'll fill you in.'

'What do you think, Peter?' I ask, as he swerves to avoid an overloaded motorbike straying into our lane. 'Are the *memsahib* and Fiona getting on alright now?'

'Oh yes,' he says. 'Yes, yes, they are much better. We don't have so many problems as before.'

'And Bwana Smyth?'

'He is okay,' says Peter, with a little more hesitation. 'He is still forgetting all the time, but he is mostly good.'

It sounds like this time around, things will be different. Good.

Fiona, Marguerite and Walt are all out when we get back to the house.

'They've gone for lunch at the Club,' Ruby explains. 'Fiona thought it would be good if Walt wasn't here when the car pulled up. He's got a real thing about the cars.'

'Oh yes. I know all about that.' I'm glad they're out – it means I can catch up properly with the staff.

Patrick is there at the gates, still with his huge smile and slingshot in hand. James and Esther and David and Khamisi come running out to the driveway as we pull up. After a scrum of hugs and handshakes and '*Karibu! Karibu! You are back! How is your sister Bridget?*' I realise there's something missing. 'Where are the dogs? Shujaa and Jua?'

Everyone falls silent, feet shifting in the dirt.

'Oh, they, ah . . .' Ruby starts.

'They died,' James says sorrowfully.

'Both of them!?'

'Yes.' Poor James – the dogs were always by his side in the garden.

The sunroom – where Millicent used to sleep – is to be mine this time around. It's small and narrow, with two entrances: one to the dining room, and one to the hallway that leads to the other bedrooms. I'm happy to have my own space, but I doubt it will come with much privacy, given the huge glass windows that look onto the washing line and staff quarters, and the fact that it's often used as a thoroughfare to avoid disturbing Walt when he's sitting in the living room.

I'm in there unpacking when Walt, Fiona and Marguerite get back from lunch. I poke my head out to say hello as Fiona walks Walt down to his room. 'Hi, Walt!' I say. He's thinner than when I left him, looks more vacant and tired.

He stares at me, blank.

'It's Kirsten, Dad,' Fiona prompts. 'One of your young *Or-stray-lyan* girlfriends. She's come back for a while.'

'Oh, hello there,' he says, smiling and nodding politely. But there's no recognition whatsoever, not a flicker. 'Just going to put my feet up for a few minutes,' he says, waving as he moves on. I try not to feel offended.

I didn't think he'd last more than a few months when I first arrived – now, it seems he'll be kept alive indefinitely.

Having put him down for a nap, Fiona comes back to my room and quickly gets down to business. 'Hiya, hope the flight was okay. I want you to read this excellent book.' She hands me *Contented Dementia* by psychologist Oliver James. 'This is how we should deal with Dad from now on.'

I flip through the pages as Fiona summarises the book's lessons. It details what's known as the 'SPECAL' method of dementia care: SPECAL being an amalgam of 'Specialised Early Care for Alzheimer's'.

'It's all about how to work *with* dementia rather than against it,' she says, as I land on a chapter about how dementia carers should 'make a present of the past' by going along with whatever delusion a sufferer is experiencing at any given moment, rather than constantly trying to reorient them and consequently causing them unnecessary stress and anxiety.

'Oh,' I say, 'I think I saw a documentary about this! It's like in Denmark where they've got those nursing homes with fake bus stations and post boxes and shops and things, so the residents just think they're all going about their old lives.'

'Yes, exactly,' says Fiona. 'Lots of places are doing this now – it's very effective. But the Alzheimer's Society aren't behind it – they say it's unethical.'

'Why?'

'They say that it's "systematic deception". Which I suppose it is in a way. But the point is it focuses on the emotional wellbeing of patients, which really is the most important thing as far as I'm concerned. Dad's been much happier since we started doing it.'

When I read up on it later, I see that the Alzheimer's Society's position is based on the principle that people should have choice and control or influence over decisions about their lives. The organisation says that SPECAL's intentions are good, but that the method ultimately disempowers people. I can see where they're coming from – but I also think there comes a point in a person's cognitive decline where their happiness and serenity is more important than trying to give them an agency they're incapable of exercising (provided they have trusted guardians overseeing that care). That's what I would want for myself should I be in that state.

A squeaking wheel on the laundry trolley draws my eye through the window, to where Esther is wheeling out a load of washing. She pegs Walt's sheets to the line, bright white and billowing in the sunny afternoon breeze.

'Dad's sheets should be changed every second day now,' Fiona says. 'There's a plastic liner on the mattress. We've only had the one accident so far, but it will probably become more common as time goes on.'

Then I return to the book, which stresses that we are to follow the method's three 'golden rules':

1. **Don't ask direct questions.** Open-ended enquiries can be overwhelming for someone with cognitive impairment. Instead, give the patient options. 'Would you like a sandwich or a salad for lunch?' is a much simpler proposition than the blank slate of 'What would you like for lunch?'
2. **Listen and learn from the patient.** Listen to the kinds of things a patient repeatedly asks about – this will often reveal a source of anxiety for them – and try answering with information that is best from *their* perspective. Instead of telling someone a loved one is dead when they're asked after, say they've just popped out to the shops. If you find a response that works – use it, re-use it, and tell everyone else to use it too.
3. **Don't contradict.** Challenging someone's sense of reality can only result in distress for them. Agree with whatever they're saying, roll with it. Think of it like theatre improv – become a character in their world!

All of this makes sense to me. I realise I was already doing it at times during my first stint. Playing along when Walt thought we were 'on the train', or that I was his latest mistress.

But we won't just be doing standard SPECAL. As with everything in Walt's life, Fiona wants his SPECAL care to be gold-plated: we are to learn the details of his entire life story, so that whatever era he may find himself in, we're fully equipped to make it real.

So begins my crash course on the life and times of Walter Smyth. Fiona hands me a small green notebook. 'This is now "the Bible". It should be with whichever carer is on duty. And you should make a note in it every time you find something that works or doesn't work.'

'What do you mean "works"?'

'Like, say you come up with a response for a repetitive question that seems to placate him. Also, make sure you record it if you notice a new "trigger" – we already know the main ones: dogs barking, car engines, car keys – you record it in here. The other day he heard the microwave bell ring and it set him off on a whole thing, wanting to know what the alarm was all about. So, I've asked Esther and Khamisi to make sure they stop the microwave before the timer's up from now on.'

The Bible already has a page with the names of his best friends from school. Another with the kinds of flowers his mother grew around the house. The names of his neighbours near the highlands tea farm in the 1960s and '70s, his neighbours in the UK in the 1980s and '90s, the dog he had thirty years ago, the fishing trip he took in 1993, the kind of car he drove in 1984, the name of the nearest town to the farm he managed in 'Tanganyika'.

The notebook is filled with the skeletons of memories. How as a schoolboy in England, Walt and his friends used to ride around the fields collecting shrapnel from bombs dropped during the Second World War. How as a young man, he served with the King's African Rifles, helping to 'kick the Italians out of Somalia'. How he was attacked by that lion, crushed by a buffalo, had a close call with a hippo. What it was like during the Mau Mau Emergency, living in constant fear of being attacked, of being disembowelled and left to rot on the front lawn. Where he and Marguerite were when

TOUCHDOWN TAKE 2

Al Qaeda bombed the US Embassy in Nairobi in 1998 (having lunch with friends on the other side of town, in Karen). How he had known Daniel arap Moi – long before he became Kenya's second president – before he entered politics, when he'd been a teacher in a nearby village.

Walt's whole life is a proxy history lesson. And SPECAL, I hope, will be our saviour.

~

I crash early, waking – just as I did on my very first morning in Kenya – to the muezzin's call to prayer and the smoky dawn sky. It's a welcome change from the sounds that normally wake me in my flat in Redfern: the clanging and beeping of a garbage truck, or drunks staggering home past my room.

I use the quiet of the morning to start laying plans for my productive stint in Kenya. Marguerite and Fiona know I'm keen to get some real work done this time, and have assured me I'll be able to get decent chunks of time off to do it. I let Sarah and Jack and Claire know that I'm back and would love to catch up. I send Alex an email to let him know I've touched down and am keen to arrange a visit to Dadaab for the video workshops. I research the logistics of getting to the deformed animal sanctuary in Kitale; it looks like there's a series of buses and *matatus* I could take – but I've been warned against doing that on my own. I'll need to find a fellow traveller. Ideally, someone with a vehicle.

Breakfast that morning is interrupted by an unexpected visitor – we hear Patrick's keys jangling and the gates swing open, as Magda pulls into the driveway. I love that she's familiar enough to just march on into the house and join us mid-meal. 'Hello, hello,' she says, circling the room to give everyone a kiss on the cheek, before taking a seat at the other end of the table. 'Walt! You are looking very well.' Walt is evidently put at ease by her confidence. 'And you! You are back!' she says to me, arms up in amazement.

'Yep!' I say.

'Very good,' she says. 'There is much more of Kenya for you to see still.' Esther sets another place for Magda and she pours herself a cup of coffee. 'Oh, *asante sana*. Well, we have no power again. Since last night. The whole street. Can I shower here? I have brought my things.'

'Oh no, is the power out?' Walt says, looking up at the light in the ceiling.

'No, Dad, ours is fine,' Fiona says, seemingly annoyed by the disruption. Magda is oblivious.

'No, Walt, it is only my street,' she says, through a mouthful of marmalade toast. 'They were all day putting the new lines in, as it were, for the new fast internet. Kenya Power and Telkom. In the trench, you know, by the side of the road? And in the night the thieves came and dug it all up. For the copper. Yes.'

'The copper?' Ruby asks.

'They sell it on the black market,' Fiona explains. 'To people who export it to China, apparently.'

'Yes,' Magda says. 'It's become a big problem. The government is talking about banning the trade.'

'Have we had something stolen?' Walt asks, getting more and more confused.

'No, Dad, you've nothing to worry about.' Fiona makes a point of changing the subject. 'I think we should talk about getting you another dog!'

'A dog?' Marguerite says. A new family pet is evidently news to her.

'A proper dog. A labrador or something.'

'Labradors are *lovely* dogs. We've got two lovely labradors, don't we, darling?' says Walt, putting his hand on Marguerite's wrist.

'Yes, back in the UK we do, darling, but none here in *Keen-ya*,' says Marguerite.

'What do you mean "none here"? You silly old fool. They're *here*, I can hear them barking!' Walt looks at me and rolls his eyes at his batty wife. The neighbour's dogs are yapping from over the fence. 'I'll go and call them in after breakfast.'

'See? This is why we need a dog,' Fiona says in a low voice to me and Ruby. 'Every time he hears a bark, he wants to get up to find it. Or to find his guns to "shut the bloody thing up!" Then there's hours of trying to bring him back around.'

I have to admit, she's right – things would be much simpler if there was an actual dog we could produce in these moments. Fiona has also read that pets can help reduce stress and anxiety in dementia patients, especially in those with a fondness for animals.

That much was certainly true for my own grandmother. My mother swears that the miniature dachshund we gave her and convinced the nursing home to make a special allowance for, bought her at least an extra five years of life and happiness.

'Oh! The KSPCA?' says Magda, hitting the table for emphasis. 'Yes, yes! The KSPCA. You should go to them. You know where they are? In Karen. On Langata Road. Just past the hospital.'

'Who's in hospital?' says Walt.

'No one, darling,' says Marguerite. 'Magda is telling us where to find a nice rescue dog.'

'Yes, they are wonderful there. And they make sure the animals are all, you know, clean and have had their needles and all the rest of it.'

'We'll go down to the KSPCA today and see what they've got,' says Fiona.

'Well, I can't go today – I've got bridge with Dolly!' says Marguerite.

I detect a hint of irritation. Ruby glances at me – she's noticed it too.

'Who's Dolly?' says Walt.

'*Dolly!* You remember Dolly. My friend Dolly Sutton. Your friend George's wife.'

'Oh, *George!*'

'Yes, but he's long dead.'

'Oh dear. Dead? Poor George. When!?'

'Twenty years ago!'

Fiona steps in. 'That's fine, Marguerite. You go to bridge and I'll organise the dog. Kirsten and Ruby can come with me – we'll take Dad.'

'Well now, hold on, I shouldn't mind a say given we'll be the ones living with it.' There's an edge to Marguerite's voice now, a faint threat that she's going to assert her authority – or challenge Fiona's, depending on how you look at it.

'But I think it will be a good arrangement for you, Marguerite,' says Magda. 'The KSPCA will give you a two-week trial. You can see if you and Walt like the dog before you are taking it for good.'

Walt's still muttering to himself about poor old George. 'How did he die?' he asks.

'Heart attack,' Marguerite says. Then, in an instant, the tension vanishes as she lights up with gossipy glee, leaning forward on the table and stage whispering for us all, '*In bed with Dolly!* Ha! Don't you remember? She always did send men's hearts racing. Hoo! What a way to go, really.'

'Okay now, Dad, let's have you take your pills,' Fiona says, trying to bring the morning's focus back to Walt. But he's not interested in pills. He's still laughing with Marguerite. Fiona pours the half-dozen tablets resting on the little soapstone dish back into the weekly pill dispenser on the sideboard. 'I'll try again once he's brushed his teeth.'

I see some things haven't changed much at all.

The Kenya Society for the Protection & Care of Animals is a small complex on Langata Road in Karen, on the south-western side of the city. It was started around 1910 by three women who took pity on the overworked oxen that delivered goods from surrounding districts to the fledgling city of Nairobi. One hundred years later, the shelter is home to dozens of abandoned cats, dogs, goats and donkeys, with a small team of staff employed to run sterilisation and vaccination campaigns, and to respond to reports of animal cruelty.

We pull into a gravel driveway just past the edge of a fir forest. In a pen near the entrance is a donkey bearing the faint but distinct black-and-white markings of a zebra. A softly spoken guy with short, spiky dreadlocks named Dominic emerges from the small office building to greet us. He tells us the donkey was painted by a restaurant owner looking to attract the attention of passing motorists. Apparently, 'being painted' (usually with business logos or political slogans) is one of the most common – albeit inadvertent – forms of donkey abuse the group deals with. The paint is corrosive to the animal's skin and, if not removed carefully, can cause chemical burns and lesions.

'That is why we are always trying to educate people. We tell them, "Please, do not paint the donkey. He is an animal, not a sign!"' Dominic says, before leading us to the kennels where a cacophony of howls fills the air and hopeful pink tongues poke through the fence.

Chiku stands out as the pick of the bunch immediately. She's not a labrador – not even close. It's hard to tell what she is: a solid little thing, with short tan hair and chocolate-brown eyes. 'Possibly part-beagle?' says Fiona.

But her pedigree doesn't matter. She's by far the sweetest dog there, and Walt – bending down to scratch her behind the ears – is already smitten.

'She was rescued from a construction site,' Dominic says. 'Someone called us to say the Chinese workers were slaughtering the street dogs for food, but we have not found any evidence of that. I think they are just bad rumours.' Some stereotypes go global, I guess.

Chiku recently had a litter but is now spayed and vaccinated and ready to be taken to a new home. She wags her tail, bores her muzzle into our laps, licks our knees, sits on command. A few times, she is so unable to contain her excitement she jumps in the air like a spring lamb, then runs in fast, tight circles around us before rolling over to expose her tummy for a scratch.

'Oh, hell*ooooooo* there you cheeky little curr,' coos Walt, rubbing her with the sole of his foot, as Ruby helps him keep his balance. 'And who are *you*?' He scratches Chiku under her chin, roughs up the fur on her flank. 'You're a lovely little mutt, aren't you? Ohhhh, you like that, don't you! Now, who do you belong to?' He looks at Dominic. 'Is she yours, is she?' he asks.

'She's yours, Dad,' Fiona says.

'Mine!?' Walt says, shocked, delighted, like a kid being given a present he'd never dreamed of asking for. He looks at Ruby, then at me, in joyous disbelief. 'This isn't my dog, is it?'

'Yes, Dad, she's all yours. Her name's Chiku.' Fiona turns to Dominic. 'We'll take her.'

'Yes?' says Dominic, seemingly surprised by our keenness. 'Right now?'

'If we can?'

'Yes, yes, no problem. There will just be some forms to fill out and an adoption fee but ah, yes – of course, she is yours!'

If the look on Walt's face is anything to go by, Chiku – the mutt of mysterious origin – is going to be the most powerful tool we've got.

The following afternoon, Patrick swings open the gates to the Smyths' house and salutes Walt's eighth new carer in a year. Annette – Fiona's friend from the UK – has agreed to stay for two months.

Once her bags have been brought through and she's been introduced to all the staff, we all — Walt, Marguerite, Fiona, Ruby and I — sit together on the patio with tea and scones and get to know each other. Annette seems kind, and honest. I suspect she'll be very good with Walt — and that she's way too sweet for the other demands of this job.

When Chiku alerts Walt to the monkeys invading the garden on their afternoon raid, he marches off to sort them out. Fiona goes after him, and Marguerite takes a phone call inside, leaving Annette with me and Ruby for a moment.

'Is Fiona always this bossy with Marguerite?' she asks us, incredulous. It seems this is a side of her friend she hasn't seen before.

I have to think about it for a moment; I suppose I've become used to seeing Fiona nitpicking Marguerite over how she pours Walt's tea, or where she's put his chair, or that she shouldn't have given him *that* particular scone with *that* much jam on it because the sugar will rot his teeth and give him diabetes.

'Oh, yeah,' says Ruby. 'That's pretty standard.'

'And Marguerite just puts up with it?' Annette seems shocked, and I realise that's something else I've stopped being surprised by. That Marguerite rarely objects to being told what to do in her own home.

We watch Patrick run down to the back fence with his slingshot out, while Walt tells him which monkey to line up and Fiona tries to hold Chiku back from jumping too close to him.

'Yeah, pretty much,' I say. 'Every now and then she pushes back. But I think she's realised that for the most part, it's just easier to do what Fiona says.'

Patrick ducks as a barrage of berries is thrown back down from the canopy in return fire.

'You bastards!' Walt yells, shaking his fists impotently at his simian tormentors.

'And she said something about keeping notes on who Marguerite talks to on the phone and where she goes every day?' Annette says, in a tone suggesting she hopes she simply misheard.

'Yeah, she wants us to "keep tabs" on her,' Ruby says.

So, Fiona hasn't entirely given up on her subterfuge – she just knows not to try it on with me.

'I strongly advise you stay as far out of that as possible,' I say. 'Just stick to looking after Walt, and we'll be fine.'

'Yes . . . I mean, I thought I was just here to be a babysitter, really!'

Poor Annette. Her friend hasn't given her the full story either.

I sneak away to visit the staff while Fiona takes Annette through Walt's pre-dinner routine. They're all still just getting on with life, doing their thing, oblivious or indifferent to the goings-on of the *mzungu* madhouse.

James proudly updates me on Rebecca's progress. She's at a teachers' college now, in their hometown of Machakos, and uses a computer every day. Little William has grown another foot, and is always wanting to visit from the village. It must be terribly difficult for families to be divided like this – to have to leave them behind in order to earn money in the city.

David has lost a lot of weight – he's been very unwell but is apparently on the mend. Marguerite took him to see a doctor, and Fiona has brought over some creams from England to treat a strange skin condition he's developed. He seems very grateful that they've helped him get better.

Patrick doesn't have much to say, other than to smile and declare 'Yes, yes, madam! *Mzuri sana, mzuri sana*,' when I ask him if he's well. I've brought him back some magazines from Australia. He can't read, but loves to browse the pictures.

Esther still doesn't share much about her home life. Her two sons are doing well, and her husband has a good job. I wish I could get to know her better, but feel it would be rude to press her much further.

I head back inside near dinner time. There's Khamisi, in his apron and hat, presiding over the stove.

'*Jambo*, Khamisi!' I say, 'What's cooking?'

'Mmm,' he murmurs gently, smiling as he checks on a pot of simmering stew, 'tonight you will enjoy "beef stroganoff", with vegetables and rice.' I swear the guy meditates while he stirs.

Annette gets another taste of the underlying family tension the next morning. I take her through Walt's morning routine — the precise turning of the taps, the careful placement of the razor, the laying of his clothes on the bed in reverse order. While we're in there, Fiona tells Marguerite she should really use the main bathroom to get ready, so as not to get in Walt's way in their ensuite. And that she shouldn't turn her clock radio on in the morning, because the news updates are a distraction.

Then, while we're all sitting down to breakfast, Marguerite's mobile phone rings.

'Oooooh it's my friend *Deborah!*' she says, looking at the caller ID and giving us all a knowing nod. I don't remember any friend called 'Deborah' from my first stint, and there's no look of recognition on Ruby's or Fiona's face either. '*Jambooooooo* Deborah!' Marguerite stands up from the table, chatting as she walks around the room. 'Yes, shall we!? At the little café next to the Italian place. Yes. Well, *you* say when.'

Walt watches her anxiously, as Fiona tries to redirect his attention to the slices of pawpaw and mango on his plate. 'Who's she talking to?' he mutters.

'Never mind, Dad. Just one of her many ladies-in-waiting,' Fiona says, with a roll of her eyes that Walt mirrors back. 'Marguerite – must you take phone calls while we're eating?'

Marguerite puts a hand over the end of her Nokia. 'Well *I* can't know when someone might be wanting to speak with *me!*' She pulls her hand away, returns to her call. 'Ten o'clock then. Very good. Yes. See you then. *Kwaheri!*' Marguerite puts her phone back into her pocket and sits down again.

'Who was that then, darling?' Walt says.

'That was *Deborah*,' says Marguerite, piling stewed prunes onto her cereal. 'That marvellous lady who runs the sewing shop down by the MiniMart.' None of us know who she's talking about. Walt's got no hope, but he pretends to know who she means.

'Oh I see,' he says. 'Is she well?'

'Yes. Well, I hope so. I'll soon find out, won't I? We're having tea at ten. She's *very* clever, you know. A seamstress and an *ont-ra-pra-newer!* She's making me a lovely pair of pink trousers.' Then, Marguerite leans across the table, apparently to tell Ruby and me especially, 'She's my *African* friend.'

I didn't know she had any.

Deborah's phone call is the last straw for Fiona. She installs a signal jammer in the dining room.

'If Marguerite won't stop disrupting meals with phone calls, we'll just have to stop her phone from working in there at all,' she says. She plugs the contraption into the wall socket behind the sideboard, where it's hidden from view. 'It only blocks the signal for a few metres. Outside this room you should still get reception. And you'll need to pull the cord out of the landline too. Just remember to put it back in again once meal times are over.'

Annette is not entirely down with this, but Ruby and I can see the logic. The phone calls and texting at the table *are* a distraction for Walt, and Marguerite can't seem to help herself. We decide we'll let this little deception stand.

Then, Fiona flies back to England and we're left to it. For a time, everything goes smoothly.

Ruby, Annette and I work out a roster that's split into three eight-hour shifts a day: each carer rotates between duties, being 'on' for one shift, doing 'household errands' for another, and fully 'off' for the third. It means Marguerite is able to maintain her social engagements, while the three of us can arrange some of our own – Annette visits friends across town in Karen, Ruby starts taking dance classes at a studio in Westlands, and I'm able to catch up with my cousins and Sarah and Jack.

A few weeks into my second stint with the Smyths, I even manage to get to a music festival.

Sarah and Jack have invited me. We set out early in the morning for Lake Naivasha, up the escarpment out of Nairobi and past that astonishing view you can never, ever tire of. We buy chapatis from the side of the road, listen to some Kenyan pop to get into the mood, and watch the blur of verdant green go by as we pass the tea and coffee plantations of Limuru and Kiambu.

The Rift Valley Music Festival – a 'musical experience in the cradle of mankind', as the bill puts it – is at Fisherman's Camp on the edge of the lake, beside a shaded area of tent sites and fire pits and toilet blocks. A honking, bass-thumping procession of cars and *matatus* snakes down the dirt road through the yellow fever trees, all the way back to the main highway. The vehicles are full of families and young people in high spirits, bright clothes and silly hats. The vibe is like at any festival back home – only here there are baboons and monkeys and zebras and giraffes walking around the place, and bad-tempered hippos snorting at the edge of the water, just their flaring nostrils and twitchy ears breaking the surface.

We have a beer while we set up our tent and then wander over to the main festival site, where tall Masai men wrapped in red *shukas* patrol the crowd, the event's official security team. Hipsters hand out street press and promo cards. Cliques of hot girls and buff guys circle each other coyly and cluster together to take pouting selfies. The members of a Kenyan graffiti artist collective – Spray Uzi – are working on a bank of easels by the bar.

We buy a round of beers and find ourselves a spot on the grass in front of the main stage, where a man in a *dashiki* and jeans blasts the saxophone, and a drum team stirs the air with a steady reggae beat. The alcohol hits my bloodstream, the breeze kisses my face, a fish eagle cries, and I'm intoxicated by the sheer loveliness of being here.

The afternoon ripples by, full of guitars and rhythm and chorus, then as dusk falls one of the headliners takes the stage: Ayub Ogada, a Mombasa-born singer-songwriter. The crowd falls quiet as Ogada, dressed head to toe in embroidered periwinkle blue, sits on a stool and plays the *nyatiti*, a traditional eight-stringed lyre made of cow skin stretched over a hollow wooden bowl. It makes a haunting sound I recognise from the soundtrack to *The Constant Gardener*, and it turns out Ogada provided the music for that film and many others. What a moment, to sit with five thousand people and see him sing the stars into the African sky.

We decide to wait for the traffic to clear before heading back to Nairobi the next morning. We fill the time with a trek up nearby Mount Longonot, the dormant volcano overlooking Lake Naivasha, its name derived from the Masai word *oloonong'ot*, meaning 'mountains of many spurs' or 'steep ridges'. It's about an hour's hike to the top, then another to walk around the rim of the yawning crater that reaches almost ten thousand feet at its highest peak. We sit on a ledge and take turns peering through binoculars at the miniature world inside the caldera – home to its own oblivious ecosystem teeming with wildlife: zebras and giraffe and antelope – and make a hasty descent when a passing guide points out fresh leopard tracks on the dirt path beside us.

When I get back to the house just after lunchtime, the lion is off the wall. It's stretched out in the afternoon sun on the patio steps, one front leg resting on the top of the handrail, its scruffy maned head propped up on a table. It looks, from behind, like a drunk man leaning against a urinal. Chiku is keeping a sensible distance.

'Marguerite's idea,' says Annette, sitting with the baby monitor in her lap. Walt must still be having his afternoon sleep. Marguerite, on her laptop in the study, overhears and comes out to explain.

'Yes, well, I *do* feel it's a bit confusing for Walt when we're playing along with the idea that he's in England. So I'm putting it into storage. Just want to air it out first. Give the *simba* a bit of a tan!' She snorts with laughter.

I'm impressed Marguerite has given it that much thought. She's never – as far as I've seen – done anything as malicious as Fiona would have us believe. But nor has she been especially attuned to what might help make Walt's care run more smoothly. This is a positive development.

'Now, which of you girls is my "helper" today?' she asks.

'I think that must be me,' I say. Ruby is off duty and Annette is on with Walt, meaning I'm in charge of errands for the afternoon.

'Very good. Would you mind going down to Village Market – the fellow there knows to expect you – and picking up some fabric samples for me? I'm getting new curtains made up.'

I don't see what's wrong with the old ones, but Marguerite is insistent they need replacing and plans to give them to Esther.

'She'll be *thrilled*, I dare say! They can do such marvellous things with old bits of fabric, you know. *Oooh!* Maybe she'll make one of those lovely head-wrap things? They do look splendid.'

I haven't seen an African head wrap made out of floral chintz before, but hey, maybe Esther can start a new trend.

So I take the Peugeot and drive down to Village Market, past families walking home from church in their Sunday best, past tethered goats and cattle and Masai shepherds dozing upright nearby, leaning on slender sticks.

I find the fabric shop, where the man expecting someone for 'Lady Marguerite' gives me a folder full of swatches in sensible colours like taupe and maroon and moss green, and I head back out to the car park.

But I stop in my tracks when I see a semi-naked man staring at me from a noticeboard.

The bodybuilder is standing on a stage, holding a trophy and grinning. His flexed and oiled muscles reflect the light at all angles, an ebony Adonis in budgie smugglers. He draws me in closer. I remember my trip to Mombasa, all those months ago, and the Mr Tembo competition I'd wanted to see. This flyer is for the Mr Kenya Junior Bodybuilding Championship to be held the following week at the National Theatre, across the road from the Norfolk Hotel – one of Nairobi's most iconic colonial-era relics.

Maybe it's just the novelty of physical perfection when I've been spending so much time confronted with the bodily deprivations of ageing and frailty, but I start to feel inspired. *There might be a story in this*, I think. *And I've got a good camera with me this time – I could get a few decent shots. Surely someone would be interested in an article about it.*

Back at the house, I email the Kenyan Bodybuilding Federation contact listed on the flyer, asking if I might come along to the competition with a view to writing an article about the sport. Annette and Ruby are happy to juggle the carers' roster so I can have the day off, and Marguerite – who finds the whole concept hilarious – kindly offers to let me borrow the Peugeot to get there and back.

A reply is waiting for me the next morning.

Hi Kristen
We received a brief about your interest in a meeting last evening.
Kindly come in the morning hours for a meeting with us before the finals.
Members agreed the publicity of international level is a (+).
See you later.

The expectation of 'international publicity' makes me nervous but also committed. I don't want to mess these people around; if they're going to give me access, I have to make sure I make something of it. I have to do this properly.

But when the day comes, Marguerite's forgotten about our plan.

'Where are you off to?' she demands, as I race through the kitchen with my camera bag and take the keys out of their hiding place in the back of the cutlery drawer. 'You're taking a car, are you?' She looks cross.

'I – I'm going to the bodybuilding thing,' I say, wondering whether I dreamed the conversation we had about it last night, when I checked that it was still okay to take the car. *Maybe she thinks I'm skiving off work?* 'I'm not on duty until tonight – Ruby and Annette are on today.'

'What bodybuilding thing?'

Esther puts her head down and concentrates on washing the dishes. She seems embarrassed to be witnessing this.

'The competition,' I say, 'at the National Theatre. Remember? I'm hoping it could be good for a story.'

'*Ohhhhh*, the muscle men!' Marguerite shrieks, then cackles with delight like she did when I first explained the whole concept to her. 'With their teeny-tiny costumes!'

'Yes!' I say, relieved it's come back to her. 'The muscle men! So . . . should I call a cab instead?'

'Ohhh, I know! Why don't you take the Peugeot if you like? We won't need it today.'

The fuck . . . 'Yes, that's what I – never mind. Okay. Thanks so much – I'll put fuel in it, and I'll be back this afternoon.'

Even Esther – who normally wouldn't dare express any frustration with our capricious *memsahib* – offers me an understanding eye roll as I wave goodbye.

Then traffic almost thwarts my plans. A Coca-Cola truck has broken down on the Meru-Nairobi Highway where the new flyover is being built. Another vehicle overturns as it drives off-road to get around it, and cars that try to get around *that* one start getting bogged in the sludge on the siding, after a water pipe bursts. I drive like a *matatu*, honk and wave and nose the Peugeot through the melee, arriving with only a few minutes to spare.

The Kenya National Theatre is a little past its prime. A strange, silt-stained, blocky brick building, it sits beside the University of Nairobi campus as part of the Kenya Cultural Centre. Across the way is the Nairobi Snake Park, the Kenya Conservatoire of Music and the National Museum, where you can see the fossilised skulls of some of the earliest known hominids in the 'Cradle of Humankind' exhibition. Discovered in the rich soils of the Olduvai Gorge in the Serengeti in Tanzania, and in the northern lakes of Kenya by archaeologists Louis and Mary Leakey, these ancient skeletal faces now sit encased in glass cubes, as the future peers back at them. A short walk away, their distant descendants are putting their own mortal flesh on display, trying to become superhuman.

As I climb the steps to the building, the only sign of life is a blue-coated janitor listlessly mopping the verandah. He apparently neither knows nor cares that there's an event on inside, or that I'm entering without a ticket. '*Sawa sawa*,' he says, shrugging, when I ask if it's alright to go in.

I push through the heavy wooden doors and stumble into a darkened hall, where I'm smacked in the face with musty-cool air, the laughter and applause of decades of audiences hanging in the ether.

This was where Kipanga — Kenya's first stand-up comic — performed in the 1950s in the midst of the Mau Mau uprising, delighting crowds with his goofy impressions of a retired Mau Mau leader. His routine so impressed the colonial authorities of the time that they played recordings of his shows to the inmates at rebel detention camps as part of their 'rehabilitation'. (This was certainly not indicative of the way hundreds of thousands of prisoners were otherwise treated by the British in what were essentially gulags — the true horrors of which are excruciatingly documented in Caroline Elkins' Pulitzer Prize–winning book *Imperial Reckoning*.) Twenty years later, post-Independence, a very different kind of performance about the Mau Mau graced the stage: Kenyan writer Ngugi wa Thiong'o's play *The Trial of Dedan Kimathi*, a drama about the movement's executed leader from the point of view of Kenyan nationalists. I suspect white audiences weren't quite as enamoured with that piece of theatre.

As my eyes adjust to the light, I feel my way past rows of empty vinyl seats with dog-eared seams towards the front of the stage, where a couple of floor-mounted spotlights illuminate a huge white 'Kenya Bodybuilding Federation' banner, strung up across red velvet curtains.

A few contestants are milling around the wings, rubbing oil on each other and doing push-ups, pumping themselves full of fresh blood.

One of the judges waves me over. 'Hello! Miss Kristen?' It's George, the secretary who replied to my email. He introduces me to his colleagues as 'the Australian journalist here to cover the event'. Again, I feel a pang of guilt and pressure.

'Well, I'm *hoping* to,' I said, anxious to lower expectations, 'but I'm freelancing, I haven't actually been commissioned by a publisher yet.'

'Sure, sure, you'll have no problem,' George assures me, unfazed by my lack of confidence. I'm realising that I'll have to contend with the assumption that as a wealthy white foreigner, I can get anything I want. 'We're just about to go through the next qualification round, but, please – feel free to go backstage and interview our contestants in the break. I have advised them of your work.'

I get chatting to Wilson Munene, an agricultural science student and semi-pro bodybuilder who would go on to become one of Kenya's most recognised male models, featured in advertisements for everything from body lotion and cooking oil to mobile phone companies.

Wilson tells me he's been bodybuilding since he was in high school. That as a teenager, he cut out pictures of Arnold Schwarzenegger and Ronnie Coleman from magazines and stuck them to his bedroom wall as inspiration. 'At school, I was discouraged from getting into it. The teachers thought it was aggressive and violent, so I used to hide my training. There was no gym in our town anyway. I used stones as weights and used the rafters to do chin-ups.' Wilson laments that the sport is so misunderstood in Kenya. He says he wants to change that public perception – to help people see that far from being a thug's pursuit, bodybuilding is a discipline. 'Too many young men are idle these days,' he tells me. 'They are wasting time with drugs and drinking and promiscuous sex. Bodybuilding is a good way to focus energy and be healthy. I encourage them to come to the gym with me and get into bodybuilding instead.'

Today, he's supporting his younger brother, Joseph, who is competing in the bantam-weight division. 'That's him there –'

Wilson points to a tall, lean figure at the end of the line-up on stage, just as the judges request a hamstring display: all six men turn and bend over, lycra-clad derrières pointing high in the air.

Backstage, I'm swarmed. I have no shortage of willing subjects – they're all happy to have their photograph taken, as long as I promise to email them copies to include in their budding portfolios, and to introduce them to any talent scouts I might know. ('I really don't know any!' I try to explain, as I scribble down dozens of email addresses in my notebook, but I can tell they don't believe me.) The bodybuilders cavort in the hallway, show off their lats, their obliques, their glutes. They jostle for position in the front and centre of group shots, grinning so hard tendons pop out of their necks, shouting at me and pointing out their best bits: *Here! Look! My biceps! My triceps! My abs!* At one point, an organiser has to interrupt us and corral the heavyweights on stage – they're so preoccupied with our photo shoot, they've missed the call for their set.

By the end of the day, I have some great shots and have made some good contacts – but I have a problem. Today's competition really isn't a big deal. It was poorly attended and, in any case, not an official circuit event – it doesn't make for much of a story in and of itself. But I *can* see a story in the competition Wilson mentions he's entering in a couple of months' time: the Mr Kericho Championship, one of the East African bodybuilding scene's most prestigious titles, complete with prize money and a chance to attract sponsorship. Many of the men I've met backstage will be competing; I can follow up with them there, where the stakes will be much higher. It will be an unexpected window to modern Africa.

13

SHORTCOMINGS

Annette, Ruby and I enjoy about a month of relative calm, lulling us into a false sense of security, feeling like finally we've worked it all out. SPECAL seems to be delivering on everything it promises. Walt is, as predicted, far more relaxed wallowing in happy memories than he is being dragged from the past into the present. And, as a bonus, we are far more stimulated in his company by the improvisational challenge of working out which world to apply to each moment.

'Are you here with the army, too?' he might ask, peering at me curiously, trying to place my face.

Aha, I'll think, *it's King's African Rifles time.*

'Yes,' I'll say. 'Well, I'm with the administration. I believe you're fresh back from Ethiopia, is that right? Wasn't it you who oversaw the construction of that marvellous bridge?'

Walt loves it if I bring up the bridge in Ethiopia. It sparks a twenty-minute recounting of the time he and a friend, though both of them were officers, nonetheless pitched in with their subordinates, labouring in the sun for months to help open up a crucial supply route for the troops. Whenever Walt is done reminiscing about that particular engineering accomplishment, he launches into stories about the time he just spent in the desert, fondly recalling what a 'beautiful people' and 'noble race' the Somalis are, and how 'the Wogs should really just give up now; they're fighting a losing battle'. (The Italians didn't, in fact, give up until 1960.)

If Walt sees a bill lying around, we no longer spend hours trying to convince him he doesn't need to worry about paying it. Instead, we give him an expired chequebook and help him fill one out, put it in an envelope, and drive him down to the Club to put it in the mailbox. The Club staff play along and know to throw it in the bin once we've left.

Chiku, lovely little Chiku, brings great happiness to us all. She's always there, waiting and wagging her tail, when Esther comes through in the mornings to unlock the internal security gate. Then she sprints laps up and down the hallway, nose nudging each door on the way until she finds one she can push open to burst into the room and jump onto the end of a bed, twisting blankets as she spins in excitement and licking the snoozy hands that reach to contain her before springing away to find her next willing victim. It means Walt wakes up to laughter – his own, or others' – most mornings.

Marguerite goes away for a week: back to England, to have her cataracts looked at. For the first few days without her, things with Walt go fairly smoothly.

Ruby, Annette and I take him on seaside holidays, have secret affairs, pack his suitcase for trips to New Zealand that we never depart for. Almost nothing Walt experiences is real, but his quality of life is, and surely that's what really matters?

Life in the Smyths' house is as close as it's ever been to relaxed.

Until we go hunting in 1975.

All three of us are home for dinner. Khamisi has made a roast chicken stuffed with lemon and thyme – he brings it out to the table surrounded by golden potatoes and mint peas, a gravy boat on the side.

Walt claps with delight in his seat. 'Oh my, that *is* a fair size, isn't it?' He leans in towards the chicken, examining it from all angles. 'Whose is it?'

'It is for everyone, *bwana*,' Khamisi says, beaming with pride. 'It is your dinner.'

'Well yes, I can see that, but *who shot it*? It's one from today, isn't it?'

Walt looks at the three of us, expectantly. Khamisi looks confused. Annette winks at him, then he gets it. 'Ah, yes, *bwana*, it is from today,' he says, making his way back to the kitchen. 'I hope you enjoy.'

We all click into SPECAL mode, playing off each other's cues. That isn't a chicken on the table: it's a pheasant, dragged out of a foggy swamp that morning by one of the gun dogs Walt could hear barking outside.

Ruby is first to get into character. 'I believe this one's *mine*, Walt,' she claims proudly, standing up to take charge of the carving knife. Ruby is made for this, what with her theatre training.

I imagine us all marching through the marshlands of North Yorkshire, grouse beaters up ahead, roused springer spaniels at our feet, gun smoke hanging in the air.

'Oh, ho-ho, you always were an excellent shot, weren't you?' Walt says, twirling a flirtatious finger in Ruby's direction.

'Thank you for noticing,' she replies.

'And did you dress the bird yourself?' he challenges.

'Of course she did, Walt!' Annette exclaims, feigning indignation on Ruby's behalf.

'You know I like to see things through,' Ruby adds.

'I don't believe it! You women don't like to get your hands dirty ...' Walt says, a mischievous expression flickering over his face, a smile tickling his cheeks.

'She did, Walt!' I step in to defend Ruby. '*And* she caught a fair few more birds than you today, so I'd be careful how cheeky you get, *mzee!*'

Walt roars with laughter at that. He laughs throughout most of dinner, as we take turns recounting the highlights from our day in the dales, teasing each other over who had the poorest aim, who slipped most in the mud. By the time we've finished dessert – an apple and cinnamon tart with custard – we've tallied four partridges, two pheasants and a duck.

'Well, that was a splendid meal, thank you all.' Walt leans back in his chair and slaps his palms down on the armrests. 'Now if you'll excuse me, I must go and clean my guns.'

Guns. *Ruh-roh.* I shoot Ruby and Annette a panicked look.

'Oh, no need to worry about that, Walt – we cleaned them earlier, remember?' Ruby offers.

'How about we finish off this wine?' I suggest, pouring the dregs of the re-bottled Ribena into his glass.

It's not going to work. Walt is fixated. And we are all trapped with him, in a hallucination of our own creation.

He gets sterner. 'No, I don't believe I have cleaned my guns yet. I must clean them before tomorrow. I just can't think where I've put them . . .' He stands up from the table, starting to look around the room as he tries to figure out which door to go through.

Ruby tries to distract Walt by dancing. Annette feigns a coughing fit. I can't think of anything better to do than to guilt him over bad manners. I sneak another slice of apple tart into my bowl. 'Walt, please. It's terribly rude to leave when the ladies are still eating, isn't it?'

He sits reluctantly, grinding his teeth.

Then I make the mistake of pouring him some more custard.

'I don't want any bloody custard! I want you to tell me, right now,' he pounds the table and sends the spoon flying, warm yellow globs flung everywhere, '*right this instant*, where my guns are!'

There's nothing for it but to come clean – only we can't. He won't believe us. He can't accept that our day of hunting has been a fantasy, or that we're on another continent decades in the future. If only that lion was still on the wall.

It's clear to him what's happened: his guns have been stolen, and we're all in on the cover-up. Not even bringing Esther and Khamisi in from the kitchen, or calling Frank over to tap on the window with his guard torch, or turning on the radio for the BBC Africa news updates brings Walt back to reality.

In the end, we have to barricade ourselves in Ruby's bedroom and leave Walt to stalk around the house opening and closing cupboards until midnight, when his rage finally drops to a simmer. He puts himself to bed cursing his dastardly foes, swearing to 'sort the swines out' in the morning.

I make a note in the carers' 'Bible' to avoid conversations about hunting.

Talk of guns = MAJOR trigger! Perhaps stick with fishing trips.

When Fiona calls the next day to check in, I fill her in on the hunting incident.

Although I fear it's a sign that Walt's dementia is progressing, in a way I think it's a good thing that it happened when it did – Fiona can't try to pin any of the blame on something Marguerite 'triggered', when Marguerite wasn't even there. Though Fiona does try to suggest *we* could have done more to control it. 'You should have called the staff in – he'd recognise them and realise he was in Kenya.'

'We did. That didn't work.'

'What about Chiku? You could have used her as a distraction.'

'We considered that, but thought it might make things worse given he was already convinced that any dogs around the place were his hunting dogs.'

'Okay, well, I think we're just going to have to become more creative about how we deal with Dad when he gets difficult.'

Easy for you to say from a distance, I think.

'And I think we need to have a back-up carer on each shift. To be on hand to help if Dad gets difficult, and to cover for whoever is on duty when they need to go to the toilet. He shouldn't be left alone for even the briefest of moments. There should always, *always*, be someone in the room with him – no more than three metres away,' she says. 'He's starting to lose strength. We can't have him standing up and losing his balance with no one around to catch him.'

And so, to his obvious annoyance, we become Walt's shadows. Although he doesn't fully grasp it, he seems aware of the fact that he's never truly given a moment alone. He becomes more fidgety – wanting to get up and walk around the house or the garden, trying to lose whoever is tailing him that day. By the time Marguerite gets back from England, we are feeling trapped all over again.

A few days later, Fiona calls back with the results of her latest research. Ruby and I sit on Skype in the living room while Annette takes Walt for a walk around the garden.

'I don't think it's any old dementia,' Fiona tells us.

I tend to agree. His isn't the sort of sweetly screwy senility that saw my grandmother stuff her handbag full of leftover lamb chops wrapped in serviettes. His is more paranoid, more intense. More of a torment than a simple loss of memory.

Fiona thinks he's got what's known as 'Lewy body dementia' or 'LBD'. The only way to confirm a diagnosis is a post-mortem autopsy, where through a microscope the brain will reveal itself to be riddled with sticky balls of protein: the 'Lewy bodies' of the disease's name, which appear inside nerve cells as small, spherical masses. Eventually these balls colonise the grey matter, leaving no room for the biological processes that facilitate regular thought. Perhaps most tragically they are thought to cause the loss of dopamine neurons – the cells that help us experience life's pleasures.

For now we can only speculate, look at Walt from the outside and try to pinpoint his pathology, but his daughter says the doctors agree that LBD is the most likely explanation for his behaviour. And he fits the pattern of decline: unlike Alzheimer's disease, which tends to be slow and steady, LBD advances in a 'step-like' progression. After a time of seeming stability, a sufferer will just wake up one day unable to walk properly or to remember people's names.

Fiona rattles through a list of symptoms she found online.

All of this, Ruby and I agree, is Walt to a T.

Years later, I'll read a heartbreaking essay by Robin Williams' widow, Susan Schneider Williams, published in the journal of the American Academy of Neurology. Titled 'The Terrorist Inside My Husband's Brain', it vividly describes the everyday effects of Lewy body dementia as her husband suffered it before taking his own life. I'm struck by how closely her story details the type of trauma Walt was experiencing.

Susan writes of how Robin's illness – a mystery at the time; he'd only been diagnosed with Parkinson's disease – started with seemingly unrelated symptoms: 'Constipation, urinary difficulty, heartburn, sleeplessness and insomnia . . . a poor sense of smell – and lots of stress.' She tells of how his fear and anxiety 'skyrocketed to a point that was alarming' – something she later learned was an early indication of LBD – and that his condition soon progressed to 'problems with paranoia, delusions and looping, insomnia, memory, and high cortisol levels'.

Everything Susan writes about her husband's experience mirrors Walt's. Especially her observation of the unpredictability of it all, the way the 'plethora of LBD symptoms appear and disappear at random times – even throughout the course of a day'. It was only once Robin had died that doctors were able to confirm that his mind had, as they'd suspected, been invaded by Lewy bodies. Experts declared his 'one of the worst LBD pathologies they had seen' and told Susan there was nothing else anyone could have done. Robin, it seemed, knew he was losing his mind, and found that agony too much to bear.

The moments that Walt knows his own grasp on reality has slipped are by far his worst, too. I understand that. A few times, he's sat me on the edge of his bed, looked me in the eye and said he's had enough. To have to witness yourself unravelling, watch your wit coming undone like old rope, knowing that very soon you'll be floating out at sea in the nothingness, adrift and alone in the dark. The thought of it is undoubtedly terrifying. Surely that's the cruellest way of all to turn the lights out on someone?

But a key difference between Robin Williams' story and Walt's is the environment they each found themselves in when the disease struck. Robin was on a movie set. Walt is in the middle of a dangerous city in Africa. His fight-or-flight instinct sees him reach for confiscated guns, or wanting to drive away into Nairobi traffic. The terrorists in his brain are real: memories of Mau Mau fighters breaking into his house, of people trying to rob him, trying to *kill* him.

In Walt's case, it's hard for anyone to draw the line between paranoid delusion and traumatic flashback – and it's almost as frightening for us as it is for him. We have to ensure his wellbeing, but our own physical safety also becomes a very real concern. Over the next week he grabs me a couple of times, trying to prise car keys out of my grip, and I'm stunned by his strength. Anger seems to nullify his physical frailty — I know he could really hurt us if he wanted to.

One morning, I'm kneeling on the ground in Walt's bedroom, trying to fit the little piece of pink bubblegum between his toes. Another corn is forming — we'll need to take him to the podiatrist if it gets any worse.

He keeps kicking the gum away just as I'm about to put his socks on. 'What's that horrid lump of muck?' he says. He's grumbly today because it's grey outside. Or maybe he's just grumbly because he's grumbly.

'Please, Walt!' I beg, when he kicks the toe separator for the third time. 'I'm trying to help you. This will make your foot feel better.'

Annette overhears us as she's walking past. She's off duty, but she pops in to help anyway. 'Hello there, handsome man!' she says, distracting him while I fiddle with the bubblegum again. 'Well, you *would* be a very handsome man if you had a tie on, wouldn't you?' She takes a tie from the dresser and sits beside him to put it on.

Walt relishes the flirtatious attention. Annette natters away at him, doing his tie up and straightening his hair just long enough for me to finish with his shoes and socks.

'Thanks so much,' I say when it's finally done. Her time with us is nearly up; it'll be a huge loss when she's gone. She's been very good with Walt, but has found the tension between Fiona and Marguerite hard to cope with.

Ruby's mum knows a lady who knows a girl in Gladstone who might be a good replacement. As I take Walt through to sit by the fire in the living room, I hear Ruby and her mum talking on Skype in the study.

'She's only nineteen,' Ruby's mum is saying, 'but she's actually been working in an old folks' home. She wants to take a gap year and do some travel – it's perfect!'

'Mum, are you *sure* she'd be up for it? We really need to make sure we've got the right kind of person. It's not as simple as it sounds.'

'Yeah, course! She'd be great, Ruby!'

'Have you explained the situation to her? Like, in full? All the crazy family drama and everything? What Walt's like?' Ruby really does want to make sure this girl has the full story before she comes.

'Pffft, Ruby, she says she's seen plenty of that in the nursing home. People squabbling over inheritance and that sort of thing. She knows what she's in for.'

But Jade does *not* know what she is in for.

Two weeks later, those iron gates are swinging open again for Carer Number Nine. I have never seen culture shock writ so large across a person's face as the moment Jade pulls up in the driveway only to be berated by Walt for stealing his car and by Marguerite for having smudged eyeliner.

'I say, did somebody punch you on the plane? You've got a horrid big bruise on your face.'

'Ummm, hi,' Jade says awkwardly, trying to wipe her eyes clean. *God, she's just a kid!* I realise. Then she screams, 'Argh! What's that?!' as Chiku races past, chasing a monkey that's been stealing scraps from the rubbish pit at the back of the staff quarters.

It turns out that until now, nineteen-year-old Jade from Gladstone has never been out of Queensland. She'd been dreaming of going to Melbourne for a weekend – that was going to be her big adventure. Now she's in a Nairobi nuthouse, a return flight booked for three months' time. And despite Ruby's and my best efforts to put her at ease that night of her arrival, her second day on the job dashes any hopes she might have had for a soft landing.

It starts off simply enough. I'm on duty so I talk her through the bed alarm, getting Walt dressed and the morning routine of breakfast and pills and papers on the patio.

But then Walt goes to the loo and doesn't come back.

And when we check the baby monitor, he's not there.

And then Esther comes out to the patio looking alarmed. 'Kirsten, please, come quickly. The *bwana* is very cross.'

We follow her through to the garage, where Walt's found himself a garden hoe. 'These bloody people!' he roars when he sees us. He rattles the bonnet, trying to pop it open.

'Hi, Walt, what's going on?' I ask tentatively, keeping Jade behind me.

'I'm disconnecting the batteries to all of these vehicles. Sick to *bloody death* of people driving them around without my permission! I can see how many miles you've clocked up. You've got a bloody cheek.' He rattles the bonnet harder. 'But I've got *no fucking keys* to get into them.' He looks at me, puts his hand out. 'Give me the keys.'

'Walt, I don't have the keys.'

'You *bloody well give them to me now, you bitch!*'

'Go inside,' I tell Jade. She's not equipped to deal with this level of Walt-fuckery just yet. 'Okay, Walt, I'll give you the keys but I have to find them first.'

He comes closer and swats at the sides of my shorts to check I'm not stashing them in my pockets. I hold an arm out defensively, then pull my pockets inside out to prove I don't have them on me as I backtrack into the driveway. 'Esther, get James, please, and Ruby – and see if you can find the keys.'

By the time they all come tearing out of the house, Walt is holding the garden hoe over his head and chasing me in circles around the driveway. Chiku thinks it's a game and is running between us barking, nipping our heels. A crowd has gathered: James, Esther, Khamisi, David, Peter, Patrick, Jade and Ruby are all now standing around on the gravel, helpless in the morning sun.

Peter's got the keys to the Peugeot. He jangles them before tossing them carefully on the ground at Walt's feet. Walt snatches them up, walks over to the Mazda, finds they don't fit.

'*Bwana! Bwana*, that is the wrong car. Please – try this one,' James says, trying to lure him over to the garage.

But the *bwana* is now incandescent. He comes at me again.

He's about to strike, when Ruby saves the day. She runs between us, then stages a 'fall': lies groaning on the gravel, clutching a knee to her chest, screaming for help. The staff all run over, not realising it's a ruse until they get close enough to see her giving the thumbs up and they twig to play along.

'Oh madam, madam,' Patrick cries, hands over his head in pantomime despair, 'are you alright?'

Walt stops in his tracks, torn between his chivalrous and murderous instincts.

'I will get you a bandage,' Esther says, racing inside, trying to stifle her giggles.

'Quickly,' James tells the others, 'send for help!'

I crouch beside Ruby to play the damsel in distress. 'Oh no, Walt, can you help us? Please! She's hurt herself badly.'

It works.

Walt drops the hoe and walks over to where Ruby lies crumpled on the ground. 'You took a terrible tumble, there, young lady,' he says, looking down at her tenderly. 'Now, where does it hurt?'

Ruby even manages to squeeze some tears out. 'My leg – I think I've broken it!'

Walt takes charge, starts clicking his fingers, issuing orders. 'Okay, let's get you inside. *Kuja hapa*, James – call for a doctor. You two,' he points at Patrick and Peter, 'help carry this young lass inside.'

'Yes, *bwana*,' they say, taking an arm each, Khamisi rushing in to help me support her legs. By the time we get her inside and laid out on the couch, we're all of us nearly in stitches.

But Ruby has fully committed to her role. She lays a hand across her head, rolls her eyes back. 'Oh dear, I think I might faint!'

Esther arrives with a wet washer and a glass of water, while Walt sits holding Ruby's hand. 'Where's that bloody doctor?' he asks.

'I think they've just arrived, Walt,' I say. 'I'll go bring her in.'

I find Jade in the dining room, biting her nails. 'Hey, mate – we need you to pretend to be a doctor for a bit.'

'Huh?' she says.

'Just – come through to the living room and pretend to take Ruby's pulse and stuff. I dunno, act professional.' I spy my gym bag on the end of my bed through the open sunroom door; I duck in to grab it, then pick up my headphones on the way back. 'Here, use these, pretend they're a stethoscope. And maybe tell Ruby to take one of these.' I hand Jade the tub of Marguerite's multivitamins from the sideboard and put the gym bag into her hands to be carried like a doctor's satchel.

'Okay . . .' Jade smiles nervously and follows me through to the living room.

At first, I worry this is going to backfire – that she won't be able to do a good enough job to fool Walt. But she rises to the occasion and puts in a turn as the best hammy soap-opera doctor that a woman-pretending-to-have-broken-her-leg-to-stop-a-crazy-old-man-from-assaulting-her-friend could hope for.

Bravo, Jade, I think. *I shouldn't have underestimated you.*

I send Fiona an email that night to let her know about the day's events. I don't think she needs to be updated on Walt's every breath, burp and fart – but I *do* think she should know when he turns landscaping implements into weapons of mass destruction. Her response is to have me instruct all carers and staff, and Marguerite, to ensure that all 'potential weapons' be locked away or removed from his reach. The trouble is, Fiona can have us lock away the golf clubs and the fire poker and the kitchen knives, but *any* loose object heavy or pointy enough to do damage is a potential weapon to Walt's enraged eyes. We can't lock down the whole world.

∼

I manage to juggle some shifts with Ruby and Jade so that I have time to go out the following Saturday. Claire's invited me around for a barbecue and to stay the night – her girls think a sleepover with their Aussie cousin will be 'super'.

I arrive to the happy squeals and indignant cries of children playing in the yard. The girls race over and drag me onto the trampoline to show me their new tricks. I try and fail to repeat their tumbling, then I chase them around the house, and throw a tennis ball for the dogs.

I head over to the patio where the adults are huddled together, hushed tones, brave faces – something's up. I remember Claire's friends – Prisha and Sandeep – from a night we were introduced at the bar. There, they were the kind of boisterous good company I missed so much from home. Today they're just as welcoming, but clearly weighed down with worry.

'*Jambo, jambo!*' Claire gives me a warm hug. 'Here, what can we get you – a beer? A wine? Come through, I'll grab you a glass.' In the kitchen she fills me in. 'So,' she says, pouring us both a glass of white, 'we've had a bit of drama. I'm trying not to let the kids figure it out.'

'Okay . . .'

'Henry – Robert's dad – was shot yesterday.'

'What!?'

'He's fine, he's fine. He was hit in the leg, but he'll be fine.'

'What happened?'

'He was ambushed. Hijackers. In the middle of the road in broad daylight. Driving right past the Korean Embassy – can you believe it? He was on his way to the bank, with the cash from the bar. Two in the afternoon. So he's driving along and this car overtakes him, and there's another one behind him, then the one in front pulls up across the road and they block him in. And then these guys all get out – five or six Somalis, we think – and they've all got AKs and they start firing at his car. One of the bullets went through the bonnet, hit the chassis then ricocheted back up through his seat and hit him in the back of the leg. He was bloody lucky – or bloody unlucky, depending on how you look at it.'

'So what? Just to rob him?'

'*Jah!* They grabbed the money and took off.'

'Is he okay? I mean, apart from the bullet?'

'He's shaken up. But he'll be fine. I was with him just now at the hospital – they've bandaged him up, and he's going home this afternoon. He won't be able to walk for a little while but he'll be fine. But shit, you know – we're just . . . it seems like an inside job. It had to be. It's just devastating – it means one of our staff has betrayed us. These guys – they had to know what he had and where he was going. You know, we're even careful to change the route each week. So they knew his car. They were following him.'

'Oh no.'

'That's really the worst part. To think we can't trust the people who work for us. It's bloody awful.'

But Claire has some good news for me too. An old school friend of Robert's is heading 'up country' the following weekend to visit a friend, just past Kitale. Claire had remembered that I'd been wanting to visit the deformed animal sanctuary in Kitale and asked him whether he could take me with him – he'd never heard of the place and was immediately as intrigued as I was.

'Marcus prides himself on knowing the country inside out,' Claire explains. 'So he's happy to take you somewhere he's never been before. He's kind of what we call a "KC" here. Have you heard of a "KC" before?'

'That's a "Kenya Cowboy", right?' I haven't met any in the flesh yet, but I know what to expect. Sarah and Jack have filled me in, pointed out a few of the Crocodile Dundee types when we've been out and about in Nairobi. A 'KC' is a white man who considers himself native to Africa, with bloodlines in the continent running several generations deep. He'll speak Swahili fluently, probably other tribal languages too. He prefers to spend his time in the bush, as far from the bustle of the city as possible and wears tatty khakis and a dusty tan no matter the place or occasion. He smokes. Drinks. Is a sometimes boorish type who hasn't yet figured out that you can't just do whatever you like because you're a white guy with money anymore – although, more often than not, he gets away with bad behaviour. KCs generally don't have 'a job', instead making ends meet through a series of on-the-ground logistics contracts – helping set up safari camps and managing ranches, that sort of thing.

Marcus, Claire tells me, being the son of a French hunter and – more importantly – the owner of an apparently indestructible Land Rover – is the ultimate KC.

'Come, he's outside – I'll introduce you.'

Marcus is standing at the edge of the patio, smoking. He has the matter-of-fact manner of a man from another time. I tell him I want to see the two-headed cow.

'So do I. I'll take you there,' he says. 'We can stay with my friend in Mount Elgon. He's got a flower farm. A greenhouse of a million roses. Would you like to see that too?'

Of course I want to see a greenhouse of a million roses in the middle of Kenya – but the trip will take four days. I'll have to beg Jade and Ruby to jointly cover me while I'm gone, which means doing a run of back-to-back shifts with Walt through the week to buy the time. It'll be worth it, though, I'm sure.

It had better be worth it. I spend night after night up with Walt, the bed alarm alerting me to his nocturnal wanderings. He's either terrified because he doesn't know where he is, or furious because he thinks he *does* and that people are out to get him. He thinks Marguerite is his mother most times, which only fuels the confusion, so she takes to sleeping in the study while I sit on the bed with him for hours calming him down.

The days aren't much better. There are moments of calm, but many more of agitation and anxiety. Car engines, chequebooks, empty jerry cans, dogs barking. The list of triggers in Walt's carers' notebook grows longer and less avoidable. Marguerite takes her frustrations out on us and finds reasons to leave the house as much as possible, which leaves us with one less tool in our arsenal to manage Walt's difficult turns.

By the time Marcus picks me up early on the Friday morning, I'm ready for *any* kind of escape.

I climb into a Land Rover that's clocked more than half a million kilometres, much of it on the corrugated stretch to Lake Turkana in the Ethiopian end of northern Kenya. This has left it with a chronic, all-over rattle and more than a few battle scars. The doors don't close properly. The brakes have to be pumped twice to take effect. Loose screws and grimy cigarette tins dance across the dashboard as we climb down the escarpment road out of Nairobi, and the Great Rift Valley opens up to our left in that breathtaking roar. We don't talk much, at first.

For miles ahead on the road, a snaking line of banked-up trucks hugs the cliff face, puffing black smoke and groaning with effort as impatient cars pinball through impossible gaps in the oncoming traffic to get past them. At every bend is a cluster of souvenir stalls and lookouts flagged by faded red Coca-Cola signs, rickety old slab-and-tin shacks teetering on the lip of a sheer drop, looking like they might be swallowed whole by the valley at any moment.

'You know, apart from the traffic, this road hasn't changed much in the last seventy years,' Marcus says. I find that very easy to believe. 'They made Italian prisoners build it during the Second World War. There's a tiny chapel up ahead on one of the corners. It looks like something out of the Amalfi Coast, in miniature.'

I watch him change gears with an arm streaked with jagged scars.

'Are you looking at my arm?'

'Yes. Sorry,' I say, embarrassed to have been caught, though it doesn't seem to have bothered him at all.

'I fell through a glass door when I was twenty-five. Severed a bunch of tendons and nerves, all the way from my shoulder to my wrist. Lucky to live, really. I lost a lot of blood. Anyway. It works well enough.' He flexes his hand and grins. I take it he's not easily offended. 'So what's old Walter Smyth like?' he asks. 'He must be an interesting guy.'

'Oh, you know,' I say. *'Colonial.'*

Marcus laughs. 'Ah, well – you can't hold that against him. We're all a product of our time. You realise his early years in Kenya, most people were still wearing animal skins. And now look! They're selling sheepskin hats to tourists and using the money to buy Levi's jeans. That's an extraordinary change for a person to witness in a lifetime. It's an even more extraordinary change for the Africans! I'm not sure it's been for the best, either. Who says our way of doing things is better?'

A *matatu* screams past on the right, fishtailing as it pulls back into the lane in front of us at such late notice that by the time the oncoming truck blasts its horn it's accusing innocent drivers behind us. I brace myself against the dash for the impact – but none comes. We slow up with mere inches to spare before we plough into the back of the van. Marcus doesn't seem anywhere near as alarmed as I think he should be. Nor do the *matatu* passengers – not even the woman holding a sleeping baby against the back window seems to realise how firmly she just brushed shoulders with Death.

'Jesus Christ,' I gasp. Marcus holds the steering wheel with his elbows as he lights another cigarette.

'How old did you say Walt is? Eighty-something? Hell, he must have seen some things. You should ask him to tell you some stories.'

I really don't want to talk about Walt.

'Why don't you tell me about what you do up in Lake Turkana?' I say.

'The World Bank is funding a wind farm up there. Slowly. Very slowly. Anyway. I'm doing logistics for them.'

'What does that *actually* mean though?'

'It means I help make things happen. That part of the country is virtually lawless. The tribes up there – the Turkanas and the Pokots – are constantly at war. They're always raiding each other's cattle. It's a huge problem. But you know – that's their world. They're desert nomads. They've always carried on like that. To them it's not theft – it's tradition. Problem is, they've got guns now. So it's all a lot bloodier than it needs to be. When you go up there, the locals walk around with AK47s slung over their shoulders and just about nothing else on. So when the World Bank or whoever it is wants to send some equipment through their territory – turbine blades, say – I go in to help negotiate the passage with the locals. You need to know the right people to get things done. It's diplomacy, really.'

'And you enjoy it?'

'I love it. Well, I love the work. I'm not so sure about some of the people I work *for*. The wind farm thing is fine. And I like collecting soil samples from remote areas for researchers. But there are all sorts of prospecting companies out there, who I must help from time to time. They're all very quiet about it, but they've been looking for oil, and I'm fairly sure they've found it. Just a matter of piping it out now. And I'm not sure they – or the government – have the best of intentions when it comes to the locals. There'll be land grabs soon. Things will get nasty. They always do.'

SHORTCOMINGS

Marcus's prophecy will take five years to come true. By 2016, the value of virtually barren land in northern Kenya skyrockets when it becomes known a billion barrels of oil is sitting beneath it. Gangs of young men armed with machetes and guns tear through Turkana in convoys of trucks. They are land cartels, headed by elite Turkanas who take advantage of poorly kept paperwork, out-of-date land registries and corruptible administrators to snatch parcels of community-held grazing land, then subdivide it and sell it off for themselves.

We drive through Naivasha, Gilgil, Lake Nakuru. I remember the lake from the safari I took at the end of my first stint with the Smyths. It's a soda lake – alkaline – home to millions of flamingos. At Molo, we follow the highway as it swings north, heading for Kitale.

The drive is exhausting. Parts of the road are so bad that rather than avoiding the potholes, we simply aim for the smallest ones. I have to hold on to the door handle with one hand and brace against the roof with the other, to stop myself from being thrown around the cab. There's no air conditioning so we have the windows down, hot dust collecting in the corners of my eyes and mouth, filling my nose and ears. I could not be happier.

We pull up, finally, in Kitale. The town's population is supposedly 100,000, though it looks to me only a fraction the size. On the main street, Marcus asks several passers-by for directions to the Kitale Nature Conservancy, but nobody has heard of the place.

'*Ng'ombe na vichwa viwili?*' he says to a group of men outside a mechanic's garage. They keel over with laughter.

'A cow with two heads?' one repeats in English. 'Ach, no! No, no, no, no. We have nothing like that here in Kitale.'

I start to wonder whether the whole thing is just a myth – whether the girl who told me about it had been misled – but Marcus isn't disheartened.

'It'll be here. Don't worry. We'll find it,' he says. And eventually we do. On the A1 road heading north out of town, where on a fifteen-foot-high red wall painted with a mural of animals is a sign in big white lettering which reads:

KNC
KITALE NATURE CONSERVANCY
FOR: – ECO-TOURISM – BIODIVERSITY CONSERVATION –
EDUCATIONAL TOURS – RECREATION AND MEETINGS.

Behind an imposing set of iron gates is a 250-acre complex, fronted by a sprawling, lumpy pile of brightly painted, hand-moulded concrete with thick thatched roofs. It's like something out of *The Flintstones*.

The place looks deserted. A three-legged dog sits tied to a multi-pronged signpost directing visitors to 'BUTTERFLY VIEWING' and 'PICNICS'. Just as we're about to head for the 'DEFORMED ANIMALS' a guide appears, shakes our hands, and beckons us to follow him the other way.

'This way, this way please!' he orders, leading us through to the botanical gardens.

'My name is Denis,' he says formally, as we stand among a smattering of native shrubs and trees, small wooden tags inscribed with their Latin names wired to their branches. 'I am here at your service, to guide you through the wonders of our park. Please, if you have any questions, do not hesitate to ask.'

Marcus and I follow Denis around the plantation, coming to a stop at each and every specimen for him to run through his didactic spiels by rote, eyes closed. *Latin name / common name / geographical region / traditional medicinal use*. It becomes apparent that just about anything that grows out of the ground has been considered a cure for stomach ache or a potent aphrodisiac, by some tribe, at some point in time.

'The man can go for six hours with this one,' Denis says, holding out the leaves from one thorny bush. 'Twelve hours,' at another. Then, the gold standard: 'This one – *twenty-four hours!* Mmhmm. Yes. Like Viagra. A whole day! His wife will get very tired. So maybe this is why he has to have many wives.' Denis laughs, but I don't think he actually meant it as a joke.

One of the trees has papery bark that men grind up to brew a tea that makes their penises grow longer. 'The women sometime make it in secret,' Denis says. 'If their husbands cannot satisfy them.' He doesn't seem to find any of this embarrassing or amusing. Kenyans in general, I've found, are not at all shy when it comes to discussing sexual matters.

Then he leads us to the Biblical Mountains exhibit – a dirt trail flanked by a series of colourful cement dioramas, depicting each and every Bible story that takes place on a mountain. We walk past piles of rocks topped with gruesome tableaus that look as though they were created by a pre-schooler having a bad acid trip in a church.

Here's Noah's Ark, beached beneath a rainbow, and Aaron worshipping the golden calf. Here's Moses on Mount Horeb with the burning bush, and again on Mount Sinai reading the Ten Commandments from stone tablets. Abraham, on Mount Moriah, holds a knife to the neck of a child. The hand-painted caption on a piece of slate propped up in front of the awful scene reads 'Abraham about to sacrifice his son Isaac, Gen 22:1-15'. A terrifying giant King Og, barrel-chested and smeared in blood, holds a dagger behind a white shield with a red skull and crossbones.

'Why *mountains?*' I ask Denis.

'Mountains are very important in the Bible,' he says, as though it's obvious. It turns out the man who runs the park, Mr Ndura – a former teacher – is deeply religious. He has built the whole place with his own hands and money, and this holy gauntlet is his personal tribute to God. It's an admirable effort, but it must be said: these figures are the stuff of nightmares, with their crude, out-of-proportion heads and tiny hands, lumpy eyes and jagged-toothed mouths screaming at the sky. I'm glad to leave the monstrous visions behind us and move on to the monstrous animals I've come to see.

At first, nothing seems out of the ordinary. There's a perfectly normal horse, a couple of Ankole cows with their magnificent horns reaching skyward, a shaggy ostrich in a pen. Then a dwarfed billy-goat hobbles over, his whiskers almost reaching the ground on account of his short, stocky bowed legs. Denis gives him a handful of pellets, and points out a nearby bull. A mass the size and shape of a large pumpkin hangs down behind his tick-riddled pizzle.

'It's a hernia,' Denis says. 'It doesn't cause him any pain, but it does stop him from mating.'

Beside the bull is another cow, with a horse-like tail and a flap of skin that looks like a deflated balloon laying slack over one side of its hump. Denis says the horse-cow is just that, a 'horse-cow'.

I grew up on a farm. As far as I know, horse–cow crossbreeds are not a real thing. 'Really?' I ask, doubtful.

'Yes. It's a half-horse, half-cow. From an interspecies mating. And the piece of skin on its back is a semi-formed male sex organ.'

I start to doubt Denis's expertise.

There's a calf with the bovine version of Down syndrome and inverted knees, a hermaphrodite sheep with a thick, matted tail that looks like a beaver hanging off its back, and a cow and a donkey with no tails at all. There are all kinds of creatures with only three legs and a goat with five, the spare hanging limp from the side of its chest. And stomping, snorting, mounting everything in sight is a cow with what I recognise as freemartinism – a condition where the female twin of a male calf is born sterile, hormonally affected by her brother's development in the womb. So Denis isn't far off when he tells us 'this cow is crazy – she thinks she's a bull'.

He shows us down to a small lake we can go rowing in, if we like? It's more of a pond, really. Still, we climb into the little blue dinghy pulled up on the bank and paddle happy figure-eights in the sun. We pull up in the reeds at the bank, just as a black cow has come down for a drink.

Oh god, oh Jesus on a mountain, the horror.

Here it is. But the cow doesn't have two heads. It's worse than that. It has one head with two distorted faces. Three eyes and three horns on one side of its skull, one of each on the other. Twisted nostrils and an upturned mouth that opens sideways and looks like a shucked abalone with teeth. The oral disfigurement is so severe the poor thing can't graze — can't grip the grass tight enough with its jaw. The park staff have to feed it by hand. Five times a day, someone comes and sits on a small stool beside that beastly head with a bucket of hay and grains, patiently guiding handfuls of food into its mangled mouth and speaking softly to the hole where one of its ears should be, those three black eyes blinking back with gratitude. The kindness overwhelms me. I choke up. I weep.

I ask Denis if I can meet Mr Ndura, the owner. He's out of town at the moment, but Denis gives me his phone number.

When I follow up with Mr Ndura a few days later, he tells me: 'These are God's creatures. We have a duty to look after them. If some scientists wish to come and study them here I welcome them, but that is not the purpose of the conservancy.' The park is funded mostly from the money he's made in business. I ask whether he thinks there is something causing these deformities? Contamination of some kind? He can't be sure, but doesn't think so. The animals are from all over the region. Their defects are seemingly random occurrences in otherwise healthy herds, or sometimes the result of inbreeding. Word of his sanctuary has spread through the towns and the villages. He has convinced people to send defective animals his way to be cared for, instead of slaughtering them out of a fear of evil spirits. 'I am an educator,' he tells me. 'That is my passion.'

Mr Ndura's passion for education is clear in the final section of his park: the Climate Change and Environmental Education Centre.

A twelve-foot-high cement installation, bright with fresh poster paint, shows men working a patch of green grass with machetes and hoes and cutting down trees, while sorrowful animals watch on. Lettering along the base of the scene reads 'UNITED IN GRIEF MOURNING THE LOSS OF THEIR HABITAT', and then a sign on a giraffe-patterned rock 'DESTRUCTION OF WETLANDS LEADS TO LOSS OF BIODIVERSITY'. A huge concrete half-dome representing Earth is hollowed out, the opening covered with chicken wire. Across the span of the mantle reads 'The 11TH COMMANDMENT: Thou Shall not destroy PLANET EARTH – IT IS OUR ONLY HOME'. Inside the globe, a three-dimensional model of the apocalypse has been constructed out of junkyard knick-knacks. Among the toy cars carrying coffins and beaches flooded with blue paint is an armless lady mannequin, blood dripping from one eye, a gluggy explosion of yellow-brown goop smothering her left breast – the result of 'SKIN CANCER', according to the laminated label stuck to her chest.

All over the place are signs listing the consequences of global warming. 'A rise in sea levels, upsurge of diseases and the collapse of economies and ecosystem' warns one. Another shows a woman and child walking across the bare earth carrying bundles of firewood on their heads, the sun shining pointedly from above them and a caption reading 'USE ALTERNATIVE SOURCE OF FUEL'.

Then the pièce de résistance – a statue of Wangari Maathai, the renowned Kenyan environmentalist and first female African Nobel Peace Prize winner, standing in a bright orange dress and matching headscarf, her hands clasped above another entreaty: 'STOP BLAME GAME ON GLOBAL WARMING AND CLIMATE CHANGE: WE EITHER ACT TOGETHER OR PERISH TOGETHER'.

At a time when climate change scepticism is taking hold in the Western world, the enthusiasm seems futile. The average Kenyan is lucky to have electric light at night, let alone an SUV to drive around town, or ducted air conditioning. Kenyans — like all people in the developing world — are the least responsible for what's happening to the planet, and the most vulnerable to its consequences. But here they are, campaigning for action, pleading for cooperation to avert a global catastrophe.

Marcus and I thank Denis for his tour and leave him with a good tip before hitting the road. It's another hour and a half to his friend's farm, right on the Ugandan border at the foot of Mount Elgon, and we're keen to get there before dark.

We drive in the dying light past people walking away from the road, towards huts in the dry middle distance. Their homes are silhouetted against the sunset, as are the acacia trees and flocks of roosting birds, shadows before a blood red glow diffused through orange dust.

We arrive at Pat Reynolds' property just as the sun dips behind the mountain. He and his Norwegian wife, Siri, a doctor, welcome us into their home — their verandah looks over a valley and across to Uganda's hills on the other side.

Pat grew up here. Over dinner, he tells us how he remembers being a kid in 1976 and waking up in the night to a roar that rattled the windows. Palestinian and German terrorists had hijacked an Air France plane and Ugandan President Idi Amin had allowed them to land at Entebbe Airport, where they'd taken over a hundred Jewish hostages. The noise that woke Pat was Israeli commandos flying in to rescue the passengers after a two-week standoff — 'Operation Thunderbolt' would go down as one of the most audacious raids in history, and would not have been possible had Kenya not allowed the Israelis to refuel their Hercules planes in Nairobi first.

On this side of the border, the history is a little more placid. The property is one of the oldest in Kenya. Since 1920 it's grown all manner of horticultural products — coffee, peaches, avocados — but for the last twenty years Pat has focused on roses. He sells them to the European market by the millions. (He's not alone — Kenya is one of the world's biggest exporters of flowers.)

In the morning he takes us through the greenhouse where in the cool crisp air, rows upon rows of roses — in all colours and varieties — are suspended in hydroponic troughs and lovingly tended to by a busy team of Kenyans in red sweaters. (The farm isn't simply a commercial endeavour — it funds a number of community projects, including a medical centre, an HIV clinic, a home for AIDS orphans and schools.) In the sorting room, the cut roses are separated according to quality, type and stage of bloom: a worker explains that the English prefer their petals opened wide; continental Europeans tend to want them tucked up tight. Every day, a plane lands on the property's dirt airstrip to be filled to the brim with blooms which, mere hours later, are for sale on the streets of Amsterdam.

Yet again, I'm struck by how much of Africa's role on the world stage is hidden from the West, drowned out by the spectacle of tragedy.

A couple of days after I get back from my road trip, Marguerite is off to the coast again. This time to a beach resort in Diani, just south of Mombasa, with 'Cousin Frances' and her teenage daughter. 'A *girls'* weekend,' she says. 'Perhaps we'll find the young one a suitor.'

'Watch out for the beach boys,' I say, as I help load her bags into the back of a taxi.

'Why's that?' she asks.

'Well, they're *gigolos!*'

'*Are they!?*' She seems shocked. Then mischievous. 'Well! Perhaps they ought to watch out for us! Ha!'

The pair of them admire themselves in the mirror on the back of the door.

'We're going to a fancy-dress party tonight,' Ruby explains. 'One of Sean's friends from the UN.'

'It was my idea,' Sean confesses.

My heart skips a beat as the door swings open – it's Esther, carrying a pile of fresh sheets to change Walt's bed over. She gasps at the sight of us, then starts to apologise and back out of the room.

'No, no – it's okay, it's okay, Esther,' says Ruby, pulling the maid back in and closing the door behind her. 'We're just – *shhhhhh*,' she puts her fingers to her lips, bringing poor Esther into the conspiracy. 'We're borrowing some of their clothes for the night. You can't tell anyone.'

Esther relaxes enough to ask, 'You are pretending to be the *memsahib*? And the *bwana*?'

'Yeah, what do you think? Have we pulled it off?' Ruby clears her throat, adopting a regal stance. '*Yoo-hoo! Yoooo-hooooooo!*'

Esther hides her face behind her hands, then slaps her thigh with delight. 'Yes!' she says, almost crying with laughter. 'Yes! That is very good!'

'Okay, sweet,' says Ruby, stripping their layers off and shoving them into her backpack. 'Let's go before Walt comes back inside.'

I help them sneak around the far side of the house and run down to where their cab is waiting by the corner, and feel a pang of jealousy at the fun they're having.

Though I also feel pretty smug when, at about three in the morning, I wake up to hear Ruby retching in the bathroom. I go in to check on her, turn the light on, and see she's doing it all wrong.

She's sitting on the toilet, and vomiting forward. A violent spray of red wine and mystery chunks, all over Marguerite's shoes.

Ruby manages to clean the spew off the shoes enough that you can only smell it when you lift them close to your face. They're in the wardrobe again by the time Marguerite returns from her holiday, none the wiser. She's come back with a new pair of shoes anyway: a pair of Bata 'flip-flops' with rainbow straps. There are Bata shoe shops all over Kenya – their thongs are as ubiquitous as Havaianas back home – though I'm not sure septuagenarian colonial women are the target market.

'Aren't they fun!' she says, twirling around the living room and doing ballet poses as she models them for Walt.

'Oh yes, yes, marvellous,' he says, with faux sincerity, then pretends to try not to let her see him pulling a disgusted face behind her back. It's playful moments like these that show how even through the murkiness of the disease, he's still capable of wit and fun.

As a treat, Marguerite grants Ruby and me a rare night off together. We reach a group decision – that Jade will be fine on her own, and that Fiona doesn't need to know we left just one carer on with Walt.

Ruby and I arrange to rent the Kirbys' flat.

We drive the Peugeot over and the Kirbys' *askari*, Charles, lets us in. The Kirbys are out of town so it's only us and their staff here tonight. He walks us through the lush gardens to the cottage at the back of the property. It's a cosy little log cabin with a double bed, a bathroom, and a small landing overlooking a lily pond.

As the sun goes down we sit on the deck watching the monkeys squabble, relishing the silence and the relief at not having to consider how our every move might disturb Walt. I close my eyes and listen to the night birds harmonise with the last call of prayer for the day. It's the first time I've felt truly relaxed in weeks. When it gets dark we move inside, lock the doors, and settle into the pillows, watching a movie on Ruby's laptop. Around eleven, we start to drift off.

Around eleven-thirty, we shit our pants.

Someone's on the deck. We both feel the room shake with the weight of heavy footsteps and sit up in bed at the same time, hearts pumping, ears open, gone from near slumber to high alert in an instant.

I turn the bedside lamp off. I don't want them seeing in when we can't see out.

We sit dead still in the dark, straining to hear. There's shuffling. There's a man's voice. There's the door handle jiggling against the lock.

'Fuck this,' Ruby whispers. There's a panic button on a key chain on the bedside table. She presses it. Nothing happens.

'How do we know it's worked?' I say. 'Shouldn't it beep or flash?'

'I don't know. Maybe the battery's flat?'

Fuck. This. I grab the switch knife I keep in my bag and flick the blade open, holding it the way I've been shown to stop it being pushed back into my own hand, my thumb behind the handle. I know how pathetic it is – that this won't save me, that nothing will if whoever is outside wants to hurt us – but fuck it, I'll at least try to do some damage on the way down.

But nothing happens – there's silence. We sit there for minutes, frozen still, starting to wonder whether we imagined the whole thing. Ruby gets up and looks through the window. She can't see anything. 'Maybe they've gone?'

Nope, they've just moved around the cottage – we can hear low voices on the bathroom-window side.

Ruby jumps back into bed and pulls out her phone. 'Should I call Charles?'

'Yep, and I'll call G4S.' I start googling the number.

'Charles?' Ruby whispers. 'Can you come to the cottage, please? There's someone outside. They're trying to get in.'

It feels like hours pass as we sit there waiting, holding hands tight, wondering if we're going to die together tonight.

The cottage shudders again with the weight of a man leaping up the stairs. 'Hello! Hello? Miss Ruby – it's Charles.' He raps at the door. 'Hello?'

I feel my grip tighten around the knife. *What if he's in on it? What if it was him all along? An inside job like the hijackers that got Claire's father-in-law?*

Ruby pulls the curtain across. We can see the long, curved glint of a panga in the moonlight. His knife is much bigger than mine.

We stand there together, looking at each other, trying to work out if we can trust the guy.

'Of course he has a panga,' Ruby points out. 'They all carry them around. And he's come down here expecting intruders.'

'True,' I concede.

We don't have much choice, gotta go with our gut. We unlock the door, and Charles doesn't kill us.

'Hello, madams, are you okay?' He looks through to the cottage, checking that nobody else is inside.

'We're okay, we're okay – but there's somebody out there. More than one.'

'I couldn't find anybody,' Charles says. 'I went all around the gardens – there's no one here. But maybe you should come to the main house. I think you will feel safer in there.'

'Yep, let's go.' We grab our things and follow him up the path.

We lie awake with the lights on in the Kirbys' guestroom for the rest of the night, my rage slowly morphing into a fatigue-dulled terror.

By sunrise, the fear's gone. It seems like an overreaction. The dew shimmers on the lawn; the ducks paddle across the pond. That said, I'm shaken and exhausted as we drive back to the house to clock on for the next session with Walt.

And when we get inside, there's more drama to deal with.

The door to my room is closed, and we can hear the vacuum cleaner going. Ruby and I look at each other. It's odd. Esther never closes the doors when she's in the bedrooms. It's an unspoken rule of the house – a demonstration or assurance of honesty, I guess.

I open it cautiously, hoping we're not about to walk in on something we shouldn't, but in no way prepared for the absolute shit tip we encounter.

A layer of white dust blankets everything. Broken pieces of plasterboard lie scattered across the bed, my desk, the floor. Chunks of wood sit atop a pile of swept-up dirt and cobwebs. The painting of a gerenuk (from the Somali word *garanuug* meaning 'giraffe-necked' antelope) has fallen off the wall and lies smashed in the corner. Goddammit, I loved that painting. Such a funny little creature, standing on its hind legs to eat the leaves off an acacia tree.

Esther freezes, wide-eyed, dustpan and brush in hand. She stares at me in anticipatory terror, like a child caught trying to cover up smashed china.

I haven't quite figured out what's happened yet but know enough to shut the door quickly behind us so that no one else need know. We don't need Walt in here thinking someone's fired a cannon through the window. We don't need Marguerite shrieking about the filth on her duvet.

Esther says nothing, but slowly raises a finger to the ceiling. We look up at a hole the size of a bathtub in the gypsum board and see four sets of eyes peering back down from the darkness. As my eyes adjust to the light, I make out James's and David's faces. Two other men are huddled beside them. One of them I recognise is the *fundi* (handyman) Michael Kirby arranges for us, to fix bits and pieces around the house. The fourth guy must be his offsider. Turns out they're up there to repair the hot water tank, which has been leaking. They appear to be shitting themselves.

'Hello, Kirsten, hello, Ruby!' David says, nervously. 'Sorry, *pole* – we had an accident.'

'But is everyone okay? Nobody's hurt?' Ruby asks.

'No, we are fine!' James assures us. 'David landed on the bed!'

We look back at Esther, and explode with laughter. We can't stop laughing. Then Esther laughs, and James and David and the *fundi* and his mate laugh, and I feel terrible that these guys were bracing themselves for a serve.

'Let's get this all cleaned up before anyone else sees it,' I say. And together we sweep and vacuum and pick up the pieces and laugh until the room is back together, and it's only if you look up that you see a big hole in the ceiling and wonder who or what fell through it.

Later that afternoon, I hear Michael Kirby yelling in the kitchen. I assume he's here to talk about the intruders on his property last night. But he's not.

He's tearing strips off the *fundi* and his offsider, and James and David. What-the-bloody-hell-were-they-doing and how-utterly-useless-could-they-be and how-many-times-does-he-have-to-tell-them.

A hot fury ignites in my stomach and works its way up my throat. I find myself storming through the house until I'm standing in front of him, tingling with rage.

'Hey! There's no need to speak to people like that! It was an accident. These things happen,' I say.

'This is none of your business,' Michael says, as seemingly shocked to have been spoken to like this by a young woman as I'm shocked at myself.

'Actually, it is my business,' I say. 'It was my room. No harm's been done. No one was hurt. It's all cleaned up and we'll be able to fix the ceiling.'

'Does Marguerite know yet?'

'Not yet. We'll tell her when she gets home.'

'You just wait and see how happy she is about it,' he wags his finger in my face.

'I'm sure she won't be happy about it but I'll explain what happened.'

Michael glares like he wants to punch me. I glare back, daring him to.

'Righto, then. You take care of it.'

'I will.'

'And tell Marguerite I'm done helping you lot.'

'Okey-dokey. See ya,' I say, faux cheery, waving him out the door, enjoying – just a bit – that I've made him as angry as he's made me.

The staff are silent, staring. I realise I might have put them in an awkward position – maybe they'll face repercussions for my little outburst, and it may seem like they're partly responsible for the transgression.

'Don't worry about it, guys, I'll sort it out with Marguerite.'

Still, they just stare. I realise they might also think I've been terribly disrespectful, even if it was in their defence.

'I'm really sorry about all that,' I say.

Ruby and I are stoned. She managed to score a joint at the dress-up party and stashed it for 'emergency use'. We've just shared it outside after dinner, standing between dew-damp sheets on the washing line, gazing up at an enormous full moon. After the night of waking terror, and the incident with the plumbers and Michael Kirby, and another long day with Walt, we felt we could do with some help unwinding.

Marguerite is out. Jade's on duty. Why not?

When we go back inside, all the details of our small, bizarre world are suddenly more consequential.

Walt is sitting in his green velvet wingback chair in front of a roaring fire in the hearth. He's holding a crystal whisky tumbler full of soda water stained amber with Angostura bitters; he thinks it's Scotch. He's smiling and laughing and shaking his head at us. He's wearing his paisley silk robe – the one Sean wore to the dress-up party.

Ruby and I are sitting on the couch across from him, in flannelette pyjamas. It's not a couch, actually. It's a 'sofa'. It's one of those rosewood ones, with lattice panels on either end, covered in beige upholstery with a moss and maroon floral pattern. A burgundy Persian rug is spread across the parquetry floor between us. Chiku stretches out with her tummy towards the fire.

Jade looks at us from her chair beside Walt. We blink back, smiling like dolts. She knows we're high.

We say we'll watch Walt for Jade while she has a shower. We don't really mind – in the state we're in, it doesn't feel like work. And Walt is having a grand old time. He finds our Australian accents very amusing. He thinks we're at a raucous dinner party.

'Go on, then – why don't you pair sing something for us?' he dares.

'Righto!' Ruby says. She pulls the opera CD out of the player and frisbees it across the room. Walt loves that move almost as much as I do. We've already heard the overture from *The Marriage of Figaro* three times tonight.

Ruby plugs her laptop into the stereo, and I turn the lights down until it's just the soft glow of flickering firelight.

'Oooooh,' Walt coos, all camp and corny, leaning forward in his chair, 'this is starting to feel very cabaret!'

A swirling, swelling string section starts up. I recognise it immediately as the introduction to 'A Whole New World' from Disney's *Aladdin*.

'Yes!' I scream. 'Great choice!' I know just where Ruby is going with this.

We push the coffee table to the side, turning the space into a stage. Ruby takes the part of Aladdin, and I sing Jasmine's lines.

And Walt *bloody loves it*. He's clapping and laughing and cheering. 'Very good, I say, that's very good indeed!'

We drop to our knees and pull up the end of the Persian rug, steer it around like we're on our 'magic carpet ride', peer over the edges in mock terror. Neither of us is hitting the notes; it's all just atonal wailing, now with Chiku howling along, though whether in protest or solidarity I can't be sure.

Jade emerges from the bathroom just as we bring in some interpretive dance. I attempt a somersault. Ruby does a cartwheel and knocks a vase off the bookshelf. The fallen flowers become props – we tuck them into Walt's collar and carry on, crescendoing through to the end then bringing it right back down for the gentle, intimate finale, with Ruby slowly lowering herself into the splits, while I bend over and look back at Walt through my legs.

Walt gives us a standing ovation as we collapse in a sweaty heap, out of breath. 'Bravo!' he says. 'Bravo!' He tosses the roses from his neck at our feet.

Fiona would have an absolute fit if she knew about this.

'What the actual fuck?' Jade says, standing at the doorway with her wet hair wrapped up in a towel. She puts her hands on her hips in mock outrage, as though we're naughty children, but is smiling, appreciating the fun.

'We're broadening Walt's musical horizons,' Ruby says, lining up the next track on her laptop.

'It's Aussie hip-hop, Walt!' we shriek over the Hilltop Hoods.

'It's bloody awful, is what it is!' he says, wincing as we garble-rap the lyrics to 'The Nosebleed Section'.

'Alright, guys,' says Jade, sensing it's probably time to shut this down. 'Bedtime, I reckon?'

I guess there are some cultural barriers that can't be crossed.

Next morning, head a little foggy, still humming the refrain from 'The Nosebleed Section', I'm kneeling on the tiles in Walt's bathroom, having just helped him dry off after a shower. The cold, hard floor presses sharply against my bones as the old man sits wrapped in a towel on the chair in front of me. I pat down the slack between his knees, rub creams all over his body, and change a bandaid on his elbow where he nicked it on a rosebush.

After making sure I've wiped out all the moisture from between his toes so that the webbing doesn't rot and split, I notice that his nails need to be filed back. They're starting to curl into the skin; they must be pressing against the end of his shoes.

'Just bring your left foot forward a little for me, would you please, Walt?' I ask, cradling it beneath his heel.

'No!' he spits from nowhere, kicking out so that I lose my balance and throw a hand down to steady myself. It lands on the pointy end of the nail file. 'Get your hands off me!' he snarls.

A reflexive anger rises sharply from the pit of my stomach, partly from the pain and partly from the unexpected nastiness. I push it back down, reason it away. *He doesn't mean it*, I remind myself. *It's the disease.*

I take a deep breath, pull the file out of my hand, and cautiously lean away from him as I wipe the blood onto the bathmat. I'm in a vulnerable position — he could kick me in the teeth if he wanted to. 'Please, Walt, look how long they're getting! You'll get an ingrown toenail if we don't sort them out soon. We don't want that.'

'Don't you dare touch me, you nasty little bitch!' he says, pulling both feet back under the chair. 'I've had a gutful of all you people and your constant interfering.'

The viciousness feels too personal, so ungrateful that it stings. I wonder whether this is, in fact, a moment of clarity — a genuine response to what's been happening around him, not just a symptom of his unravelling mind.

'Okay,' I say, defeated. 'We'll leave it for another time. Come on, let's get you dressed.'

Walt stands up from his chair, clutching the ends of the towel together at his waist, and takes a menacing step towards me. 'I don't need your help – get out!' he says. 'Go on, get out of my bloody sight!' The venom in his voice belies his frail, shrivelled body.

I leave him alone in his bedroom. I sit at the end of the living-room couch, so that I can see down the hallway to his door. On the monitor I watch him pacing, opening and closing drawers, clutching his head, muttering to no one.

An hour later he emerges, agitated and disorientated, wearing his dirty clothes. He looks distraught. 'Excuse me,' he says, holding out a scrap of scribbled paper, 'could you help me make a phone call? I need to speak with my mother.'

He is desperately lost and, in the weeks that follow, only becomes more so.

'Absolutely not,' says Fiona over Skype.

I've taken Walt in for his monthly check-up with Dr Andrews, who suggested – on being apprised of Walt's deteriorating mental state and increasingly aggressive behaviour – that we consider placing him on a low dose of Risperidone, an antipsychotic sometimes prescribed to dementia patients.

'He is not to be put on any form of psychiatric drug whatsoever,' Fiona says. 'It's bad for his heart, for one thing.'

'But Fiona, his ECG results are excellent,' I say. 'Dr Andrews says it's the best he's seen Walt – physically, at least – since he came back to Kenya. He can't believe how much he's improved. All his blood results too. Everything is looking great.'

'No. I don't care. We saw what happened last time, with the Citalopram. It's too great a risk.'

'Fiona,' I beg, 'we need to try something. He's becoming unmanageable. It's dangerous for him *and* us. Yesterday he threatened Patrick with a kitchen knife because he wouldn't open the gate for him!'

'Well, that's because he's feeling trapped. And he *is* trapped, when you think about it. He obviously feels that on some level. He's very perceptive, you know. You must tell Patrick to open the gate for him next time!'

'And then what? Just let him walk all the way out to the main road?'

'He won't get that far. Just let him stroll for a bit and he'll come back soon enough. Follow at a safe distance to keep an eye on him. Look, I am very aware that we need to do something to improve things, but I think we should take a step back first to try to see what's gone wrong. Has there been a change in his routine or sleep patterns? If Marguerite is keeping him up at night, she might have to sleep in the study. Have you all been on top of avoiding triggers?'

'Yes, Fiona,' I say, exasperated. 'As much as we possibly can – but we can't control everything. We can't stop other dogs in the neighbourhood from barking. We can't stop passing cars from beeping their horns. We stick to the routine, we stick to sleep patterns. None of it makes any difference. I don't know what to tell you. He is highly anxious pretty much all the time these days. He's not happy.'

'You know,' Fiona says, sounding like a new theory has dawned on her, 'it could be his prostate playing up. If he's not emptying his bladder properly, he's at risk of getting a UTI and that's known to cause sudden changes in behaviour in the elderly, especially dementia sufferers.'

Annoyingly, I know she's right. My family went through the same thing with my grandmother. She'd have sudden episodes of severe confusion, which would be miraculously cleared up with a course of antibiotics. There's some bizarre connection between bladder health and cognition in the elderly.

'There are some sample pots in the cupboard,' Fiona tells me. 'Get him to wee in one for you tomorrow and take it in for testing, just to be sure. It'll be a bit tricky, though – you'll need to get it midstream.'

Early the next morning, I hide behind Walt's bathroom door. I wait to hear that splash. Then I dart in with a plastic jar to intercept his piss.

Walt's wee isn't great.

There's no sign of a UTI but there *is* too much creatine in it, which Fiona says means his kidneys might not be processing protein properly. This, she says, is likely to be the cause of his recent distress and difficult behaviour, as confusion is one of the symptoms of kidney dysfunction. So, we are to cut red meat out of his diet entirely, and in addition to having his urine sampled we are to start getting his bloods done twice a week. *Walt loves steak and hates needles – this is going to be fun.*

Fiona has me enter the results into a spreadsheet, including all past results from his medical file, so that we can generate graphs and identify any long-term trends. Within a week or so, Walt's creatine levels drop and he remains UTI free – but Fiona now has an entire data set to play with. She decides we should 'be more responsive' to his metabolic profile with strategic dietary adjustments.

When his blood glucose creeps up by a fraction of a percentage point, Fiona warns of impending diabetes and tells us to cut down on sweets. When Walt's 'hs-CRP' results go up – whatever that means – we're told to cut back on salt. When his phosphate goes up, she worries it's another sign of failing kidneys, and tells us to cut down on cheese and milk. But she doesn't want him to become deficient in calcium, so we are to introduce more broccoli and almonds to compensate. But then she worries about the almonds getting stuck in his teeth and causing cavities or gum disease, so we have to stop that and reintroduce dairy products. Unfortunately, natural Greek yoghurt is the only type that's high in calcium but low in phosphorus, and Walt won't eat it unless it's covered in honey, so we're back to fretting over blood glucose again.

Marguerite is getting the shits as she tries to keep up with our constantly changing dietary demands. I don't blame her. Fiona refuses to communicate with her about anything to do with Walt's health, so she's being told what she can feed her husband by three unrelated Australian girls fifty years her junior, and none of it is making him any happier.

Physically we have Walt humming like a fine-tuned vintage car (albeit one being slowly eaten away by rust), but despite his five-star piss and first-class nutrition plan, his violence and aggression increases.

I'm sitting on the patio with Walt one morning, reading the papers. So far, so good. He took his tablets at breakfast without protest. He even brushed his teeth of his own accord. We sit, with the birds and the sunshine and the breeze.

Then a slow but steady rhythm begins to permeate the air. Chiku's ears prick up. A drum beat. Growing stronger, closer. Coming over the fence. Then voices – whooping, cheering. Singing?

Walt hasn't seemed to notice yet, so I duck inside to where Jade – on back-up duty – is sitting in her room on her laptop.

'Are you playing music?' I ask, and she shakes her head. 'Can you hear that?'

She looks down, eyes shut, concentrating for a moment. Shakes her head again. 'Nope?'

From inside the house, we can't hear anything.

'Never mind,' I say, racing back out to the patio. A newspaper sits draped over the arm of Walt's empty chair. He's gone. *Shit, shit, shit.*

I hear Patrick at the gate. '*Pole, bwana, pole* – I am not allowed.'

I run out the front.

'What do you mean "not allowed"!?' Walt yells. '*I* bloody well say what is and is not allowed around here. Now open that bloody gate at once!'

The noise is growing closer: it's a mob of some kind, that much seems clear.

Patrick looks at me, panicked.

Walt looks at me, angry. 'Is this your *askari*? Tell him to let me out at once – I want to see what the hell is going on out there.' He's got that look on his face. Teeth clenched. Jaw set. There'll be no talking him out of this one.

'It's okay, Patrick, open the gates,' I tell him. *Fuck it. If this is what Fiona thinks we should do when Walt gets wound up, let's do it.*

Patrick unlocks the padlock, loosens the chain, pulls the gate open. Walt marches through and charges off down the road towards the noise, Chiku trotting along beside him, tail wagging.

'See if you can get James, please, Patrick?' I say. 'Just tell him to follow us, in case I need his help. And leave the gates unlocked, so we can get back in easily.'

'Yes, madam, yes, yes,' Patrick says, running off to find James in the garden.

I follow Walt at a safe distance, several paces behind. This is much further than Fiona's three-metre rule, but I'm making an executive decision – he doesn't want to be shadowed right now.

The drums are rumbling, the voices undulating in some kind of call and response. The pattern puts me at ease – it sounds dramatic but not aggressive, and suggests an organised demonstration of some kind, not a riot.

Walt rounds the corner ahead of me and slows. Chiku runs a few yards ahead, barks, and circles back beside Walt, where they both just stand and watch. As I catch up, I see a mass of hundreds of people in bright orange shirts, marching down the main road. They wave banners and balloons, blow horns and whistles, sing and dance and twirl.

I stand beside Walt. He's already calmer, but slightly baffled by the spectacle. 'What on earth do they want?'

'It's an AIDS awareness march,' I say, catching sight of a sign that reads 'HIV – towards zero'.

'Oh, right,' he says. 'Yes. The Church has a lot to answer for when it comes to all that business, what with their anti-prophylactic preaching.'

'*Jambo, mzee!*' a couple of women at the edge of the procession shout to Walt. Then a whole group of them join in. '*Jambo, mzee! Jambo, jambo!*'

A young guy comes over, shakes Walt's hand and puts a sticker on his collar, saying something in Swahili that Walt laughs at. '*Asante!*' he says.

After a few minutes, the tail end of the march passes us, and a long, slow snake of honking traffic drags behind it.

'Can I interest you in a pot of tea, Walt?' I ask, wanting to get him back home while he's still smiling, before the frustration of delayed motorists changes his mood.

'Oh-ho, I never say no to a pot of tea!' he says, whistling for Chiku to follow as we make our way back to the iron gates, where Patrick, James and Ruby are all anxiously waiting.

The day Walt chases me with the nine iron feels like it should be a turning point. The moment when our physical safety is so seriously compromised that something has to be done. I tell Fiona how the morning had started smoothly enough, but took a turn when the diesel generator kicked in during a power cut. How Walt had gone through to the garage to investigate the sound of the engine, then seen the keys to the Peugeot sitting on the kitchen window ledge. How I'd snatched them up just in time, and how he'd become enraged, grabbing one of the golf clubs from the bag that had been left leaning against the deep freeze.

Marguerite is getting especially anxious about being responsible should anything happen to us. She begs Fiona to do something. Fiona refuses. She says that our poor control of his 'triggers' is letting us down – the car keys should never have been left on the ledge, the golf clubs should have been put away. She says that Marguerite is to blame for most of his upsets.

I can't stand it any longer. I arrange a Skype meeting to discuss what can be done one day while Walt's down having a nap.

'I don't know why you didn't just show Dad his passport,' Fiona says, when Marguerite tells her about the time Walt became so furious at not being able to fly out of Kenya that he refused to eat lunch.

Poor Marguerite. That woman just cannot win. She fires back: 'You said *not* to let him see that sort of thing! You said it would "set him off" about having all his documents in order!'

'Yes, but if he *asks* for something and you can't distract him from it, then you *should* give it to him,' Fiona says. 'In fact, you girls should mock up an e-ticket for a flight to England and keep it with his passport at all times. You'll have to print out a new one every few days, updated so the dates line up.'

'This is getting impossibly tricky to keep up with,' Marguerite says. 'And it's getting very unsafe around here, for me and the girls and the staff. You know, I'm legally responsible for everyone here – what if something happens, if somebody gets hurt?'

'Dad won't hurt anyone,' Fiona says.

Ruby, Jade and I all look at each other. We know otherwise.

'He *might*, Fiona!' says Marguerite. 'Dr Andrews says there's a drug called Risperidone we can try.'

'Marguerite, you know you are *not* to change his medication without consulting me and the Trust!'

'I understand that, but you simply cannot leave us in this situation. Something must be done.' She storms out of the room.

I really don't want to get involved in this debate, but I want even less to be attacked by Walt wielding a blunt object. I've done a bit of research, and it is true that people with Lewy body dementia in particular are sensitive to antipsychotic drugs, and that they can come with undesirable side effects. Even so, we're at the point where I think it's worth at least a trial of the drug, to see if it helps. So, I enter the fray. 'Listen, Fiona, I really do think we have to try *something*. He's getting out of control. First we had the garden hoe incident. Then the golf club. He's getting worse.'

'You should have just given him the keys.'

'I did in the end! He nearly drove through the back fence! You can't seriously suggest letting him behind the wheel is safe. There are other people here too, you know.'

The bed alarm goes off. Ruby and Jade go to check on Walt.

With just me on the line, Fiona relents. 'Listen, I've got an old friend who's just moved back to Nairobi. Suzanne. She's a psychiatric nurse, running some sort of mental health clinic there. Marguerite should remember her from when we were at school together. I'll ask her to go around and assess the situation, see how Dad's going. It would be good to get an independent opinion anyway. I'm not sure I trust Dr Andrews when he's only got Marguerite in his ear.'

'That sounds great,' I say. 'Tell her to come as soon as she can.'

As I hang up, I see Walt through the window, marching back and forth between the three locked cars in the driveway, Ruby by his side as she desperately tries to convince him to come inside.

Fiona's friend Suzanne comes around to assess Walt, and he thinks Marguerite is his mother.

We're sitting out on the patio when he beckons us into the living room with a finger held to his lips, while Marguerite is sorting through files at her desk in the study. 'My poor old mother through there,' he whispers. 'She's gone completely barmy – thinks *I'm* her *husband!*'

'Oh dear,' I reply, 'she must be getting a bit confused in her old age.'

'I've tried to set her straight but every time I tell her I'm her son, she insists her name is "Marguerite" and says we're married!' He holds out a Post-it note that has been stuck to her desk since her last visit to Dr Andrews. It reads 'ADD LIFE TO YEARS – NOT YEARS TO LIFE'.

'Jolly good advice, I'd say!' Walt says, not realising it's for him, not her.

'I suppose there's no harm in letting her think you're her husband, don't you?' Suzanne says, immediately seeing the need to play along.

'Yes, I think you're probably right,' he agrees. 'I don't want to fuss the poor dear anymore.'

Marguerite calls out from the study – some tennis is on TV. 'Are you coming to watch the tennis, darling? One of those big black American girls is playing. I never know which one it is. Mars or Venus? Or is it Saturn? My *word* she can give that ball a thwack! *Ooof!*'

Suzanne raises her eyebrows at me. I get the sense she's come across people like Marguerite before – that it's a British thing. A Prince Philip kind of thing.

'Coming, dear!' Walt calls back. Then to Suzanne and me, with a conspiratorial wink, 'I think this is going to be a very, *very* tricky day.'

Suzanne sees right away that Walt's dementia is much more severe than Fiona will admit. She sits with him for an hour, running through some basic cognitive screening tests to come up with an overall assessment. 'I'd place him somewhere between moderate and advanced phase dementia,' she says to me. 'Closer to advanced, really. He's mixing up family members, experiencing hallucinations, becoming aggressive when he gets frustrated – this is certainly the point in time at which many people would start to consider psychiatric medication.'

'So do you know much about Risperidone?' I ask. 'That's what the doctor has suggested – but Fiona's dead against it.'

'Look, it's very commonly prescribed and quite effective. I can't see any reason not to try it out. You should just start at a low dose and see how he responds. It's for his sake as much as yours – he's experiencing quite bad anxiety, and being wound up like that so much of the time isn't good for anyone. It's no wonder he's starting to lash out.'

'Yeah, we've been trying to explain that to Fiona, but she doesn't get it. She's not around enough to see how bad it gets.'

'I'll talk to her about it,' Suzanne says. 'She trusts me. I don't know what's going on between her and Marguerite, but I don't want to get involved.'

'Trust me,' I say, 'don't.'

'Honestly, Walt could not possibly be any better looked after. The way he's being cared for here is beyond gold standard. To be in his own home, with this many people around to monitor him – really, there is nothing more anyone can do.'

Suzanne, as it turns out, knows better than anyone just how lucky Walt is. She's recently set up an NGO to provide affordable mental health services in a country where, understandably, the whole concept of 'mental health' is poorly understood and takes a back seat to the more tangible concerns of physical diseases and hardships. The clinic runs from a tiny shack on the north-western edge of the city and is open to the public twice a week. Word of the clinic has spread, and hundreds of people now travel hours – some on foot – to be treated for afflictions ranging from depression and anxiety through to schizophrenia, Alzheimer's and epilepsy. Until it opened, Nairobi only had one dedicated mental health facility: the notorious Mathari Hospital, a concrete asylum where chronic under-resourcing and overcrowding meant patients were routinely neglected, exposed to abuse and deprivation, and very rarely – if ever – received the care they needed.

One report, by the Kenya National Commission on Human Rights, estimated there were 8.5 million Kenyans with untreated mental health issues. Suzanne wants to change that. In addition to providing diagnosis, treatment and support to patients and their families, she's working to increase awareness of mental health issues more generally. Each year, she offers nursing scholarships to train counsellors who can then take their skills back to their communities and establish outreach clinics of their own. Her passion is palpable – this isn't some half-hearted, do-gooder effort, the sort of 'dig-a-well-and-go-home' charity that gives so many foreign aid projects a bad name. Suzanne sees the organisation as the beginning of something much bigger and longer term: the foundation for a better mental healthcare system throughout the country.

'You should come along and see what it's all about some time,' she says.

I will, I say, I will.

I'm on back-up duty one morning, sitting in the computer room at the Club. Ruby is having morning tea with Walt in the garden room, while Marguerite has a round of golf on the course next door. I get a Skype message from Fiona:

Hiya, urgent. Can u talk?

It's always urgent with her. I take my laptop into the booth and dial in.

'Okay, so,' she says, 'I've had a good chat with Suzanne. And she's convinced me it's worth trialling the Risperidone with Dad. But he will need to be *very* closely monitored – and only on the smallest dose, 0.25 milligrams. For no more than two weeks to begin with.'

'Okay,' I say, relieved she's at least come around to trying something. 'But is two weeks going to be enough to know whether it helps? I thought it took several weeks for that sort of thing to kick in.'

'Look, it's a serious psychiatric drug, and Dad is very sensitive to any kind of drug, as you know. And it increases the likelihood of stroke. So we need to be sure it's well worth the risk if we're going to use it.'

'Okay.'

'Dr Andrews has written a prescription. Marguerite isn't to know about it.'

'Well, I won't be lying to her if she asks about it,' I say. Fiona clearly needs some reminding that I'm not getting dragged into that shit again.

'Just please be very careful with him once you start with it,' she says.

'Yes, of course we will,' I promise. I understand her reluctance – I wouldn't want my dad put onto unnecessary drugs either, I don't think anyone should be. But I really do believe we need to at least try this.

When I head through to the garden room to give Ruby the update, Magda has joined her and Walt. 'Kirsten! Hello! I was just telling Ruby – did you see on the noticeboard? There is a fun run in the Karura Forest in a few weeks. A corporate thing. You girls should go! It is lovely through there! Yes, because you know there are the walking paths, but it *is* a bit too dangerous to go on your own even during the day because of the bandits, as it were, but with all the people and a big event like this it will be very good. Don't you agree, Walt?'

'Oh yes, very good,' he says, spooning more jam onto his scone before Ruby can stop him. I don't think he's followed anything since 'noticeboard'.

'I will put your names down on the list, yes?' Magda asks. 'It is just one-thousand shillings to enter.'

'Jeez, Magda, are you getting commissions on the people you sign up or something?' I tease.

'No.' She frowns, confused. 'A commission? But why would that be?'

'Never mind, it was a joke,' I say.

'Sure, sign us up,' Ruby says. 'I'm sure Jade won't mind covering for us that morning.'

'Okay, well, I'm just off to pick up some things from the pharmacy for the *mzee*,' I say. 'I'll see you back at home.'

But I see something curious when I go down to the shops after picking up Walt's new prescription.

It's Marguerite. Sitting at a café. With an African woman. *Wasn't she meant to be playing golf?*

'Kirsten! *Yoohooo!* Over here!' she waves me over. 'This is my friend Deborah.' Ahhhhh, so this is the famous Deborah.

'Hi, how are you?' Deborah smiles, shakes my hand. She has a slight British accent, short cropped hair, and is stylish as heck in a bold print dress and matching headband.

'Hi! Good thanks, nice to meet you,' I say. She looks about forty-something. *Why is she friends with Marguerite? Why is Marguerite friends with her?* Maybe I'm the one being ignorant, or unfair to both women. It's perfectly feasible that they could enjoy one another's company.

'We thought we'd have some cake, given how well I went at golf today,' Marguerite says, pointing to the remaining crumbs on the plate in front of her. 'Only nine holes, but I was very quick.' I look at her shoes. They're not wet with dew. She doesn't look pink in the face. I don't think she's been playing golf this morning at all.

'Marguerite loves telling me how well she goes at golf,' Deborah teases.

'Now, what are you doing here anyway? Shouldn't you be at the Club with Walt?' Marguerite suddenly becomes terse.

'Oh, I'm ... ah ...' I hesitate, unsure whether to tell her here and now about the Risperidone. I decide it's best not to. 'I've come to pick up some more of Walt's pills.'

'Well, run along then. You ought to get back to the other girl. In case she needs help.'

Marguerite's not normally this bossy. I can't tell whether she's showing off in front of her friend, or trying to get rid of me.

I open the newspapers the next morning to find I won't be going to Dadaab any time soon.

Two Spanish aid workers, with Médicins Sans Frontières, have been kidnapped – grabbed as they left a health centre set up to treat the thousand Somalis who stream across the border each day, fleeing famine and the Al-Shabaab militants who won't let Western aid groups into its territory to feed them. The women's Kenyan driver was shot and wounded in the attack, the first one to have occurred inside the confines of the camp.

NGOs are pulling out all over the shop; even the UNHCR is considering recalling staff. Everyone is rattled. Alex emails me to say the FilmAid project is on hold indefinitely.

The whole north-east part of the country is facing a security crisis now – only a few weeks ago, a quadriplegic Frenchwoman was kidnapped from her holiday home at Lamu. Somali gunmen pulled up out the front of her house in a speedboat, then carried her off without her wheelchair or cancer medication. She died in captivity a few weeks later. A month before that, a British man was shot dead and his wife taken from a resort on Kiwayu Island, further north. Aside from the obvious human cost, the economic hit to the region will be devastating. The Lamu archipelago, an ancient Swahili settlement with a number of significant historical and archaeological sites, is one of Kenya's most popular tourist attractions – now it's a tropical gauntlet.

Later in the morning I get a text from Suzanne asking if I'd like to visit her clinic today.

I drive the Peugeot out to Lower Kabete Road, where I find a tiny cement block with a tin roof, on a small grass plot across the road from a post office. Close to a hundred people are sitting around the building, some waiting on the verandah, others resting in the shade of the trees. Some left their homes at dawn, travelling hundreds of kilometres to reach this place they have heard about – the place that helps 'the troubled'.

One young woman has brought her older brother with her: she says that every time she cooks the family dinner, he snatches the pot from the *jiko* and tips it down the toilet, claiming the food is poisoned. Another man has brought his fourteen-year-old daughter, who's been disappearing in the night, setting off for Nairobi from their village on foot. Friends and neighbours sometimes catch her along the way; at other times she simply turns up again in the morning, refusing to say where she's been or what she's been doing. Her father worries about her ending up pregnant – or worse. Yet another has brought his mother. Only sixty-something, she's becoming very forgetful. 'She only talks about people from the past,' he says. 'I think she is seeing ghosts.'

Suzanne takes me inside, where the clinic is separated into two rooms: one where patients sit for consultations with a psychiatric nurse, the other a makeshift dispensary, where trainees and counsellors are filling prescriptions and manually counting out pills. She introduces me to Steven, a thirteen-year-old boy with a seemingly permanent smile who is helping her manage the waiting list.

He has epilepsy and was kicked out of school because of his fits – the villagers thought he was possessed by demons.

'I know epilepsy isn't really a "mental health" issue,' Suzanne tells me. 'But it's so poorly understood here, we're really the only people who can help him.'

All Steven needs to manage his condition is a one-cent tablet, phenobarbital, taken once a day. Phenobarbital has been used in low doses as an anticonvulsant for epileptics for over a hundred years. Though a number of other drugs have since superseded it, it remains cheap and highly effective, and is endorsed by the World Health Organization, making it a particularly suitable drug for the developing world – where 80 per cent of the globe's epilepsy sufferers live. The problem is, it's a narcotic that's subject to strict international controls and regulations, so not too many pharmacies around here will stock it. Suzanne has sourced all of her medications at cost price or cheaper through pharmaceutical companies and only charges patients here what they can afford.

Since he's been medicated, Steven has only had one seizure. If it wasn't for Suzanne's clinic, this kid might have been denied an education. But now he's back at school. 'I'm going to be an engineer,' he tells me proudly.

'He probably will be – he gets jolly good marks,' Suzanne says.

Over the course of the morning I meet a number of grateful clients – some with great success stories, others still works in progress. There's a young woman with schizophrenia who hasn't had an episode since taking her medication but is having troubling side effects: stiffness and cramping in her neck, severe enough that her head rests on a permanent tilt. She's on a 'typical antipsychotic', first used in the 1950s but since mostly out of favour due to this sort of Parkinsonism and similar adverse effects. The clinic has sourced her a newer drug, and are counselling her and her carer – her brother – on how to phase it in.

There's a teenage boy with depression who has made great progress – every two weeks he comes for talk therapy. At first he wouldn't even make eye contact; today, for the first time, he laughed.

The man with the forgetful mother is told that she most likely has Alzheimer's. That she is seeing ghosts, in a way, but that there's no drug they can give her to stop that. The staff tell him to keep her in her village, where she's surrounded by the people and places she knows best. That as long as she's safe and supervised, she'll be okay. The man seems dissatisfied. He leaves saying he will consult a *mganga* – a witch doctor – instead.

The nurses count pills and give injections. I help Steven tick names off the list and watch the crowd outside shrink. But there aren't enough hours in the day; the clinic doesn't have time to see everybody. There are still a few dozen tortured souls who've missed out. They put their names at the top of the list for next time, then shuffle off on their long journeys home, back to the slums, or the townships, or the country.

Suzanne hates having to turn anyone away. 'But you can only do what you can,' she says with a sigh, sweeping the last of the red dirt off the long grey verandah.

On the way home, I stop in at the other end of the spectrum of fortune in Nairobi: East Africa's first-ever KFC, a drive-through and dine-in restaurant at the Junction Mall on Ngong Road, the shopping centre closest to Sarah and Jack's place. Robert's been involved with helping get it set up, so I decide to head down for the opening.

The queue is over a hundred people long. They've lined up for hours to sample the Colonel's secret herbs and spices. The crowd is made up of fashionable teenagers on school holidays, women in business suits, and working dads with children who fill the booths in the diner.

I strike up a conversation with the man in front of me, Huzefa. He works for a global telco and reckons the huge turnout is the result of 'major buzz on social networking sites'. There's been virtually no official advertising for the event, just word-of-mouth gossip and net-savvy Kenyans spewing status updates and tweets in the lead-up.

The Nairobi store is just the first of dozens planned across Kenya, Uganda, Ethiopia and Tanzania over the next few years. I note the paradox: that the fast-food industry is taking off here while in other parts of the region people starve. Huzefa has a different take. He expresses frustration at being pitied by Westerners for the perceived hopelessness of his homeland. He hates that no one's covering the country's own efforts to help those affected by the drought in the north, and tells me that a 'Kenyans4Kenya' campaign currently saturating FM airwaves and social media has so far raised more than 240 million shillings. Much of that money's come in ten-shilling donations transferred by the mobile phone–based transaction service M-Pesa: a Kenyan innovation, and the precursor to Apple Pay. I take Huzefa's point. His countrymen buy badges and turn out in their thousands to send off truckloads of donated food to Turkana, but all we see on the international pages are pictures of dead cows and thirsty kids.

That's the story, I realise, and I successfully pitch it to a news outlet back home.

It's a tiny little thing, but it feels like it counts as some sort of an accomplishment.

Fiona's back again. She's staying for two weeks. She wants to do an overall health assessment of Walt, see for herself how he's handling the Risperidone, and overhaul the caring regime if necessary.

When she arrives, she notices the new curtains, and that the lion is gone from the wall, and develops a theory: Marguerite is planning to sell the house and move Walt into a local aged care home. She decides *that's* what Marguerite's friend Deborah is all about: she's a real estate agent. I'll never find out if she is right about that.

Two days into her visit, I have an afternoon off. I spend it in the computer room at the Club filing my KFC story. I've gone out of my way to be inconspicuous, walking back to the house, so that I can slip in through the gates quietly and not trigger Walt with the sound of a car pulling into the driveway. I creep around to the side of the house, wanting to come in through the sunroom instead of the front door, in an effort not to disturb him. But lunch must have run later than usual – I realise too late that they're still in the dining room, and the door through to the sunroom is open.

Walt spots me. I freeze.

'Who the devil is that?' he demands.

'Hi, Walt – only me!' I call cheerily, hoping the moment might pass him by.

Fiona shoots me a filthy look. She jumps up from her seat and pulls the door shut.

I'm livid. My entire being goes white-hot as I quietly, violently rage. I swing my fists, stamp my feet, roar silently at the sky, flip her the bird through the closed door with such force I actually strain a muscle in my hand.

Then I turn to see Esther and David staring at me from the clothesline outside my window.

I stare back for a moment, mortified to have been caught in such a childish act. Then we all collapse into laughter.

'These people are fucking *crazy*!' I hiss at them from the doorway.

'So are you!' David points out. Fair call.

I remain trapped in the sunroom until Fiona has put Walt down for his nap.

'This can't go on,' I tell her when she comes back down the hallway. 'You just cannot treat us like this. We live here. We need to be able to relax when we're not "on duty" with Walt. You can't control every little bump and squeak in the house!'

'I know, I know,' she says, stopping short of actually apologising, 'but Dad's comfort is the whole point of you all being here, so we're going to have to come up with an alternative arrangement.'

'Like what?'

'Can you and Ruby stay with your friends from the High Commission?'

For a moment, this seems like an appealing solution. I'm sure they'd be happy to have us stay. Then the reality of the logistics sets in. Nairobi is not a city made for commuting, and my friends' apartment is on the other side of town.

'But how would we get here for our shifts?' I ask. 'And what about when we're on night duty?'

'You'd obviously have to sleep here on those nights. And maybe we could get you girls a car to share. Or have Peter collect you each day.'

'It's a good hour away in the morning traffic. And the person who's on in the morning needs to be here when Walt wakes up. And even if we did have our own car, we'd only get home for a few hours before having to turn around and come back again. And what about driving at night? I thought it wasn't safe to?'

In a flash, Fiona has a plan B. 'I'm going to find a flat for you girls. Somewhere nearby. Somewhere you could walk to if you had to.'

By the end of the week, Jade, Ruby and I are moving into our own place: a three-bedroom guesthouse at the back of a property a few streets away, backing onto a forest. Fiona had seen it advertised for rent on the noticeboard at the shops.

The 'Maharaja flat', so nicknamed by Marguerite because it's owned by an Indian-Kenyan artist, is perfect in *almost* every way. The place looks like something straight out of *Vogue Living*. The shelves are decorated with beautiful stone carvings and sculptures, much of the furniture is custom-made from reclaimed wood of old dhows and the brass-studded Gujarati doors I saw in Mombasa, the living room features plush rugs and a huge leather couch and armchairs piled high with soft throws and cushions and poufs. A striking series of paintings and photographs, much of it the artist-owner's work, adorns the walls, while the bathroom – full of light and greenery and scented candles – is like a day spa.

Here, we have our own kitchen. Sure, it means buying our own groceries and preparing our own meals, but having that level of control over our lives feels more like a privilege than a chore. If we want to have baked beans on toast for dinner, in our underwear, watching TV, we can. There's no dressing up for dinner at seven, no need to eat politely and make tired conversation with Walt or Marguerite, no tiptoeing around the house to get a glass of water lest you disturb Walt in another room. We only have to stay over at the house with Walt on the nights we're on duty. We have our own bedrooms. No need for the constant interruption of people coming in to get Walt's medicine, or to charge the pagers, or to use the shared laptop for Fiona's regular Skype calls. No having to wear earplugs to block out the *Songs of Ireland* or the ninety-fifth rendition of Mozart's *The Magic Flute*.

But there is something, which I can't quite put my finger on, that makes me feel uneasy about the place. When I close the glass doors at the end of the day, and look out through the gardens in the fading light, even with the resident *askari* patrolling the grounds I somehow feel less safe.

Ruby and Jade don't seem to share my concerns, so I push them aside and settle in. We go to work. We come home from work. And we don't have to think about work when we're not there. Almost like having a normal job.

Almost.

SHORTCOMINGS

Walt is asleep when his daughter calls me and Jess into the dining room. He's having his afternoon nap. I've just set his bed at all the right angles, propped up the three pillows *just so* – the thickest under his left shoulder, the other two cradling his head. He tried to pull me into bed with him, but I wriggled out of his grip and shut his bedroom door behind me in a flurry of flirtatious *tsk-tsk*-ing.

Fiona's flying back to England in a few days and wants to make sure that if he 'goes' while she's not here, he 'goes well'. She produces a rolled-up woolly green sock. Every time I opened the suitcase to restock Walt's pills, I saw the green sock in there, and only now do I realise that I've always vaguely wondered about it.

'I need to ask something of you girls,' Fiona says. Calm as ever.

Jess and I look at each other, wondering where this is going.

Fiona unrolls the sock, reaches down into the end of it, and withdraws a small glass ampoule of clear liquid and a sterile syringe sealed in a plastic and wax-paper pouch. 'I'm taking Dad off the Risperidone. I don't think it's helping him at all. Increasing the risk of him having a stroke or heart attack just isn't worth it. And the reality is that's *already* the most likely way Dad will go, when the time comes.'

She puts the vial on the table. A cough splutters out of the baby monitor in shallow treble tones. I tap the screen on, see Walt hasn't stirred, tap it off again.

'Now, if or when that happens,' Fiona continues, 'it could all be over very quickly for him, which would be a blessing. But it could just as easily go the other way and be a horribly prolonged process. If he survives an attack, he will be in a great deal of pain. And that's what I want to avoid.'

I sense Jess shift in her seat. *Is this going where I think it's going?*

Fiona continues, her words careful and clear. 'This is morphine,' she says, placing a fingertip down on the table in front of the glass tube. 'I want you to use it if he is struggling or in distress. You'll know when. If he has a heart attack and stops breathing, he'll turn blue. He's too fragile to be resuscitated – you'll most likely just break his ribs if you try. He will probably be in pain. If he has a stroke, he may just spasm for a bit. It'll be like a seizure. It'll look awful, but he won't feel any pain at the time. The thing is, in either case he won't recover well. It'll be the start of months of decline. It will be awful for him.'

She looks us each in the eye. 'If I'm not here and you find yourself faced with one of these scenarios, I'm asking you to inject him with this.'

She taps the spot on the table. The curve of the meniscus flinches inside the glass tube.

When Fiona sees that we understand what she is asking, she continues. 'You'll need to roll him onto his side to get at his back. Let me show you.'

Fiona demonstrates on Jess's back for me, then on my back for Jess. She pulls our shirts up and points out where, between the scapula and the spine, we are to push the needle through his skin and inject an amount of liquid morphine. She asks us to inject it a half-inch deep, subcutaneously, then to place several drops under his tongue to give him more immediate relief. Then to sit with him, to comfort him.

'Please,' she says, 'I don't want him to be afraid, and I don't want him to be alone.'

Neither Jess nor I agree to do it.

But I'm sympathetic.

From the moment I was first able to fathom death, I've been somewhat obsessed by it. I'm terrified of dying slowly – of being diagnosed with terminal cancer or some awful degenerative disease and having to endure years of pain and indignity. The anxiety of that knowledge seems like it would be even more torturous than the physical suffering itself. I watched my own grandmother take several cruel weeks to die. Starvation and organ collapse claimed her in the end, which is usually how these things go. The experience made me surer than ever that having the ability to manage your own end on your own terms means being able to quell that existential panic – a right everyone should be afforded but never compelled to exercise, nor invoked by anyone but that individual.

I want to explain all of this to Fiona, but when I begin to she shakes her head and raises a hand to stop me, as though she doesn't expect a response. I see that she felt she simply had to ask, knowing her request would almost certainly be refused, on the off-chance one of us might agree to carry it out for her.

My pager starts beeping – Walt is out of bed.

'I'll go,' Fiona says, leaving Jess and I to sit there in shock. We just look at each other in silence.

Fiona doesn't ever mention the vial or her request again.

14

FUN RUN

Ruby and I arrive at the Karura Forest at seven, driving the old Peugeot along a dirt road through the trees until we reach a car park full of gleaming Mercedes and BMWs in a grassy clearing marked out with bunting. An officious race warden tells us to follow the lycra-clad queue into a squash court where we register and are issued with competitor numbers to stick to our shirts. As far as I can tell, we're the only individuals running; everyone else seems to be a member of a corporate or charity team.

Oddly, the whole scene reminds me of home – it's like the marshalling area for the City2Surf race in Sydney, full of middle-class health nuts, the kind of people who have to schedule exercise into their otherwise sedentary lives, and who run for the networking opportunities as much as the 'fun'.

Ruby and I puff along through the greenery for ten kilometres, birds and monkeys scattering and converging again around us as we jog, overtaken every so often by a trio of long, lean African semi-pros who lap us twice before we're even halfway through. I remember what a pleasure it is to be outdoors, to be in the thick of dirt and trees and nature, to feel and breathe the rawness of a place. But there's also something about the forest that makes me uneasy. I wouldn't want to be here alone, or at night. We reach the finish line in a respectable time, middle of the pack, then lay ourselves out in the shade to recover.

We're sipping iced Lucozades from one of the food vans set up near the show ring where G4S – the security company that sponsors the event – is demonstrating the prowess of its canine team. A pack of snarling German shepherds strain on their leashes. A man in a padded suit runs out into the open. 'One . . . two . . . three . . . four . . . five . . .' the announcer counts. 'Release the dogs!'

The crowd applauds as the dogs launch themselves at the puffy man and drag him to the ground, jaws set tight on his arms and legs.

'There you have it, folks, the intruder is brought down in under ten seconds,' says the man on the PA. 'For more information about the G4S canine squad and your private security needs, please come and enquire at our stand, just to the right of the main stage.'

'I guess this is the Nairobi version of Boost Juice handing out free smoothies, huh?' says Ruby.

I realise the group sprawled out beside us is from the *Nairobi Star*, one of the local newspapers.

I introduce myself to the nearest of them, a bearded man in his fifties trying to scrape the mud out of the tread of his shoes. As luck would have it, he's the editor. I tell him I've been following the bodybuilding scene a bit, and pitch him a report on the Mr Kericho competition. He's into it.

And that's that. I've finally got a real job to focus on.

Magda thinks this is just wonderful news. We're all out to dinner at the Club for her birthday that night – Walt and Marguerite, Ruby and Jade and me.

'Excellent! Excellent!' Magda says, clanging the side of her wineglass with her knife when I tell her about the serendipitous ending to our fun run through the forest. 'A toast to the new correspondent!' We all raise our wine – well, Walt raises his Ribena – and send cheers around the table. 'It is very good that you went on this run. Yes.'

'Well done, well done indeed,' says Walt with enthusiasm – then quietly to Ruby sitting beside him, 'What is it that she's supposed to have done?'

I have the sudden realisation as we leave that I'm nervous about going back to the flat.

'Do you get a funny vibe from the flat?' I ask Ruby, when we make our way out to the car park afterwards.

'What do you mean? It's *awesome*! So much better than being stuck at the house.'

'No – I know it's nice. I just . . . I don't feel safe there. I can't quite put my finger on why. It just feels isolated and vulnerable.'

When Peter drops us home after dinner, we sit at the gates, the motor idling, waiting for the *askari* to appear. Nothing. Peter taps the horn. Nothing.

Walt starts to get agitated. 'What the devil is going on?'

'*Sijui, bwana.*' Peter clicks his tongue. 'This is not good.'

I start to get nervous. I'm still no more comfortable with the whole sitting-at-the-gates-in-your-car-at-night thing.

Finally, the *askari* turns up. Peers through the window of the guard hut, unlocks and opens the gate.

Peter pulls up beside him.

The man's eyes are bloodshot; he reeks of booze – I can smell it from the back seat.

'Are you drunk!?' Marguerite exclaims.

'No, madam,' he replies, thick-tongued and woozy.

'You are! I can smell it! You've been drinking, haven't you? Were you asleep just now?'

'No, madam, I was . . . I was on patrol.'

Peter and Walt interrogate the *askari* in Swahili, as he mumbles back with pathetic excuses.

'Enough!' Marguerite says. 'You need to be here to let these girls in!'

'Yes, madam.'

'Don't let this happen again!' says Walt.

'Yes, *bwana*.'

I don't sleep much that night. I've never had a good vibe from the *askari*. Now I worry about him being so passed-out drunk that he won't stop any intruders, *and* I worry that he might be so angered by his dressing-down that he might seek revenge on us.

A few days later, I'm at Claire's place and tell her where we've been staying.

Her eyes widen. 'You must be careful there, hey?' She drags me away from the living room, to be out of earshot of the girls. 'I don't like them hearing too much of this stuff. But you should know – that area along the forest, it's a bit dicey. There was a home invasion there not so long ago – they really flogged the family up. Brutal stuff. Tied up the father and cut off his ears, beat him badly. The gangs come in and out through the forest, it's hard to catch them in there.'

'I take it having a drunk *askari* isn't a great idea either?'

'No, it's really not. Honestly, you should tell Marguerite to find you somewhere else to stay.'

I don't have to – Marguerite figures that out on her own. She's heard the same story from some friends at the Club and immediately fired off an all-points email, addressed to Fiona, the lawyers and the family Trust, and cc'ing the carers. She says she's been told that there have been disturbances around the area recently, and that she isn't comfortable making us stay there. She thinks it's too easy for 'the baddies' to get in and apparently picked up on the vibe I did, claiming she also felt spooked when she went to see the cottage.

And so, less than three weeks after moving into our boutique hotel, we're back in the asylum.

If Walt isn't going to be medicated, we are. With the best benzodiazepines we can get our hands on. The house is unbearably tense; I'm on edge all the time, jumping out of my skin at sudden noises, waking up in the night in cold sweats. I don't think I've ever experienced this kind of stress. Ruby is in the same state. We really do *need* some pharmacological assistance. Or so we tell ourselves.

It starts out innocently enough: a temazepam here and there, begged from Marguerite to help with 'trouble sleeping'. Then a few gobbled down in daylight hours, to help 'take the edge off'.

But then, just as Marguerite's supply runs dry, we luck into a source of our own.

Ruby goes to see a local shrink, on account of her increasing anxiety. She's expecting talk therapy but comes back with a prescription for a short course of bromazepam, an anti-anxiety drug similar to Valium. 'One three-milligram tablet a day,' are the doctor's instructions. 'For a week, tops.'

Well, that's all well and good. But the pharmacist didn't have any three-milligram tablets in stock, so Ruby was issued six-milligram tablets instead. And they didn't take her script, so she has an apparently infinite supply.

We decide to try it that afternoon, while Walt's napping. It's wonderful stuff: much more suitable for our purposes than temazepam, or Valium, or Xanax. Somehow, it induces supreme relaxation without drowsiness, making us feel as though we're made of nothing but bubbles and rainbows and indifference. We float around the house in a coherent but tranquillised haze, floppy limbed and unflappable, absolutely zero shits to give about the

Smyths and their internecine sniping, immune to their provocations, infinitely patient with Walt and his circular conversations. Zen. As. Fuck.

'I say, have you seen the news?' says Marguerite, laying a thick slab of marmalade onto her toast. She's in her bright pink polo shirt and a pair of white capris today, fresh back from an early round of golf, dewy beads of sweat amassing beneath her visor. It's almost exactly the outfit Ruby dressed up in for the fancy-dress party.

'No, what's happened?' I ask Marguerite warily, as I guide Walt to his place at the end of the table. I hope whatever the 'news' is isn't going to ruin the good mood he's woken up in today.

'That British couple, nabbed from their *banda* in Lamu! Well, they killed the husband, actually. But they've kidnapped the wife and dragged her off to Somalia.'

There goes that hope about Walt. He starts freaking out. 'Oh, how dreadful! Who were they? Anyone we know?' This is exactly the kind of thing that shouldn't be discussed in front of him, but Marguerite can't seem to help herself.

'No one we know, darling,' she says, seemingly oblivious to the distress she's causing. 'They were on holiday from the UK. They'd just been on safari on the Mara. It was terrorists, they say!'

'Bloody Mau Mau. Shoot the lot of them, I say!'

'No, not the *Mau Mau* – that other ghastly lot from up there – "Al Shaba-Bobby" or something.'

'Al Shab-who?' says Walt.

'I think it's "Al-Shabaab",' I say.

'Yes, that's right,' says Marguerite, leaning across the table to add, sotto voce, '*Mohammedans*. And of course, they're demanding a ransom. Millions! Well, you know how those things go. Even if her family pays up they'll probably still chop her head off.'

'Sorry, whose farm was attacked?' Walt is still fretting. I distract him with a slice of pawpaw.

'No, not a farm, they were taken from *Lamu*! Can you imagine? Up on the coast there. We used to go there all the time – it's a lovely spot, isn't it, Walt?'

'Oh, *Lamu*. Yes, that is a lovel–' Walt begins, but Marguerite barrels on over him.

'They just came through the window in the night. Shot him. Threw her into a boat, and took off. *Shocking*. And I tell you what, this is the last thing those resorts need coming into the holiday season. It's all over the news in England. People are cancelling their trips already! Well, I can hardly blame them. Wouldn't you?' Then, out of nowhere, she jumps up from the table shrieking.

'What? What is it?' I ask, thinking she's spotted a terrorist about to come through *our* window.

'Oooooooooooo! Oooooooooooo!' she screams, bouncing from side to side as Walt and I hold on to the edge of the table in panic and Esther comes running in from the kitchen.

Esther and I crawl around under the table, searching for the snake or the spider that must have crept up Marguerite's pants, but there isn't one. All we can see are her bare legs and blue cotton briefs, now that she's taken her trousers off and is holding them out to Esther. 'Soak them in *hot* water, will you please, Esther? *Hot!* Make sure you use the *hot* tap!'

Esther, bewildered, takes the pants through to the laundry. Marguerite, in just her underwear, sits back at the table, takes a bite of toast, and washes it down with the last of her tea as though nothing's happened.

'What was that all about?' I ask.

'Hmm?' she says.

'With ... with your pants just now,' I say. 'I mean, you're not wearing them anymore.'

'*Ohhhhh!* So silly – I dropped some marmalade on my lap. A jolly big lump of it right down my front.'

'What a horrible mess,' mumbles Walt, going back to his pawpaw. At least he's forgotten about the jihadists on Kenya's doorstep.

When our reserves of bromazepam start running low, a Kenyan friend of Sarah and Jack's suggests we ask for it without a prescription. 'You just need to be assertive about it,' he says, amazed we bothered with prescriptions in the first place. 'This is *Kenya*. Just take a scrap of paper with the name of the drug scribbled on it. Rules here are ... you know, *flexible*. Especially for *mzungus*. You'll have no problems.'

It works. Especially at the strange little dispensaries that for some inscrutable reason are often found at petrol stations in Nairobi. 'The doctor told me to get this,' I say, handing over my note confidently with a wad of cash. (I'm astonished at how quickly I've become a practised, privileged junkie. I now understand how drug abuse can go undetected in some people for so long.)

Sometimes the attendant meekly protests. 'Sorry ... you should have a prescription for this.'

So I include it with the rest of Walt's order. 'It's for the *bwana*,' I whisper over the counter, nodding pitifully in Walt's direction as he sits bewildered on a plastic chair, asking what we're doing at the bloody travel agency again – he's had enough gallivanting for one year, thank you very much.

'Ahhh.' The pharmacist nods. 'Do you want to take two boxes?'

I give it a thoughtful beat. 'Yeah, you know what – I guess we'd better,' I reply gratefully. 'Saves us having to come back too soon.'

The small windows of time I have between shifts become grand feats of laziness. The Club becomes about as far as I can be fucked going to get out of the house. I spend hours lying next to the pool, drinking Scotch, eating bar snacks and reading current affairs magazines, telling myself it's all a way to 'stay on top of what's happening in the world'. I inevitably doze off before I get to the end of an article, and try to forget that I'm not doing very much writing of my own.

It gets to the point where Ruby and I take to washing two of those lovely pink pills down with a glass of whisky and soda at the end of an especially trying day. It turns the house into an immersive theme park, the implausibility of our situation suddenly rendered in hilarious high definition. We roll around the floor of our bedroom in stitches, having just noticed some bizarre Anglophilic details in the décor. Like the fact that in every room there's a watercolour portrait of a different breed of hunting dog, each with a dead duck in its mouth. Or that there are seven doilies in the study alone.

'I don't believe you,' Ruby slurs.

'Come on then, let's go count them,' I reply.

We stagger down to the study, where Marguerite is watching Sky News with a cup of peppermint tea, and Ruby distracts her with dumb and obvious questions about the next day's plans while I walk around the room pointing out the seven crocheted mats that sit under vases and coin trays and water jugs, counting them up with exaggerated fingers and mouthing each number in silence, and Ruby starts giggling and Marguerite notices our bleary-eyed high-drunk faces and says, 'Good gracious, you girls look *dreadful!* No wonder you have such trouble sleeping – you should go to bed when you're so tired!' And we say, 'Yes, you're right. We'll go to bed now. Goodnight!'

And we stumble back to Ruby's bedroom and flop into bed and lie in the dark doing impersonations of Marguerite, a medley of her best catchphrases and most outrageous quotes. '*Yoo-hoooo!*' we warble in our best soprano toff. 'Do you know it was the *funniest* thing . . .'

'I had a *lo-ver-ly* round of golf this morning – I won, even with all the blacks and yellows cheating, can you believe it? And they *do* cheat. They *do!*' 'Peter, *Peter!* Oh, *do* drive more smoothly over the bumps, won't you?'

We laugh so hard the noise can't escape our bellies, leaving us in tears and gasping for air. Then we sleep like the dead until morning, when Walt's mattress alarm buzzes under my pillow, and I go through to his room to lay out his clothes and tie up his shoelaces, still blissed out and giddy in the benzo-afterglow, and wondering who out of all of us here, really, is losing their mind the most.

15
NYTOL

We can't get any bromazepam. Our good luck has run out – the pharmacists just won't give it over without a prescription anymore. Maybe there's been an industry crackdown. Or maybe they're just onto us. Instead, I get an over-the-counter sleeping aid called 'Nytol'.

Nytol is diphenhydramine hydrochloride, a type of antihistamine. Given I've only ever reacted badly to antihistamines, I really should know better. This isn't a good gamble. But I figure it's 'only an over-the-counter' drug. The effects will be mild, surely.

We take four pills each. Ruby is out within half an hour. She sleeps soundly throughout the night, snoring gently, drooling a little on her pillow, having peaceful dreams.

I know this because I lie on the spare bed in her room and am awake all night enduring horrifying auditory hallucinations and heart palpitations.

A mosquito the size of a soccer ball circles my head. It buzzes and whines like an orbiting power tool, threatening to land on my ear. I try to swat it away. It swoops closer. Gets angrier. Summons a bunch of friends to taunt me, a whole swarm of bees and locusts and nasty beetles. I swear, I even hear one of them whisper my name.

For what seems like hours I lie still, trying to steady my heart rate with deep breathing, whispering mindfulness exercises. *My toes are touching the sheets . . . I have five fingers on each hand . . . I will tap each one against the next . . .*

But the buzzing persists, and my skin starts crawling, and then I start scratching myself to pieces.

The monsters become too much. I jump out of bed to turn the light on. My legs vanish. I cling to the doorframe as I search along the wall with rubber arms for the light switch, then scream as the room floods with brightness. Ruby doesn't even stir. I can't see the bugs but I can hear and feel them, dive-bombing me, wriggling down my pyjamas. I crawl along the carpet to my laptop and open it to see the drug information page I looked up earlier that night. Further down the page, under basic advice about dosages, I see 'hallucinations', 'nightmares' and 'itchy skin' listed as possible side effects. Mm, yes – things I should have thought about earlier.

I look up 'diphenhydramine' on drug review forums and read dozens of posts by people who've also been plagued by the invisible army of giant insects. There is nothing to do but wait for the effects to wear off. I spend the rest of the night in the bathroom, sitting on the tiled floor with the lights on, swatting phantom bugs away with a damp washer and slathering myself in sorbolene. Esther finds me wrapped in a mosquito net when she comes through to collect the laundry in the morning, my head between the bathtub and the toilet, my laptop between my knees.

'Kirsten! Are you okay!?' She helps me to my feet through what feels like the thick fog of a horrendous hangover.

'Yeah, thanks, Esther,' I reply, checking the room is clear, relieved the buzzing has stopped, glad to have my legs back.

I stand at the door to Ruby's room, watching as she yawns and stretches languidly in her bed. 'The rest of the Nytol is all yours,'

I say, before plodding back to my room and sitting on the end of my bed, trying to muster the energy to get dressed for the day.

When I take my plates through to the kitchen after breakfast, I try to explain to Esther what happened. 'Hey, sorry about this morning, Esther,' I say. *I'm a spoiled idiot who took too many antihistamines to try to escape the existential suffering of having an annoying job.* 'I, ah – I had an allergic reaction to some tablets I took last night. They made me a bit sick.'

'Ohhh, *pole sana*,' she says, as though there's nothing that weird about finding someone covered in moisturising cream and gauze passed out next to a flat computer. 'You are okay now?' I don't deserve her sympathy.

The Nytol horror really takes the shine off the bromazepam buzz. I realise the past month has been a blur. Despite our rules – never take it on duty, never drive while affected – we've still managed to sedate ourselves to the point that we've clearly developed a tolerance for the drug.

Besides that, my conscience has started to get to me. It's pathetic, I realise, to become a pharmaceutical junkie because life in Walt's house is 'hard'. And 'relaxing' isn't really helping me relax at all. It's certainly not helping me get anything real *done* to be spending my downtime lazing on a sun lounger by the pool at the Club, guzzling G & Ts as I develop an equatorial tan, eating samosas and picking the crumbs off my chest, reading until my arms tire of holding the book up and my eyes can't take the glare anymore, or the shade I've been dozing under shifts to the other side of the umbrella. Actually, it's truly revolting. I've never found that sort of hedonism as enjoyable as it's made out to be, and realise that getting hammered and sunburnt is only a temporary balm that sees me start my next shift with Walt even more irritable than I'd finished the last.

NYTOL

I make a promise to myself: to focus on getting the bodybuilding article written, and to stop being a sloth. Instead, to truly let off steam, I need to boil. I rededicate myself to the gym, and I get hooked on sweat instead of sedatives.

The gym is a relatively new addition to the Club's facilities. It's in a huge new annex behind the main building, with soaring ceilings and wide windows along the northern wall that look out onto the pool and open out over low hedges to let the fresh Nairobi breeze drift through the room, sweeping the sweat along with it. I sign in at the mahogany reception desk, where I'm handed a key to a locker in the change rooms. Jugs of chilled water infused with slices of lemon and mint sprigs sit on a silver tray in the hallway, tinkling with crystalline ice cubes. A wicker basket of freshly rolled towels is stationed at the door to the main room, along with bottles of spring water and wet washers. This is how I imagine North Shore mums in Sydney do 'the gym': a world away from the tin sheds cooled by pedestal fans that I grew up with in Mackay.

An attendant is walking slow lengths of the room, guiding a lamb's-wool buffer across the polished wooden floorboards, while it hums at the thick red power cord trailing behind it. I feel bad about scuffing the waxy sheen, so I tiptoe across it in my socks, only putting my shoes on once I reach the equipment.

A couple of hefty personal trainers are on duty to instruct any guest who desires it. They seem painfully bored. One is called over to spot a couple of diplomats' wives on Swiss balls. He guides them through gentle Pilates movements, and I can't help but be amused by these accented ladies with alarmingly poor balance. They seem far more interested in the trainer's company than his expertise.

I just want to run.

(This first visit would set the rules for what became a ritual: it was very important that I got the second treadmill along the northern wall. The second treadmill sat directly in front of an open window and had a clear view of the bright blue diving board at the deep end of the pool. I formed a relationship with that machine. Sometimes I'd wait twenty minutes for it to become free, even when all the others were available.)

The psychic cleansing begins with a series of soothing sounds and silent mantras. The fizzy zip of the tread on my shoes skidding over the grip of the belt. *Fuck Walt, the spoiled old bastard.* A plastic *thunk* and *slosh* as I slam my water bottle into the holder. *Fuck Marguerite, the scatty old bitch.* Towel folded over the rail, just so. Bobby pins in to hold stray hair off my face. A series of beeps as I set the incline and button up on speed. *Fuck Fiona, the paranoid schemer. Fuck all these impossible cunts.* Until a walk trips into a plodding jog and I fall into a run at thirteen kilometres per hour. And then, I just run. Run and breathe and sweat and blast music through my iPod. Run and stare in soft focus at the red numbers ticking over on the display, which shows time and distance rolling steadily forward. Run and stare at the yellow tracer creeping its way around a picture of a 400-metre oval, or Al Jazeera headlines about South Sudan becoming the world's newest country, or the results of the mid-term elections in the United States. I run and stare out the window at the Kenyan nannies looking after other people's children: broods of black and brown and white kids swirling around the pool, all squealing and laughing and crying together.

I run. At the three-minute mark, I find my rhythm. Lungs and legs sync up. At ten minutes, I feel euphoric and weightless, as though I could run forever. Seventeen minutes is when the pain sets in, and the digging begins. I rake over the slights of the previous twenty-four hours. A dirty look from Fiona because I coughed and disturbed Walt while he read his newspaper. Marguerite asking me to go and buy groceries for her, then driving off in the car she told me to take. Walt refusing to swallow his tablets at breakfast, then grabbing me by the wrist when I reached to put them back into the container, with a grip that pinched my radial nerve and sent a shock all the way up to the back of my neck. All of it burns like petrol.

From twenty-three minutes, it gets easy again. By the time the red numbers tick over to forty, I'm physically spent and spiritually renewed. I hit the stop button, take my weight on the handrails and place my feet on the sideboards until the belt whines to a stop.

I sit on my towel at the end of the machine, loosen my laces, let my arms hang from my knees and watch the sweat bead on my thighs, streak down my shinbones and drip from the end of my nose into a pool on the floor. I suck air in and blow it back out. Feel my pulse settle, and my joints ache, then finish off with a half-hour routine of body-weight exercises and stretching.

In the change rooms, none of it seems that bad anymore. Poor Walt is a dying old man. His daughter and wife just want what is best for him. My job isn't hard: it's an extraordinary chance to see Africa – I just need to make more of it.

I'm chastened, exhausted, and my life is put back into focus. Thousands of people are starving to death in a famine just a few hundred kilometres away, for fuck's sake. People are getting blown up at bus stops for following the wrong religion. I'm beyond fortunate. I return to the house restored, with a wellspring of patience and perspective.

I leave early on the Friday morning of the Mr Kericho weekend.

I've managed to talk Ruby and two of the AYAD girls we met through Sarah and Jack into coming. A road trip through the western highlands to see the world's biggest single tea plantation and some of the fittest men in the country – who'd say no to that?

Windows down, music up, we're climbing the escarpment north out of Nairobi, taking turns to control the stereo: Fleetwood Mac and Florence and the Machine wail into the Great Rift Valley. We drive north past Mount Longonot, past Lake Naivasha, and past the Olkaria geothermal power station – soon to become the largest in the world. We drive past Lake Nakuru. We carry on west, towards Molo on the northern edge of the Mau Forest, and then . . . then, we get stuck.

A storm has ripped through the area. Trees have fallen, huge craters have opened up in the ground, live powerlines are thrashing and sparking across the road. Traffic is at a standstill, *matatus* and trucks and buses honking pointlessly. But there's no way around it, no turning back. This is the only road to Kericho. It'll take as long as it takes.

We inch along, keeping our spirits up with karaoke renditions of Bruce Springsteen and Meatloaf. We play I-spy, and Ruby and I do impressions of Walt and Marguerite that have the AYAD girls in stitches. Whenever we catch up with ex-pats, we're called upon for updates on life in the house. Although we're always desperate for *their* news from the outside world – from people doing important and interesting work – they just want the latest on the colonial time-warp soap opera that all sounds too insane to actually be true.

It's dark by the time we reach a junction where a couple of local men have appointed themselves traffic wardens in return for compulsory donations. A *matatu* is stuck on the side of the road, bogged in the mud on the siding. The passengers are resigned to their fate; sleeping faces press against the windows as the driver spins the wheels. Kericho is only 250 kilometres away, and what should have been a four and a half hour journey has already stretched to at least six.

I hold a two hundred bob note out the window, and the men stop the traffic coming from the other direction, allowing us to manoeuvre around a huge log and past a snaking electrical cable spitting sparks into the air. Just as we get through, we hear an almighty crack behind us: an even bigger tree has collapsed, completely blocking the road, and some of the branches have caught fire.

I hit the accelerator, but somewhere along the way I make a wrong turn. We end up on a dirt road winding around the side of a mountain, no phone reception, no map. A couple of women at a lonely *duka* selling sheepskin hats and warm Cokes assure us that Kericho isn't much further, and so we press on, decidedly less confident than when we began the trip.

Faith pays off. Finally, around ten, we pass the Deliverance and Full Gospel tin-shed churches where Pentecostal Christian guidance is passed on to Kenya's poor and humble, as long as they give the right amount in tithings. From God's barns, we follow the lights of Kisumu-Busia Road to the Kericho Tea Hotel.

It's only when we wake up in the morning that we can appreciate our lodgings for their faded former glory. The Kericho Tea Hotel was clearly the Club of this town in its day. A grand stone building set over manicured gardens, with a bar, and a ballroom and private *bandas*, it was the centre of the social scene for pre-Independence white settlers, who farmed tea on the surrounding highlands. And although these days it caters more to travelling Kenyan businessmen than wealthy *mzungus*, it seems that nothing – no chair, no bedspread, no curtain – has been updated since 1963. The only giveaway of the modern era is a framed picture of President Mwai Kibaki, hung on the wall above reception.

On our way to the primary school where the competition is being held, we pass by lush countryside: the deep green brush of tea plantations, flecked with the white sacks of pickers and their colourful *kanga* headscarves. The town of Kericho is considered the heart of Kenya's sizeable tea industry – no other country in the world exports as much of the *Camellia sinensis* leaf. Something like half of every cup drunk in England comes from here, and a fair amount of that consumed in Egypt, Sudan and Pakistan too, making it Kenya's biggest forex earner – though little of that cash reaches the labourers on the hills, who pocket less than 10 per cent of the price their crop earns at auction. The tension between the rise of corporatised agribusiness and small-scale farms is a perennial political issue.

Kericho seems an unlikely venue for a bodybuilding event, as the region is hardly known for its gym junkies. But once we arrive at the school, I realise there's more to it than just the title.

A crowd of a few hundred people is milling around the car park. A couple of canvas booths are set up at the entrance to the main hall – they're running free HIV tests, for competitors and spectators alike. It turns out the Mr Kericho competition is sponsored by the Walter Reed Project, a US Military HIV Research Program with a local base in town, and they've scheduled the event to coincide with World AIDS Day. Kenya has had great success in tackling the epidemic: the rate of infection is down to 6.3 per cent, less than half what it was a decade ago, thanks in large part to bold public-education campaigns like this one, which aim to overcome the stigma of the disease. The social etiquette around 'knowing and disclosing your status' is now standard fare for relationship advice columns, TV panel shows and drive-time radio talkback. Newspaper classifieds feature personal ads for 'positives seeking positives', women's magazines run features titled 'How many dates before you ask the Status Q?' and despite the protestations of church groups, condoms are as widely available as Coca-Cola.

We make our way inside, where children's desks have been pushed to the side and rows of plastic chairs set up for the audience. A roving theatre group dressed up as colonial police is entertaining the crowd. They're wearing 'white face' and have stuffed their shirts to create saggy paunches, and are clowning around blowing whistles and wagging fingers in people's faces, excellent mimics of the men who told their grandparents what to do.

While my friends find a good spot to watch from, I go backstage to get set up. Through a tangle of sweaty biceps and barbells I find Wilson and Joseph: the brothers I met at the junior event in Nairobi. Wilson is giving Joseph a pep talk while smearing him with cooking oil. 'Symmetry, remember – left and right together!' he urges, holding his arms up in a double curl, 'and smile – you have to smile!'

Joseph flashes a tense grin, mirroring his brother's example.

The men hustle to be registered at the weigh-in station, then queue up at a trestle table loaded with laptops and leads. A couple of young DJs are trying to keep track of a growing pile of competitors' MP3 players and smartphones as they coordinate the playlists.

The emcee calls for a group prayer to kick off proceedings, and the hall falls silent as around fifty hulking men sit on school chairs with their heads bowed.

Finally, God acknowledged, the main event begins. Celine Dion yowls over the PA system with a medley of pop-ballad remixes as the first contestant struts onto the stage wearing a very small pair of Brisbane Broncos togs. He pirouettes away from the crowd, flexes his lats and pulls the maroon briefs taut across his clenched buttocks. 'THAT'S MY TEAM!' reads the yellow lettering – the old Australian National Rugby League slogan. Frenzy ensues. Teenage boys whoop, grown women shriek and children crouch by the stage with digital cameras while the judging panel watches on soberly, making hurried notes between poses.

Once the round is over, I go behind the curtains to find out more about the Broncos kit.

'The *mtumba*,' the man tells me. 'There are many like this here!' The word *mtumba* roughly translates from Swahili as 'sackcloth' but is more commonly used to refer to the enormous second-hand clothing market on the outskirts of Nairobi. All those bundles of outdated trends dumped at Vinnies after spring cleaning? The sad runs of commemorative hats for sporting teams that end up placing second? All that crap ends up over here, much more than anyone needs. The *mtumba* has had a devastating impact on local textile industries, with traditional garb giving way in a generation to the Nike swoosh. Recently, thanks to a 'proudly African' campaign among the continent's fashion designers, there's been a push to reclaim cultural identity, but it seems they've yet to corner the men's spandex market.

And those briefs are a big deal, too. No one wants to wear the same pair on stage twice so competitors swap between rounds, and each man saves his best pair for the finals. The men are so unfazed by my presence (or my camera) that they readily strip right down to nothing. I avert my eyes out of respect, but there are so many mirrors around the place that I soon figure it's best to leave the room until the costume changes are done.

On the bright side, the fact that they're so relaxed means I'm able to observe that the atmosphere behind the scenes is one of genuine camaraderie. The men spot each other under heavy weights, and readily share training and dietary advice. Meat is an expensive luxury and supplements totally unaffordable for most, so any tips on cheap protein alternatives are welcome. 'Eggs, peanuts and milk for breakfast,' recommends one guy. Another swears by *ugali* and beans.

The most fun – for the audience and contestants alike – comes with the two-minute 'freepose' rounds: here, each contestant shows off their best assets through choreographed moves set to cued lighting and music of their choice – more often than not, they've gone for a Backstreet Boys track. The performances fall somewhere between interpretive dance and aerobics, as the men strive to show off 'personality' and 'stage presence'.

The prize pool this year of 133,000 shillings (about $1500 almost twice Kenya's average yearly income) has drawn competitors from as far as Mombasa, 750 kilometres away on the coast, and Kampala in neighbouring Uganda. One particularly good display from Ivan Byekwaso — a twenty-six-year-old Ugandan who takes out the middleweight division — gets the crowd so worked up that the security guards are forced to remove some of the more inebriated supporters who are jealous of the interloper's attention from women in the audience. For a moment, it seems these guys might cause a scene — but in the end they agree to leave peacefully.

For the KBBF, the event seems to be shaping up as a great success. The past few years have seen their dedicated efforts to building the sport pay off. It's a great turnout, a mix of long-term supporters and a few curious passers-by for whom bodybuilding is a foreign — and evidently highly amusing — concept. There's a bit of star power in it, too. Guest judge Paul Mwangale is a former Kericho man who last year was crowned world champion at the international FAME Bodybuilding Championship and has secured the sponsorship of a leading South African sports supplements brand. To the locals he's a celebrity; to the other bodybuilders he's an idol.

That night, twenty-eight-year-old Meshack 'Priest' Ochieng is crowned Mr Kericho. His nickname honours Lee Priest, the internationally renowned Australian body builder from Newcastle. Ochieng is a well-known and respected competitor. He stands just 160 centimetres tall but boasts an astonishingly solid physique, regularly topping the field in his welter-weight division. The audience erupts when he brings his wife and children on stage to accept his prize, then quiets as he's handed the microphone.

'Discipline is a must for one to succeed,' he says. 'It's not being faithful to the Ten Commandments alone. It's being able to follow the training program as written, eat as required, and avoid what might make you perform poorly. Why do footballers camp far from their friends when preparing for games? There is a reason for that.'

Through the bustle of the departing crowd, I spot a noticeboard at the back of the hall. On it, next to a UN poster of child soldiers titled 'War Is Not Child's Play', someone has pinned up an email titled 'What a Life!' Its several printed-out pages feature a series of poignant photographs of human struggle: an old Asian man with one leg hobbling down a snowy road in bitter winter; a young Indian boy begging in the street; a small girl doing her schoolwork on a rock. Each is captioned, 'If you think you've got it tough, look at them.'

It's jolting to see the sort of sentimental tosh I see in my Facebook feed hanging in the primary school of a developing nation most Westerners are conditioned to feel sorry for. A subtle reminder that people are the same the world over: no one prefers self-pity over agency and hope.

By the time we get back from Kericho, each room has been installed with a new 'smoke detector', we're told. Only, as I later discover, the devices don't detect smoke at all.

While we've been gone, Fiona orchestrated a day with Walt and Marguerite out of the house, brought in a team of *fundis* to fit the little white units to the ceiling, and hooked them up to the wi-fi network.

Now, she can tune in from her home in the UK – from anywhere – and watch us all on her laptop.

None of us know it, but the asylum has become a panopticon.

Walt and Marguerite are fascinated by my bodybuilding photographs. I sort through them on my laptop in the living room, picking out the best shots of each category's winner to send through to the *Nairobi Star* with my report on the event.

'But what are they doing?' Walt says, peering at my laptop screen as I flick past a shot of Ochieng holding his trophy aloft, then one of a change room full of oiled-up skin, then another of a man grinning while he does the splits. 'Why aren't they wearing any clothes?'

'They're showing off, darling! Like all men do!' Marguerite says, leaning over my shoulder. 'And my word, aren't they right to. You would too if you looked like that!' She elbows Walt, squeezes his bicep.

'I certainly would not!' Walt says. 'But I do agree – they are very sturdy-looking men.'

I can't help myself. I show him a picture of the roving performers dressed up as colonial police.

'What do you think of these guys, Walt? They're playing at being cops.'

He squints, then cracks up when he realises what the costumes are meant to be. 'They've certainly got the tums right!' He's got a sense of humour, you have to grant him that.

When the newspaper boy comes to the gate the following morning with the *Star*, Patrick races it over to the house. The staff all gather round the garage as I open it up to the sports pages. There's my report – a double-page spread! But wait – *no, oh fuck, nooooo* – they've stuffed up the captions. The wrong names are under the pictures. And Meshack Ochieng – Mr Kericho himself – hasn't been featured at all.

I feel sick. When I check my emails, I find I've already got messages from some of the competitors pointing out the error. I reply to them all apologising, then let the *Star* know about the mistake. They promise to print a correction and to run a short profile on Meshack the next day to make up for it, if I can send through some text in time.

Fiona pokes her head into my room and tells me I need to come through to breakfast. She doesn't want me interrupting them halfway through.

'I'll be there in a tick,' I tell her firmly. 'I have to sort this out.'

Walter Smyth can survive with one less carer for half an hour. After all the trust these men put in me, I need to fix this up right now.

~

Fiona's found us another flat. This one, we're assured, is safe. It's on the second floor of a new apartment complex, for a start. Much harder to break into. And it's across the road from the Swedish ambassador's house, so security in the area is top-notch.

It's nowhere near as nice as the Maharaja flat, and this one only has two bedrooms – so we'll have to rotate through them depending on who's on duty – but that's fine. Any kind of private space is a welcome escape from the house.

The new apartment is a great success until Ruby and I get home one afternoon to find the place has been ransacked. There's stuff everywhere: cushions on the ground, vases knocked off the coffee table, smashed glass and a trail of muesli leading from the kitchen to the balcony door.

'Ah, fuck!' I yell, wondering what's been taken. Then I realise something's not quite right about the mess. 'But wait, what kind of burglars would take muesli?'

Monkeys, as it turns out. They've squeezed through the security bars and upended the kitchen in a hunt for sugary treats, and are now sitting on the balcony enjoying them, cackling at our expense from a pile of sucked peach stones and banana skins.

Once we realise nothing valuable's missing – aside from the sultanas and dried fruit from Ruby's cereal – the whole thing seems kind of funny. I can sleep at night with monkeys at the windows. We just have to remember to keep them closed.

16

THINGS FALL APART

It's just after lunch when Ruby's phone rings. It's Jade. On the way home from her Kenyan boyfriend's place, she's been in a car accident. We can't make any sense of what she's saying – Ruby tells her to calm down, to speak slowly.

Fiona, realising something dramatic has happened, sends us into the garden to take the call. 'Not in front of Dad!' she hisses. 'He's already asking what all the fuss is about!'

A man ran across the road in front of the taxi Jade was in. He smashed into the windscreen on the passenger side – Jade saw his head crash into the glass before he bounced off the bonnet. Their car spun into oncoming traffic, missed a head-on with a truck by a millimetre after the taxi driver turned the wheel again, swerving the other way. They finally came to a stop when they crashed into a fence.

Jade says she's okay. Her neck hurts; she has some cuts on her arm. But the man they hit is lying in the middle of the road, bleeding and unconscious. Jade thinks he might be dead. 'He's not moving!' she sobs. 'He's not moving!'

A crowd has gathered; the police are there. She has to go to hospital with the driver and the maybe-dead man, to be checked out herself and give a statement about what happened. But the taxi driver is asking her to lie – to say that they're friends. It turns out he isn't a taxi driver after all, just a guy with a car.

'I don't know what to do!' she cries.

'Jade, listen to me,' Ruby says. 'Go to the hospital. I'll meet you there. It's going to be okay. I'll see you there soon. Call me if anything happens.' Ruby hangs up and orders herself a taxi, while I go inside to tell Fiona what's happening.

'Well,' she says, 'I don't want her taking the Peugeot – Dad will get all wound up if he hears it!'

'She's not driving,' I say. 'She's catching a cab. It's coming for her now.'

Fiona looks around. Walt is gone. 'And now we've lost Dad,' she snaps, striding outside to find him.

'Lost him?' I ask. 'What do you mean "lost" him? Where could he possibly be but in the garden somewhere? Jesus, Fiona, can't you see something a little bit more serious is going on?'

But she doesn't hear me. She's found her father. He is bending down to pick a grub off a rosebush.

Ruby and Jade get back from the hospital just before dinner. Jade didn't have to give a statement in the end, so the whole perjury business has been avoided. She doesn't know if the man they hit has lived or died. He's still lying in the hospital where no one knows his name or how to find out who he is – just another one of the thousands of pedestrians hit on Nairobi's roads every year. Three or four people a day are mowed down by *matatus* coming too fast around corners or crushed under the hot-rubber weight of an eighteen-tyre semitrailer while trying to cross an eight-lane highway to avoid the thugs that loiter around the footbridge. Any one of these tragedies would be national news back home; here, they barely make the newspaper. Just another sad thing that happened. *Pole sana.*

Jade has whiplash and is wearing a foam neck brace. When she hobbles back into the house, Walt looks her up and down in alarm. 'Good Lord, what a bloody gimp you are!' he exclaims.

Jade laughs, but soon dissolves into tears. She's clearly still in shock. But when Ruby suggests the two of them go to the flat for the rest of the evening to get some rest, Fiona is annoyed. 'It's really not ideal,' she says. 'Dad's in a state and I need some time to go over a few things with Marguerite, and I want to talk with you girls about updating the job list too.'

'I'll watch Walt,' I say. 'You guys go.' I've volunteered to take over their shifts even though I know it will mean being on duty for sixteen hours straight, which is its own kind of hell.

'I can fill them in on the jobs list later,' I say. 'Jade needs a good night's rest.'

And I need to start making plans to return home. There's a job to go back to: a new consumer affairs comedy program. A world away from Kenyan bodybuilders and demented colonials and monkey raids – but it's starting to feel like the world I'm ready to return to.

The salad is sitting on the kitchen bench, covered in cling wrap, ready to be served for lunch. Like all of Khamisi's meals, it's immaculately presented: layers of crisp lettuce, wedges of bright red tomatoes, sliced black olives and a ring of halved hard-boiled eggs circling the edge of the dish.

I'm in the garage, putting the mangoes and pawpaws we bought at the markets this morning into the gauze fruit box where they'll ripen for a few days, when I hear Marguerite in the kitchen. 'Are those anchovies?' she demands. I watch through the laundry lattice as she peers down through the plastic film over the salad.

'Yes, *memsahib*,' says Khamisi.

She pulls a revolted face. 'Oh, how *disgusting!* Why have you put those in there?'

Khamisi is insulted. 'It is a nick-oy-see salad, *memsahib*.'

'A what?'

'Nick-oy-see salad,' he says, pointing at it. 'You asked me to make nick-oy-see salad. That is a nick-oy-see salad.'

Marguerite rolls her eyes. 'Ni-*swah*, you mean, Khamisi. Ni-*swah!*'

'Nick-oy-see!' Khamisi insists, dragging out the menu notes he made yesterday and pointing at the word written there in his careful biro lettering: *nicoise*.

'Well, whatever you want to call it, it shouldn't have anchovies in it!'

Khamisi isn't going to let this one slide. 'Nick-oy-see salad *always* has anchovies! A nick-oy-see salad has lettuce, tomato, olives, egg, green beans and anchovies. If you don't want anchovies, you should have told me.'

'It has *tuna*, not anchovies! And there should be potatoes in there. Why aren't there any potatoes? You could use the ones left from last night. Here you are. Look.' Marguerite takes out a plastic container of leftover potatoes from the roast dinner we had the night before and dumps it on the kitchen bench. 'Now, take those horrid things out – they're far too salty for Walt anyway – and put some of these lovely potatoes and tuna in there instead.'

To classically trained and painfully proud Khamisi, this is sacrilege. He's professional, a traditionalist, a perfectionist. Marguerite may as well have told him to serve up dishwater – she has offended his sense of identity. But he does as he's told. He picks out the anchovies. He adds the potatoes and tuna to his corrupted salad. He leaves for his afternoon break.

And he never comes back.

Esther pulls me and Ruby into the laundry the next day to tell us that he's quit. She seems sad – but not surprised. 'He was having many problems here,' she says. 'With Marguerite and Fiona. He said there were too many people in charge.' He texted Esther, asking her to say goodbye to Ruby, Jade and me, and to have his monthly pay given to her to pass on to him.

'Great, now we have to find another cook,' Fiona fumes, as though that's the great shame here.

'Yes, well, he could be very difficult, couldn't he?' says Marguerite, trying to deflect any blame from her own actions.

I'm dismayed: from the day I first arrived, Khamisi was a warm and constant presence in the house. I loved watching him cook, having him talk me through his careful processes, how clear it was that he enjoyed his work – even if the people he worked for weren't always easy. To see him pushed so far that he, despite desperately needing the job, should quit on principle, somehow bothers me more than just about anything else has so far.

More bad news comes the following morning.

Marguerite turns on the TV, and we learn that Kenya is at war. 'Oh *nooo*,' she moans. 'What a silly thing to do!'

Walt and I come in from the patio, where we've been laying out the mango skins and bird seed, to see the head of the army announce that Operation Linda Nchi – 'protect the country' in Swahili – has been launched in response to the recent spate of Al-Shabaab kidnappings and murders.

'Oh, deary me,' says Walt, lowering himself into a chair in front of the TV, chewing on the end of a finger.

Esther stops clearing the breakfast table to come through and watch from the doorway.

A map on the screen shows the plan for Kenyan troops to invade the southern conflict zones of Somalia in order to destroy the Islamist group, apparently with the consent of the Somalian government and the cooperation of their military. Though then there's a clip of the Somalian ambassador to Kenya saying they 'cannot condone any country crossing our border'. It's all very confusing, clearly a mess. The taking of the two Spanish MSF workers from Dadaab was ostensibly the final straw, but according to some reports this plan has been in the works for a while and the kidnappings are just a handy excuse. One of the experts says that Western powers – including the US and France – have been scheming to intervene in Somalia since 2010. The coverage makes Walt even more edgy.

We follow the news more discreetly from then on. I don't know how wars in Africa normally play out, but I suspect it's not something you stick around for if you can help it. As the days go by, and the Kenyan tanks get bogged thanks to a fortnight of heavy rains that have turned the desert into mud, the truth gets even murkier. There are unexploited oilfields in southern Sudan and northern Kenya. There is ten billion dollars' worth of Chinese investment waiting to fund a rail and road network to transport that oil to the coast. And there are the ports of Kismayo and Lamu, where that oil could be loaded onto tankers and shipped across the Indian Ocean . . . you know, if only the security of the region could be guaranteed.

Al-Shabaab retaliates by sending an operative to lob a grenade into Mwaura's Bar, an after-hours pub in the city, injuring thirteen people. The following day, they blow up a *matatu* at a busy bus stop, injuring ten and killing one.

The Kenyan police respond by ordering raids on Eastleigh, home to many Somalian migrants and refugees. They uncover stockpiles of explosives and ammunition and round up 'terrorist suspects'.

Security tightens across the city. Western embassies issue travel advisories warning Westerners not to visit places where Westerners congregate, which doesn't leave Westerners with many options. Sarah and Jack aren't allowed to go to their local bar anymore; it's just home or the office for them. Even the Club has taken extra precautions – now, when you pull into the driveway, you have to weave around hi-vis barrels as you approach the security gate and wait to be cleared by sniffer dogs. Marguerite feels it really ruins the whole VIP vibe.

Fiona has to go back to England – I get the sense her husband, Jonathan, has had just about enough of her absence. But she makes us promise not to go anywhere public other than the Club and shops, when we really have to.

Nairobi is nowhere near as fun when most of the city is out of bounds. I've realised my time in Kenya is nearly up anyway, but it's a shame to leave on a sour note, knowing things here have turned ugly.

And they get even uglier in the house.

Someone's been stealing money from the brown envelopes of cash that are poorly hidden all over the house: in the liquor cabinet, in the storeroom, in Walt and Marguerite's bedroom.

For a while we've suspected that money was going missing, but it's hard to keep track of it with so many different people dipping in and out of the reserves to run errands and get groceries and pay for Walt's doctors' appointments and pills. A missing hundred bob here and there – it can easily be innocently overlooked. Ruby and I set up a ledger from which cash had to be checked in and out, and receipts and change – to the shilling – provided for all purchases, in an effort to clear any suspicion that we are trying to rort the system.

Then we discover we were under surveillance all along. Fiona has been sitting in the UK watching a live feed of the house coming in via the 'smoke alarms'. Perhaps she was hoping to catch Marguerite trying to kill her husband, but instead she's caught a thief. Esther.

She flies back to Nairobi to fire her. There are a lot of tears. Marguerite is livid to discover there were 'eyes' in the ceiling, and she has them removed.

Ruby, Jade and I take Walt down to the Club, to keep away from the drama. When he dozes off in a chair by the fire in the reading room, we steal a moment to get our heads around everything that's happened.

'I cannot *believe* those things were cameras!' Jade says. 'I just – I cannot *believe* she did that.'

'I can,' I say. 'Pretty much nothing can shock me here anymore.'

'Why didn't she tell us!?'

'Probably thought she'd catch us doing something, too,' Ruby says.

'I'd say so,' I say. 'I don't think she really trusts anyone. But I can't believe Esther was stealing, either. I mean, I get it – it would be bloody hard not to. It just sucks. This all sucks so hard.'

'I'm so glad I'm outta here,' Jade says. Her time is just about up – she's leaving next week, just in time to miss Christmas with the Smyths.

17

PAMMY

When Pammy, Jade's replacement, pulls up in the driveway, I have to wonder whether she's a practical joke.

Pammy is from East London. She's in her fifties but young at heart – she's wearing a nose ring and a pink zirconia belly button ring that is proudly displayed on the fleshy fold between her singlet and trousers. Fiona recruited her through a vaguely worded advertisement for a 'dementia carer/companion' on Craigslist. She screened applicants via Skype interviews to ensure they weren't black, fat or dreadlocked. (One candidate was eliminated because of her 'ratty hair' – Walt won't have a hippie in his house.)

It's my job to take Pammy around town to show her where everything is and how things work. A Nairobi induction, of sorts. When I tell her she'll need to wear something a little more conservative for the Club, she protests. 'Bugger me, that's all I've got! It's stinkin' 'ot over 'ere!' Ruby lends her a white cardigan to cover her shoulders, and we get her to tuck her singlet into her waistband.

I begin with a tour of Village Market. As we walk through the food court, past the high-end fashion boutiques and the luxury travel agents, Pammy tells me, at great volume, the following autobiographical facts:

- She used to do 'close protection security' at a swingers' club with her ex-husband.
- She's been celibate for two and a half years, so one of the perks of working at the swingers' club is 'getting to watch'.
- She hasn't brought any of her 'toys' over but does have a 'nice little clit-tickler rabbit gizmo' at home that she thinks she'll miss, and she might need to buy a replacement while she's here.
- Her son is a 'dirty boy' with a 'big willy' who used her credit card to buy a hundred extra-large Durex condoms off the internet before she left.
- She really needs to do a big shit: 'It feels like the kick of a baby!'

At one point, she whips around to stare at a Kenyan man who just walked past and exclaims, '*Corrrr!* He's horny!'

'What, did he have a boner?' I whisper in disbelief.

No, it's not that. 'Horny', I learn, is just Pammy's word for 'attractive'. 'He's the best lookin' bloke I've seen since I got here!' she says.

Pammy excuses herself to empty her bowels after chugging a coffee 'to get things moving'. She returns from the public bathroom expressing deep satisfaction about her recent defecation. My poker face is exquisite; I tell her I am very happy for her.

Later that afternoon, we go down to the Club with Marguerite and Walt for afternoon tea. Over slices of sponge cake and scones, Pammy tells us – and everyone else in the garden room – how she hasn't been able to stop farting since she landed. 'Dunno what the heck's goin' on – must 'ave been the air pressure on the plane or somefin'!' she roars, as a Kenyan couple at the next table stare, mouths agape, tea going cold. It's the first time I've seen Marguerite lost for words.

Pammy's flatulence continues back at the house that evening. Leaving a room in a hurry as I enter it, she mutters, 'Sorry about that!'

About what? Then it whacks me in the face: a pungent, fruity steamer. I hurry back into the hallway, gasping for fresh air, and hear her telling everyone in the living room what she's done.

'I left a whoofy one for her in there – haha!'

There's a small part of me that wants to stay on, just to see how the Pammy-era pans out.

I don't get to say goodbye to anyone in Kenya properly. I'm struck, two days before I leave, with a horrific bout of food poisoning.

I'd planned on racing around Nairobi, saying goodbye and thank you to Claire and Robert and the girls, to Magda and Suzanne. Ruby and I had arranged to have lunch with the staff at the Smyths, under the jacaranda tree behind the house. Instead, I spend thirty-six hours hugging the toilet bowl at Sarah and Jack's place, having moved out of the carers' flat so that Pammy can take my place. Day and night becomes blurred, vomit and diarrhoea simultaneously explode from my body, over and over and over again. My bowels and stomach twist and cramp and spasm, expelling everything within me. The agony is beyond comprehension. There is no way I can fly home like this, I can't even stand up. I lie naked in the bottom of the shower with a folded towel for a pillow, and seriously wonder if I might be dying. *What if it's cholera?* I think. *How have I managed to live here for nearly a year and only get sick now?* I'm one retch away from calling for an ambulance when I start to feel the worst is behind me. Six hours before I'm due at the airport my insides finally settle down enough that I can walk without shitting myself if I clench tight enough, but I have Sarah get me some heavy-duty maxi pads to wear on the plane, just in case. It's a most undignified departure.

I sweat and rumble the entire way. There's a touch-and-go moment in the transit lounge in Dubai. But I make it to Sydney with a clean arse, and I have never, ever, been so happy to be home.

Jade's on duty with Walt, walking him around the house as he inspects the pavers for any unvanquished weeds. I'm on my laptop in the living room, emailing Alex about the logistics for a visit to the FilmAid project in Dadaab. It's been hard to find a time that works. I want to go for at least two weeks, so I'll have to either find a replacement while I'm gone or try to time it for when Fiona's here so that she can take on the third-carer shifts.

I see Walt tear past the window, Jade following closely behind. The man's on a mission; he can move quickly when he wants to. I hear car doors slam shut. *Oh, of course. A car.* It's just Ruby and her friend Sean from dance class, getting dropped off in a cab at the gate. They've been for a drink and are here now . . . why?

Ruby and Sean run across the driveway and come in giggling through the sunroom entrance on the side of the house, leaving Jade and Patrick to try to explain to Walt who was in the cab that's now driving away and why he's not allowed to follow it through the gates.

I go out to help calm him down, and between us, we manage to redirect Walt's attention to the burning trash pit behind the staff quarters. He busies himself poking stray bits of paper back into the heart of the flames, and telling David and James not to get too close when they start to add more.

By the time I'm back in the house, Ruby and Sean are in Walt and Marguerite's bedroom. In their wardrobe. In their clothes.

'What the fuck are you guys doing?' I say.

Ruby spins to face me. She's wearing Marguerite's pink golf visor, lemon polo shirt and white capri pants. Sean is still in his own jeans but wearing Walt's old pair of slippers and with one of his silk robes thrown on over the top.

Ruby rushes into the ensuite and comes back with pink lipstick daubed across her mouth, then grabs a tweed paddy cap from the top of the wardrobe and places it on Sean's head. 'There.'

Not long after that touchdown, I receive an email from Marguerite. She says she fired Pammy after discovering she was in cahoots with Fiona, who had hired a Nigerian to 'get rid of me'. It seems, even by the Smyth's standards, too preposterous to believe. But then I receive an email from Jack, who says they're upgrading all the security around the Smyths' house and he's heard there've been death threats against Marguerite.

It seems I got out of Africa in the nick of time. And I have one decent thing to show for myself: my feature article on the East African bodybuilding scene – complete with photographs – which is published by the *Global Mail*.

In 2015, I go to Kenya again.

Not – you'll be relieved to know – to work for the Smyths. I'm not *quite* that insane.

This time, I go for a holiday, with the man I'll later marry, Chris. I want to show him Africa, and the very strange world I spent a year in.

I organise a two-part itinerary. First, we tick off all the standard tourist-trail stuff. We take a trip to Amboseli National Park to see the elephants and gawp at Mount Kilimanjaro rising through the clouds, its snowcaps now even smaller than when I first saw them five years ago.

We go on safari in the Masai Mara, where we have the astonishing good luck to see a leopard – the most notoriously shy of all African game – drag a fresh kill up a tree. He slings half a zebra corpse over the bough, bright red entrails dripping and dangling out of the black-and-white-striped rump, then sits beside it slowly licking his paws and claws clean.

We go to the Giraffe Centre in Lang'ata and stand dead still while the fantastical creatures crane their impossible necks over the railing of the viewing platform, blue tongues probing ahead of long-lashed orbs, gently taking pellets from our own mouths.

We go to the David Sheldrick Elephant Orphanage and watch dozens of baby elephants chase their handlers around until they give up the five-litre bottles of milk they're holding. The baby jumbos wrap their tiny trunks around the plastic containers and pour the milk down their throats, then toss the empties aside and stumble and tumble and roll around in the mud, splashing, flapping, their tangled trumpets blasting in what has to be one of the most boisterous displays of pure, unbridled joy on the planet.

And once we've walked the beaten track, we spend part two of our trip reliving my time in Nairobi: we go to City Market, where I show Chris how to haggle for avocados, and where in the picnic area out the back I used to go with Peter to feed the monkeys, and where, across the road at the Aga Khan Hospital, I spent many hours in the corridors with Walt, waiting to hear whether his heart, his kidneys, his liver were holding up.

Chris and I go to Village Market. We go to the grocer and Nairobi's Sarit Centre. I show him the stationery store where Marguerite sent us to buy the staff's children's schoolbooks. We visit Suzanne's Clinic and see how far the project has come. Suzanne isn't there: the clinic – just as she'd hoped it would – runs itself now. There are four nurses on duty now, enough to make sure no one will be left unseen on the verandah.

We have dinner with Marguerite and Magda at their local Italian restaurant. I'm surprised by how much I've missed them and how happy I am to hear their voices – even if what they have to tell me isn't wonderful news.

Marguerite says that Walt is still alive, but his condition is worse than ever. He's rarely able to leave the house anymore and has very few lucid moments. Fiona has said he can't have visitors anymore, so if Marguerite wants to see any of her friends she has to go out to do so. Of course whenever she does, Fiona accuses her of abandoning Walt.

But the very worst thing Fiona has done of late – the thing that seems to upset Marguerite more than anything else – was to tell everyone in town that Marguerite 'murdered Chiku'.

'What a thing to say! I *didn't* kill her! *Chiku committed suicide.* Silly little thing.'

'She *what?*' I ask. *How does a dog commit suicide?*

Magda lends her support to Marguerite. 'Well, you know when you think about it in a way that is true, Marguerite, she did! I mean, Chiku runs behind the car while you were reversing, isn't it?'

'Yes! She topped herself!'

Chris and I meet up with Peter one afternoon at a *nyama choma* joint in Karen. Over a few *moto* Tuskers, he tells us he doesn't know what ended up happening to Esther, and that Khamisi got another job with a good family in Karen. That the Smyths have a new cook, that Patrick is still the *askari*, and that David now works in the main house, taking over Esther's role. He says at least fifty carers have been through the house since I left. *Fifty!* Some of them didn't last a month. One young girl hooked up with the Navy SEAL bodyguard Marguerite had hired to protect her from the Nigerian hitman – and they both absconded in the dead of the night.

Peter tells me the women looking after Walt now are South African. He says they're rude to the Kenyan staff and to Marguerite, that the house is a quite unhappy place. 'And the *mzee* is so very sick now. He's worse than when you were here. He doesn't remember anything much anymore. He doesn't know even who the *memsahib* is anymore!' He clicks his tongue and shakes his head. '*Pole sana.*'

'*Pole sana*,' I say. It really is all so very *pole sana*.

Chris and I meet James in his hometown of Machakos on a Sunday after church, and we go with him and Rebecca and little William to the People's Park – a new public space built beside a man-made lake, featuring gardens, restaurants and a pool. We sit near the amphitheatre where children dance on the stage, eat barbecued *kuku* and drink *moto* Cokes, and tease William and Rebecca about whether they have boyfriends or girlfriends. William is only in Grade Five but doing very well in maths. Rebecca is in her final year of college and soon to graduate as a teacher — she uses computers all the time in class. James is very proud of them both. We eat ice creams while William rides a paddleboat around an inflatable pool, squealing with delight, and James reiterates to us how sick Walt is and how difficult life in the house has become.

'Bwana Smyth cannot go out much now. Not even to the Club. He only goes out for the doctor, now.'

Chris and I go to the bar and catch up with Claire and Robert. At a *braai* in their new house, their girls — now so much older and taller — play in the garden while the adults chat on the patio.

One of their friends was caught up in the 2013 terror attack at the Westgate Mall, when Al-Shabaab militants stormed the shopping complex killing sixty-five people and leaving almost two hundred wounded. The news coverage was horrifying: footage showing bloodied bodies lying among scattered chairs at the café I'd once sat at with happy families sharing milkshakes and donuts. Claire's friend had hidden underneath a supermarket freezer with her kids while bullets and blood flew around them. The mall is reopening in a few days — it's a traumatic time for everyone. Claire looks out at her girls running around the yard.

'This is the thing about Africa. It's magic. Nobody wants to leave. Then you have children and your perspective changes. You worry about what their future holds. Hell, it must have been hard for your parents to go. But I admire them. You've no idea how lucky you are to live in a place like Australia.'

Two years later, I'm in Africa again. This time I'm sitting by the fire at a bush camp in the middle of Hwange National Park, Zimbabwe. My entire family has gone over for a three-week trip. We're on safari with one of my dad's old school friends, Eric, who now runs a walking safari company based in Victoria Falls.

Eric is telling us stories about some of the interesting clients he's had – American film stars, Middle Eastern oil sheiks . . . and a Zimbabwean woman, Lindsay, who was working for 'a mad family in Nairobi'.

'They were looking after some demented old fella there. He was totally cooked. Wanted to grab his guns every time he heard a dog bark. His wife had a personal bodyguard to protect her from the daughter, who was apparently trying to knock her off!'

After I tell Eric that there's only one family this can be, he arranges for me to meet up with Lindsay when we all return to Victoria Falls.

Over a bottle of red wine, she and I swap stories about the very strange world of the Smyth family.

Lindsay joined them a few months after I left, along with another friend of hers from Zimbabwe, Glynnis. She worked with Pammy-from-London for a time – who, when she wasn't conniving with Fiona about ways to 'bring Marguerite down', was buying hard drugs off the street and getting high in the carers' flat in her time off.

Lindsay tells me about the best night they had there: she and Glynnis organised a party to celebrate Walt and Marguerite's fortieth wedding anniversary. They decorated the house, arranged for a huge feast and cake, played music and danced all night in the living room, kicking legs up onto each other's shoulders, singing by the fire.

Lindsay and Glynnis knew Fiona could never find out about it – she'd have thought it too risky, too dangerous, too stimulating for his condition, but Walt was so happy he cried tears of joy. He went to bed smiling for the first time in months.

Epilogue
RECKONING

It's taken a while for me to work out what, if anything, I gained from this strange time in Kenya. Any lessons feel a bit like they're from a parallel universe.

I suppose I'd been curious to get a sense of the world my parents were from. To know the sights and sounds and smells of it, to experience it in a visceral way. But I think a part of me was also curious to understand how a system that we can now see is so patently unjust could have existed for as long as it did – how otherwise good people could have tolerated it. I think I get that now, a bit. Though I'm left with more questions, really.

Would, I wonder, we still be living in Zimbabwe (or 'Rhodesia') if the ruling white minority had taken the path Kenya did – had embraced a peaceful transition to independence, rather than bitterly fought a losing battle? What would *I* have done, had I been around at my parents' time? Would I have been brave enough, clear-eyed enough, to stand up and say, this can't go on? Or would I have just accepted things, as just the way the world was? Is there anything I can do now, beyond acknowledging the wrongs of the past, and understanding the advantages I've been lucky enough to be born into, and supporting moves to undo any of the structural inequities that remain?

Guilt is not a helpful emotion when it comes to grappling with these things. I do, though, feel personally responsible for accepting the racial privilege that led to my time with the Smyths in Kenya. There are small and private things I have done and continue to do in an effort to make up for this. Things that are within my power, and that I know will make a difference to people who deserve better. I have also come to realise that Africa – Kenya, at least – should not be defined by its colonial past. Its history is much longer and richer than that. Its people have agency and capacity and visions of their own future that they're busy pursuing. The rest of the world should know more about that than it does.

Despite the unpleasantness of these colonial reckonings, my love for Africa more generally – the feeling of connection I have to it – was further cemented by my time in Kenya. I don't know what to do with that. I don't know where a white descendant of colonials chased off the continent belongs. Australia is and probably always will be home for me now – but even here, I'm reminded that it's stolen land.

As for Walt – well, as far as I know, he's still going. I feel the urge to say 'against all odds', given the state I first found him in 2010, but it's not 'against' the odds at all, is it? If the odds are in anyone's favour in this world, they're in Walter Smyth's. At least, purely in the sense of his physical survival. Whether he would, if he could, appreciate the efforts being made to prolong his existence will forever remain a mystery. Would he consider the extra years he's had on this Earth to have been worth it? Is this what he would have chosen for himself? Would he have been on Marguerite's or Fiona's side, when it came to deciding which risks were worth taking to improve his happiness and wellbeing in the short term? If there is a lesson in his story, I reckon it's this: make your end-of-life wishes clearly known to those who will be responsible for carrying them out. Make sure they understand what *your* idea of quality-of-life is. WRITE AN ADVANCED CARE DIRECTIVE. Seriously, do it. Do it now. *Especially* if you've got a lot of money. Wealth might make life easier in material ways, but it can really screw with people's heads.

Walt — whether he knows it or not — has come a long way since I left him in early 2012.

Ruby visited Kenya again in early 2018, as part of a circus group tour. She had dinner one night with Marguerite, at the same Italian restaurant Chris and I had joined her at, where Marguerite filled her in on all the dramas of the intervening years, including that Fiona had taken her to court — and lost — in an attempt to gain sole control of Walt's care and estate. Afterwards, they went back to the house for a nightcap.

Ruby sent me a video of the hula-hoop performance she put on for the Smyths in their living room. It's a bizarre piece of footage. The fire is going, a new dog lies on the Persian rug, the fake wireless is playing the jazz cabaret tune Ruby's choreography was set to.

Marguerite, now eighty, is on the rosewood lattice settee, filming Ruby's dance with her iPad. Walt — nearly ninety — sits beside her in a wheelchair, with a blanket over his knees, no longer able to speak, but smiling and laughing and clapping at the *Or-stray-lyan* girl in rainbow-striped tights cavorting around his parquetry floor.

And beside him is Louis — his black, Kenyan, live-in carer.

Discover a new favourite

Visit **penguin.com.au/readmore**